THE POLITICAL HIGH COURT

THE POLITICAL HIGH COURT

How the High Court shapes politics

David Solomon

ALLEN & UNWIN

First published in 1999
Allen & Unwin Pty Ltd
9 Atchison Street, St Leonards NSW 1590 Australia
Phone: (61 2) 8425 0100
Fax: (61 2) 9906 2218
E-mail: frontdesk@allen-unwin.com.au
Web: http://www.allen-unwin.com.au

National Library of Australia
Cataloguing-in-Publication entry:

Solomon, David, 1938– .
The political High Court: how the High Court shapes politics.

Bibliography.
Includes index.
ISBN 1 86448 716 X.

1. Australia. High Court—Political activity.
2. Political questions and judicial power—Australia.
3. Courts of last resort—Political aspects—Australia.
4. Australia—Politics and government—20th century.
I. Title.

347.94035

Set in 11/13 pt Bembo by DOCUPRO, Sydney
Printed and bound in Australia by the SOS Print + Media Group.

For Jocelyn

CONTENTS

PART I

INTRODUCTION

1

'A STRUCTURAL CREATION . . . IN A VERY PARTICULAR SENSE, POLITICAL'

Since the early 1990s the High Court of Australia has been attacked frequently by politicians, lawyers and commentators, and sometimes by judges and ex-judges. It has been accused of inventing laws and rights, of changing the Constitution to the detriment of the States, of stepping over the boundary between judicial and parliamentary law-making, of bogus reasoning, of undermining democracy, of intellectual dishonesty and of plunging Australia into the abyss. Some of its detractors have called for the Court to be made more 'accountable' to politicians and the people. Immediately before the last round of appointments to the High Court the deputy prime minister, Tim Fischer, promised that the government would put three 'capital C conservatives' on the Court.

Never before has the High Court attracted such calumny. Yet throughout its history the Court has had to make decisions that have had an impact on the political process in this country and on political events. In 1951, for example, at the height of the Korean War, the Court rejected as unconstitutional a law sponsored by the government of Liberal prime minister Sir Robert Menzies, which would have outlawed the Communist Party. A few years earlier the Court rejected an attempt by the government of Labor prime minister Ben Chifley to nationalise the major trading banks in Australia. In each of those cases the government of the day attempted to overturn the High Court's decision, by trying (unsuccessfully) to change the Constitution or by appealing to the Privy Council. In neither case, however, was the Court or its any of judges vilified by political leaders or their supporters.

Current critics of the Court say that they have been provoked to express their anger by changes in the way the Court approaches its task and the nature of some of its decisions. They accuse the Court of 'judicial activism' and of becoming 'an over-mighty Court' (to use the titles of critical papers given by Ian Callinan QC, before he was appointed to the High Court). It is true that since the mid-1980s High Court Justices have been more willing to acknowledge publicly that in some of their decisions they do 'make' law (as common law judges have done for 700 years). Some politicians complain even about this aspect of the Court's work. The real problem for most of the Court's critics, however, is that they believe the Court has deliberately set itself to reform the law, well beyond anything it has previously done. Crucially, some of those decisions have affected the rights of politicians and the rights of some of their most powerful and vocal constituents. In particular, the High Court's decision in the *Mabo* case to recognise the existence in Australia of native title rights aroused anger (mainly outside the major cities), and provided a focus for more general discontent about judges and the legal system, and crime and punishment.

The predecessor of this book (Solomon, *The Political Impact of the High Court*, 1992) explored the more important ways in which the High Court has had an impact on Australian politics. There would no longer be any dispute about its general thesis that the High Court needs to be seen at least in part as a political institution that makes many decisions which can and often do have an effect on the political life of the nation. This book restates the general theme, but picks up the specific issues that have brought the High Court into controversy since 1992, particularly native title issues and civil rights, including those inferred from the Constitution by the High Court concerning political free speech, and criminal process rights.

The political role of the High Court

The High Court of Australia stands at the peak of the Australian legal system. Since 1986 it has been the ultimate court of appeal for all Australian courts. It is responsible for determining the meaning of the Commonwealth Constitution, and it has the final say on the interpretation of all laws passed by the Commonwealth parliament and the State and Territory parliaments. It also determines the common law for Australia—that mass of judge-made law inherited from Britain which still governs many aspects of the civil and criminal law in Australia.

The High Court owes its pre-eminence both to the Constitution and to some subsequent legislative developments. Chapter III of the Constitution, 'The Judicature', makes the High Court the highest court in the land. It gives it a broad jurisdiction and gives the Commonwealth parliament power to make the High Court the ultimate arbiter of most constitutional issues. The Constitution also makes the High Court an appeal court for most civil and criminal matters initially litigated in the States. But the Constitution also says that in some cases appeals can be taken from the High Court to the Privy Council. Litigants in the State courts were also able to have appeals heard by the Privy Council. Appeals in federal matters to the Privy Council were abolished by a succession of laws passed by the Commonwealth parliament, while appeals to the Privy Council from State courts in non-federal matters were finally eliminated by the Australia Acts (passed by the State, Commonwealth and British parliaments) which came into force on 1 January 1986.

The High Court had asserted its authority over the Australian court system long before the parliaments put their seal on its primacy. In the 1960s, 1970s and 1980s the Court first declared that it was not bound to follow decisions of the House of Lords, then that it was not bound by the Privy Council, and finally that State courts, if faced by conflicting decisions of the Privy Council and the High Court, must follow the judgments of the High Court.

The authority of the High Court in constitutional matters diminishes the prospective power of Commonwealth and State parliaments and governments. Australian parliaments are not 'sovereign' in the sense that, for example, the United Kingdom parliament at Westminster is sovereign. The laws that Australian parliaments can pass are limited by the terms of the Commonwealth Constitution. Exactly what those limits are is determined by the High Court. What the Court says cannot be directly overruled by parliamentary action, only by changing the Constitution. And the Constitution can be changed only by the means specified in section 128 of the Constitution, which requires the government to hold a referendum to obtain the approval of the voters for any change in its provisions sought by the Commonwealth parliament. That process, as intended by the men who wrote the Constitution, makes it very difficult to change the Constitution. By 1998, of the 38 referendums held to approve constitutional alterations only eight were approved by the people under the restrictive requirements of section 128. Of those eight, very few were seen at the time they were voted on to involve major policy issues.

Occasionally, as will be seen later, governments have tried to get around the interpretations put on particular words or parts of the Constitution by decisions of the High Court. But they cannot overturn and they cannot ignore what the High Court determines. The end result is that the Constitution means what the High Court (or, more precisely, what a majority of the Justices on the Court) says it means.

The High Court may, however, change its mind about the meaning of a particular constitutional provision, and may, over the years, change its mind several times—despite the policy to which it normally adheres, and which all courts adopt, that they should strive for certainty in the law (see chapter 13). The Court now requires good reasons for even considering an argument that one of its previous decisions is wrong and should be overturned, but it is normally persuaded to undertake such a review once or twice a year. One consequence of the Court's ability to review its own decisions is that it may be possible for the High Court to update the Constitution as circumstances dictate, even though the text of the Constitution does not change. This evolution has sometimes seemed more like revolution, and has exposed the Court to political criticism (see chapter 5 and the reaction to the

Court's expansive view of the Commonwealth's external affairs power).

That such criticism was comparatively rare before the 1990s was due in part to the exalted position of the Court. The judiciary has occupied a privileged and protected position in the Australian polity. The judges are respected in part because of their assumed non-involvement in partisan politics. They are above the hurly-burly of political life, largely insulated from public criticism and protected by contempt of court laws which the judges themselves administer with some vigour. Their high standing has generally been supported by politicians, who will sometimes try to prove their own bona fides by enlisting judges to undertake public inquiries for them, to help clothe political policy-making with a non-political, independent and judicial imprimatur. It has therefore been a matter of self-interest for politicians not to attack judges and courts. Particularly is this so in relation to the High Court. The public standing of the Court (though the public may know little about it or its work) is certain to be higher than the reputation of any politician who attacks it, particularly if the attack concerns the Court's legitimate legal and judicial work. In any conflict, the public is far more likely to impugn the motives of the politicians rather than the members of the Court. Judges are seen to be above politics—or most of them are.

This does not mean that judges do not have political views. Some may have been directly involved in politics before their appointment to the bench. The last appointment of a serving politician to the High Court (Justice Lionel Murphy) occurred in 1975. But throughout its history the High Court has included among its members many Justices who were prominent in politics before their appointment. The first High Court comprised two Justices who had served in the parliament that created the Court (Sir Edmund Barton, Australia's first prime minister, and Senator R. E. O'Connor, a minister in the first Cabinet), while the first Chief Justice, Sir Samuel Griffith, had been attorney-general and premier of Queensland and then Chief Justice of Queensland, before he moved to the High Court. But the fact that a judge has not held political office, or contested a place in parliament, does not necessarily mean he or she does not have strong political convictions. It used to be argued that in Australia the social and educational background of most practising barristers, from whom judges are normally chosen, predisposes them to have conservative political views. This argument attracted little attention and aroused little general concern, probably because most people did not regard what the High Court did as in any real sense 'political'. The judges were thought to be concerned with the application of legal principles, to be persuaded only by legal argument, and not influenced by political considerations. But times have changed. Nowadays, every vacancy on the Court is greeted with speculation in the media and among politicians about the political and judicial leanings of likely contenders and the way the government of the day will want to slant or stack the membership of the Court to meet its political interests.

Most of the Court's decisions may be neither overtly nor covertly 'political', but in some instances those decisions will have political effects. They may impact on political institutions, Commonwealth and State parliaments and governments, political parties, individual politicians, and the political process generally. They may affect the operations of other courts such as the Federal Court or the Family Court, tribunals such as the Industrial Relations Commission, and government commercial instrumentalities.

The High Court, in interpreting the Constitution, decides whether the States or the Commonwealth or neither might exercise legislative and executive power across the whole range of public affairs. In interpreting legislation it decides whether the laws the various parliaments have made are lawful and what they mean, sometimes contrary to the actual intentions of those parliaments. The Court is able to interfere with the decisions of Governors, ministers and public servants to uphold what it considers to be the relevant principles of the law.

In short, the High Court is involved in the exercise of political power. This is a power controlled only by the good sense of the Justices, Justices who are appointed, not elected, and who normally hold office until they reach the age of 70. The Court's decisions may impact on the political process at the national, State and local level, and across a vast range of institutions that are part of the political fabric of the nation. All this is to some degree inevitable in a nation where the sharing of political power is governed by a written constitution. The High Court's proper function under that constitution necessarily involves it in deciding on the distribution of political power and the legal propriety of the exercise of that power. It is itself enmeshed in the political process.

Separation of power

The fact that the High Court is involved in the exercise of political power may appear to conflict with the notion of the separation of powers, propounded by Locke and Montesquieu, which so strongly influenced the fathers of the American Constitution. They saw political liberty for the citizen flowing from the separation of the three branches of government: the executive (the Crown and its ministers, or, in the case of the United States, the President), the legislature (the parliament or Congress), and the judiciary. This doctrine was not fully incorporated into the Commonwealth Constitution, though Australia's founders separated these institutions by allocating distinct chapters to them: Chapter I, The Parliament, Chapter II, The Executive Government, Chapter III, The Judicature. The Australian Constitution was meant to be operated along the lines the Australian colonies had worked out and experienced in the preceding 50 or so years since they had begun to achieve self-government. The executive was not separate from the parliament. It was composed of members of the parliament and was responsible to the parliament. The executive was the leadership of the grouping (and eventually the political party) which could gain and maintain the support of a majority of members in the lower house of the parliament. But as political parties further developed in the 20th century, it was the executive, rather than the parliament, which was seen clearly to be the dominant force. Although the theory remained that the government was answerable to the parliament, the practice was that the government (once elected) controlled the workings of the lower house. The government did not always have a majority in the upper house, and nowadays is rarely likely to win such a majority (at least at the Commonwealth level, because of the use of a different voting system in the Senate from that used in the House of Representatives). This means that a modern government cannot always be sure of enacting all the legislation it proposes. It also means that an upper house which has the power to refuse to pass budgetary and financial legislation can force a government to the polls. It is primarily during such crises that voters are aware of a significant separation between the executive government and the parliament, though, since governments have lost the ability to control the Senate, the legislative process generally is less subsumed by executive power than was earlier the case.

Nor is the formal separation between the judicial branch of government and the other branches complete. The judges are chosen by the government, and they may be dismissed by the parliament. They are dependent on the government and the parliament for the running costs of their courts, their buildings and their salaries. Judges are prone to complain in times of financial stringency that the functioning of the courts is being affected by government cost-cutting. This, however, is normally not to be understood as an attempt by the government or the parliament directly to influence judicial decision-making. On the other hand, judges occasionally use their judgments to complain about the laws made by parliament and to try to exert pressure for their 'reform'.

The High Court has formally adhered to the separation of powers doctrine. In the *Boilermakers* case (*R v. Kirby; ex parte Boilermakers' Society of Australia* (1956) 94 CLR 254, discussed in chapter 8) it ruled that the body established to exercise the Commonwealth's power to conciliate and arbitrate industrial disputes could not also operate as a court of the kind the Commonwealth parliament may create under Chapter III of the Constitution. The government and the parliament were forced to create a new court, separate from the Conciliation and Arbitration Commission, to enforce the decisions of the Commission. The Court reached a similar conclusion in *Brandy v. Human Rights & Equal Opportunity Commission* (1995) 183 CLR 245, where it held that various powers given to the Commission were judicial in nature, and could only be exercised by a court. The Commission's decision could not be given judicial authority by being registered with the Federal Court. Yet the *Boilermakers* doctrine sits strangely alongside the now generally accepted truth that judges are not merely adjudicators but frequently law makers. The common law is a whole body of law made by successive judges, and now adapted for Australian conditions by Australian judges, led by the Justices of the High Court. In recent years, for example, the Court has been modernising and fleshing out the law of negligence and the law of contract. To some extent the work of the Court has accommodated that of the parliament. For example, the Commonwealth parliament has made a law which makes valid contracts of insurance in which an insurer undertakes to provide insurance for a third person who is not a party to the contract. The old common law doctrine of privity of contract held that such contracts were unenforceable. But the High Court held (at about the same time the parliament was considering this issue) that the privity of contract rule should cease to apply, at least in relation to insurance contracts and possibly in other areas as well. Another example can be found in the field of negligence. The States have passed laws to solve some of the problems which the courts thought were beyond their powers (in relation to contributory negligence, for example) or to overrule what the courts were doing. In a 1981 case (*Todorovic v. Waller* (1981) 150 CLR 402) the High Court decided to set a standard discount rate for courts throughout the nation to observe when calculating the amount of damages payable to a plaintiff for future economic loss—the High Court stepped in because the rate then ranged across Australia from 0 to 5 per cent. But the new uniform rate has been displaced in almost every State by State legislation. In the criminal law also, the High Court has acted in recent years to try to ensure that uniformity exists in relation to fundamental principles of the law throughout the nation, and has applied common law principles which it has developed even in those States where a criminal code has been created and enacted by the parliament to override the common law.

While the courts have performed their law-making function uninhibited by the doctrine of the separation of powers, the parliament has also crossed the divide between the two institutions by telling the courts how they should perform their function of interpreting the law. Over the centuries the courts have developed various rules of interpretation, which they apply to documents such as contracts or wills, as well as to legislation. One of the rules prevented the courts from going behind the words of an Act of Parliament to look at what the legislators had said (as recorded by Hansard) about what particular provisions of the law meant or were supposed to achieve. For example, in the late 1970s the High Court had to interpret some consumer credit legislation in South Australia. The government and the opposition in the South Australian parliament had differed over whether the new law should apply to large stores which issued their own credit cards. The government controlled the Legislative Assembly; the opposition controlled the Legislative Council. The Assembly and the Council produced different proposals, but eventually held a conference to work out a compromise. The Council's (the opposition's) view was adopted, and the Bill was amended to reflect that approach. Litigation involving one of the big stores eventually came to the High Court. There, only one Justice thought it was proper to look at Hansard to see what the compromise was supposed to mean (it was clear from the disagreements among the judges who heard the case that the amendment was open to several interpretations). The other Justices closed their eyes to the obvious intentions of the parliament and by a majority ruled that the law meant what the government and the Assembly had sought, unsuccessfully, to have passed. Needless to say, the government did not seek to correct this faulty judgment of the High Court.

In 1981 the Commonwealth parliament passed an amendment to the Acts Interpretation Act which was intended to remove the blindfold that the courts had applied to their own work. Section 15AA required federal courts to have regard to the intentions of parliament when considering the meaning of any law. In 1984 section 15AB was added, telling the courts that in discerning that intention they should have regard to any explanatory memorandum which the minister introducing legislation had provided for the parliament, and to the Hansard reports of the parliamentary debate. In an earlier era this legislative intrusion into the judicial sphere might have been resented and perhaps resisted by the courts. Instead it was taken up by some judges with enthusiasm, though the courts had to work out procedures to prevent their being overwhelmed by a mass of unnecessary or unhelpful documentation.

There is no fixed borderline between the functions of the judiciary and the parliament in the way that the separation of powers doctrine would seem to demand. But in practice most of their functions are separate and distinct and they operate independently. As will be seen later (in chapter 12), similar generalisations can be made about the interaction of the judiciary and the executive government. The pure theory of the separation of powers is not demanded by the Commonwealth Constitution. The aims of the doctrine—to prevent arbitrary rule and to distribute power among different institutions so that none exercises absolute power and each is subject to checks and balances from the others—are largely achieved in relation to the functioning of the judiciary.

The political role of the High Court takes it more into 'checking' than 'balancing'. Its function is to say 'yes' or 'no' to the validity of laws and the activities of parliaments, governments and political, judicial and other institutions and individuals. Only rarely is it involved in trying to strike a balance between the interests of others in the political arena. A rare case of the balancing function is examined in more detail in chapter 4. It concerns the High Court's interpretation of section 90 of the Constitution, which prevents the States from imposing excises. For decades the Court defied logic and its own rulings about what an excise is, to hold that licence fees imposed on the sellers of alcohol and tobacco products, calculated as a percentage of the value of sales over a prior period, are not sales taxes and are therefore not excises. The Court made it clear that it would not extend this reasoning to allow the States to tax other goods. The exception was allowed to stand, however, because the Court was conscious of the huge revenues which the States gain from these taxes, and on which they are so dependent. However, in 1997, in *Ha v. New South Wales* (1997) 189 CLR 465, the Court ruled that these licence fees were indeed excises.

The members of the Court these days reject the notion that their function in interpreting the Constitution is to maintain a federal balance. This is contrary to the initial approach of the Court to constitutional interpretation (discussed in detail in chapter 13). The modern approach has led to an ever-expanding legislative field for the Commonwealth parliament. But it has not meant inevitable success for the Commonwealth in constitutional disputes with the States. There are some real limits to the powers that the Court is prepared to grant to the Commonwealth.

Most of the cases where decisions of the Court have had a significant political impact are cases in which constitutional issues have had to be determined. But not all. As will be seen in chapter 6, the way the High Court interpreted the Income Tax Assessment Act in the 1970s and 1980s had important political consequences for the government of the day and for the bureaucracy, as well as significant fiscal consequences for the individuals involved and for a whole stratum of society.

Very occasionally a lawyer unfamiliar with the way the Court works may make a submission which suggests that the Court should take into account the political effects of a particular approach to the law. Such suggestions receive short shrift from the Court, which insists that it is only concerned with the legal effects of its decisions. This is not to say that the Court is unaware of the fact that its decisions may have a political impact. As will be seen in chapter 5, its crucial decision in the *Dams* case (*Commonwealth v. Tasmania* (1983) 158 CLR 1), holding that the Commonwealth Labor government could validly pass a law which had the effect of preventing the Tasmanian Liberal government from building several dams, was accompanied by a special statement explaining that it did not take sides on the policy issues involved, and was only concerned with deciding whether the Commonwealth had the constitutional power to act as it did. The Court apparently believes that its prestige and authority would be lessened if it were to be influenced by political considerations in making its decisions. But the Court is clearly alive to the political context of many of the cases that come before it.

Political interactions

The apparent disregard for the political impact of High Court decisions may suit the lawyers and the judges. For anyone who wants to understand the workings of the primary political institutions of the nation, it should not be acceptable. It is not just the politics of the High Court which needs to be studied; it is the political interactions of the Court and the more recognisable political organs of the state (the parliament and the government, and the informal institutions that support them—the political parties). The range and reach of the Court's decisions on political life may be seen by identifying and classifying those institutions or people who have been affected in this way.

First, and most obvious, are the institutions directly affected by decisions of the Court on federal aspects of the Constitution—the parliaments and governments of the Commonwealth and the States. The High Court's decisions in the two income tax cases in the 1940s transformed the relationship between these two tiers of government. Control of the greatest source of revenue for government allowed the Commonwealth to spread its policy control into areas such as education and housing for which it had no constitutional responsibility. The uniform tax cases cleared the way for Commonwealth governments to make (and continue to make) drastic changes in the federal balance. The Commonwealth's ability to use its financial resources to bribe State governments into carrying out Commonwealth policies was approved by the High Court as a legitimate use of section 96 of the Constitution, the grants power. More recently the Commonwealth has used its control over exports and its external affairs power to enforce its environmental policies. The political impact of the Court's decision allowing the Commonwealth some legislative power in environmental matters went beyond a redefining of Commonwealth and State powers: it became a significant (perhaps crucial) electoral issue. If the *Dams* case (see chapter 5) had not been decided in the Commonwealth's favour the Labor government would not have been able to campaign on an environmental platform and win decisive votes in marginal electorates in two subsequent (1987 and 1990) elections. But the Commonwealth is not always successful in its attempts to exert power at the expense of the States. The High Court ruled invalid an attempt by the Commonwealth to intervene in the battle between the Queensland government and the Electrical Trades Union over strong anti-union measures imposed in Queensland during the SEQEB dispute in the late 1980s. And later the Court ruled invalid an attempt by the Commonwealth to impose a national companies code over the opposition of at least half the States. The political significance of that decision was to force the Commonwealth to negotiate proper (financial) terms with the States in return for the States acceding to the Commonwealth's power grab (see chapter 7).

Occasionally the Court has rejected the attempts of both the Commonwealth and the States to legislate in a particular area. The history of the Court's interpretation of section 92 (which guarantees 'absolutely free' trade, commerce and intercourse between the States) is littered with marketing schemes that have failed the test of the day and transport regulations that were scrapped. But a new day has dawned in relation to section 92. A unanimous decision of the Court in 1988 in *Cole v. Whitfield* (1988) 165 CLR 360 (see chapter 9) reconsidered the purpose and meaning of section 92 and freed both the Commonwealth and the States from many of the constraints the Court had previously imposed on them. The implications of this change by the Court are considered further in chapter 9, while further examples of the way in which the 'federal balance' has been altered by the Court are considered in chapter 4.

The second group of institutions that has borne the political impact of High Court decisions is the political parties. The 'most dramatic example in Australian constitutional history of a judicial doctrine provoking a major change in political and legislative policy' (to quote Professor Geoffrey Sawer) occurred in relation to the *State Banking* case (*Melbourne Corporation v. The Commonwealth* (1947) 74 CLR 31; see chapter 9), in 1947. The Court held that a section of the Banking Act which prohibited private banks from doing business with the States or their agencies was invalid. This decision provoked the Commonwealth Labor government into trying to nationalise all the private banks. That legislation in turn was ruled invalid (by both the High Court and the Privy Council) on grounds which effectively gave section 92 of the Constitution a role as a permanent barrier against nationalisation of any interstate company, a decision that struck at the Labor Party's roots. From its very beginnings the Labor Party had proclaimed as one of its objectives the 'nationalisation of all sources of wealth and all means of producing and distributing wealth'. Although that objective was watered down and changed from time to time, the platform always contained some reference to a socialist objective which included the nationalisation of some key industries (see, generally, L. F. Crisp 1955). Although the Labor Party had not engaged in any concerted attempt to nationalise anything while it held effective power from 1942 to 1949, this court-imposed veto was bitterly resented. It added to the grievances Labor had about the restrictions the Constitution and the Court appeared to place on the implementation of its policies. The resentment helped shape Labor's policies over the next few decades. This can be seen in particular in the approach of Gough Whitlam, who was merely an ambitious backbencher when he delivered the Chifley Memorial Lecture in 1954, under the title 'The Constitution versus Labor', and complained (p. 4):

> Much of the frustration, and even demoralisation, in Labor ranks in recent years flows from the fact that the Australian Labor Party, unlike the British and New Zealand Parties, is unable to perform, and therefore finds it useless to promise, its basic policies. It has been handicapped, as they were not, by a Constitution framed in such a way as to make it difficult to carry out Labor objectives and interpreted in such a way as to make it impossible to carry them out.

Labor's dissatisfaction with the Constitution (which it played no part in framing), and with the Court's interpretation of it, was of long standing. The Constitution as interpreted by the High Court did not allow Labor to enact the policies it wanted in such areas as the control of working conditions. In the first eight years of the federation the electors had supported three separate political parties, providing none with an absolute majority in the House of Representatives. Labor, the Protectionists and the Free Traders took it in turns to govern. Deakin's Protectionists held power in 1907–1908 with the support of the Labor Party, because Deakin was prepared to support some of Labor's industrial policies. But in 1908 the High Court struck down the key elements of the 'new protectionism'—legislation which had created a union label and which adjusted tariffs to favour manufacturers who were not declared by the Industrial Court to have failed to provide fair and reasonable conditions of employment. The Court's decisions left the Labor Party with no reason to continue its support for Deakin and the unofficial coalition collapsed. That in turn led, within a few months, to the 'fusion' of the two non-Labor parties. This striking rearrangement of the political battlefield could be attributed largely to the High Court's rejection of the Liberal–Labor legislative scheme.

Decisions from the Court have also caused problems for the non-Labor parties, though this has occurred less frequently than for Labor. Significant political problems were created for the Fraser government by the High Court's treatment of the tax laws. In the 1970s and early 1980s the Court seemed to give the green light to tax evasion, ignoring or discounting the effect of section 260, the anti-evasion section of the Income Tax Assessment Act. The Fraser government found it almost impossible to grapple with charges that it favoured tax evasion, though it was the Court rather than the government which was causing the problem. Eventually the government introduced new anti-evasion measures, but not in time to overcome the political disability which the High Court had thrust upon it.

A third area where the High Court's decisions have influenced political changes concerns the arbitration system. The Court has transformed the power of the parliament to make laws with respect to conciliation and arbitration so that, instead of handling disputes involving a small number of itinerant workers and those involved in interstate shipping (as the founding fathers envisaged), the power is now utilised to control the working conditions of most Australians. But that control is exercised by a body set up under Commonwealth legislation. The parliament cannot make laws directly affecting most working conditions. Frustration over the increasing coverage of the Commonwealth system and the government's inability to deal directly with strikes led the Bruce–Page conservative government in 1929 to propose dismantling the system, a policy which helped bring about its defeat. Subsequent governments left the system alone to a large extent, except when the High Court said it required changes. This occurred primarily in 1956 when, in the *Boilermakers* case (see chapter 8), the Court ruled that arbitral and judicial functions could not be performed by the same body. The Court of Conciliation and Arbitration was transformed into two bodies, the Conciliation and Arbitration Commission and the Commonwealth Industrial Court. The court's functions were later taken over by the Federal Court, a transformation that allowed the government to sideline those Industrial Court judges whom it disliked. The Commission later underwent a further name change, primarily so that the government could get rid of one particular deputy president, Justice Jim Staples (see chapter 8).

Decisions by the High Court helped determine the way in which the whole superior court system in Australia was to develop. Through the 1960s, 1970s and 1980s there was considerable discussion among politicians, lawyers and judges about the development of a unified court system in Australia. Generally it was agreed that this unity should be obtained through the creation of a new court of appeal sitting above the level of the State Supreme Courts and hearing appeals from them. It would be made up of judges appointed by the States, from among existing Supreme Court judges. The Commonwealth resisted these proposals, partly because it saw for the Commonwealth-created Federal Court a role of increasing importance. The High Court boosted the Federal Court's prospects with a series of decisions that allowed the Federal Court to hear cases which otherwise would have been taken to State courts. The High Court also broadened the reach of federal jurisdiction. Armed with these decisions, the Commonwealth government was able to negotiate a new arrangement with the States. To eliminate multiple actions in different jurisdictions, the Commonwealth and the States agreed to 'cross-vesting' laws, which allowed the Federal Court to hear State matters and the State courts to hear most federal matters, the courts themselves determining which court should hear a particular case and having the power to dispatch the case to another court where appropriate. These developments killed off the proposals for the unified system, though a recent decision by the High Court in *Gould v. Brown* (1998) 72 ALJR 375 (see chapter 7) which approved the cross-vesting legislation by a bare statutory majority (3–3) suggests further changes will need to be made.

To categorise the political effects of the High Court's decisions in the manner outlined above is to introduce a somewhat artificial series of distinctions. Any one decision of the Court may have political significance across a broad range of political, social and economic institutions. The central section of this book focuses on particular policy areas where the Court has made politically significant decisions, and looks at the impact those decisions have had. Chapter 2 looks at the Court's decisions affecting Aboriginal people and their claims to native title; chapter 3 looks at the Court's record on fundamental rights and freedoms, including its recent discovery of implied rights; chapter 4 looks at the impact of the Court's decisions on the financial and political independence of the States. Chapter 5 examines the way various constitutional provisions have been utilised to create for the Commonwealth a power to enforce a wide range of environmental policies; chapter 6 looks at statutory interpretation in a non-constitutional area—taxation; chapter 7 looks at the way the Court has interpreted the corporations power. Chapter 8 examines the Court's interpretation of the limited grant of constitutional power to the Commonwealth over conciliation and arbitration; chapter 9 looks at section 92's guarantee of freedom of interstate trade and commerce. In the section devoted to Australian institutions, chapter 10 is concerned with the Court's role in the development of Australian independence and nationhood; chapter 11 deals with the relationship between the courts, parliament and the executive; chapter 12 deals with constitutional reform. Chapter 13 looks specifically at the political role of the High Court and the way in which the Court goes about its job of interpreting the Constitution. The concluding chapter briefly considers some aspects of the political functioning of the High Court.

THE FOUNDATIONS OF THE HIGH COURT

That the High Court's decisions should on occasions have significant political overtones is not surprising. The Court was partly modelled on the US Supreme Court, though that court's jurisdiction is far more limited than the High Court's as it does not act as an ultimate appeal court for State courts other than in federal matters. The US Supreme Court had been in existence for almost a century when the Australian constitution-makers began their work, and political controversy had dogged much of that history.

There was little opposition in the Conventions of the 1890s to the creation of an Australian superior court based on the United States model. There was some dispute over whether the court should be created in the constitutional document, or whether the document should outline the court's mandate leaving its formation to the parliament. The latter method was chosen, but those at the Conventions thought that the creation of the High Court was not a task the parliament could long delay, because of the clear importance they placed on it. During the Conventions the aspect of the chapter on the judiciary which caused the most problems concerned the role of the Privy Council. Many of the delegates wanted appeals to the Privy Council from the State courts and from the High Court to be completely abolished. A minority (supported by most of the colonial chief justices) wanted untrammelled appeal rights. The numbers shifted from Convention to Convention, the final wording reflecting a willingness to permit appeals only in significant cases of national importance. But this was not an issue that the British government was prepared to leave for the determination of the Australians. The Colonial Secretary, Joseph Chamberlain, supported by the Law Officers, was intent on protecting British investors, who thought their interests could not be left in the hands of colonial judges. The Australian draft was amended to allow private litigants to take appeals to the Privy Council, and to allow a wide range of appeals from the High Court to the Privy Council. This rewriting in London of the Australian Constitution was resented back in Australia, and within a few years the Court and the parliament began what turned out to be an 80-year campaign to eliminate all forms of appeal to the Privy

Council. In 1907 the Judiciary Act was amended to give the High Court exclusive (of the States) jurisdiction in constitutional cases that involved a dispute between the Commonwealth and a State over the boundary of their powers. This meant that appeals in these constitutional matters could not be taken directly from the Supreme Courts to the Privy Council. They could be appealed from the High Court only with the High Court's consent, and the High Court's policy almost invariably was not to give that consent. Over the next twenty or so years, the High Court ruled at least three times that this device was valid. The abolition of appeals to the Privy Council was not completed until the 1970s and 1980s, when the States were finally persuaded to agree to legislation abolishing appeals from the State courts to the Privy Council (see chapter 10).

Despite the high hopes of the members of the Conventions, the members of the first parliament were extremely reluctant to bring the High Court into being. There was no direct imperative to do so in section 71 of the Constitution, which states:

> The judicial power of the Commonwealth shall be vested in a Federal Supreme Court, to be called the High Court of Australia, and in such other federal courts as the Parliament creates, and in such other courts as it invests with federal jurisdiction. The High Court shall consist of a Chief Justice, and so many other Justices, not less than two, as the Parliament prescribes.

The implication was clear enough, however: the parliament should create the High Court of Australia. It was reluctant to do so mainly, if what the politicians said at the time correctly represents their beliefs, because of the money it would cost and because it was not strictly necessary. The proposal to establish the Court was criticised in the press, particularly in Melbourne, as a 'splendid luxury', and lawyers were foremost among its critics. But, as the attorney-general, Alfred Deakin, explained to the House of Representatives, this was not a court for the benefit merely of lawyers:

> It is a fundamental proposition for a structural creation which is the necessary and essential complement of a federal Constitution

> . . . Indeed, although it relates to legal machinery, the purposes to be served by that machinery are but in a fractional sense legal, are in the main general, and in a very particular sense, political—affecting directly not only the businesses and bosoms of our population, but also the representatives of the people in both Chambers of this Parliament; affecting directly the Executive of this country; affecting in fact, every portion of that Constitution of which this court is created to be the guardian [Hansard, p. 10963, 18 March 1902].

Deakin, conscious of the opposition to the proposal and the need to win support for it, did not push for an immediate decision. The Judiciary Bill to which he spoke at great length on 18 March 1902 was not brought on for debate until the following year, on 9 June, with some amendments. Two days later, after an extensive debate, the second reading was agreed to (with a majority of nine). The debate in committee continued for many days and involved substantial changes to Deakin's original proposals, some of them being carried over Deakin's objections. Nevertheless, the measure eventually went through the House and the Senate, and became law on 27 August 1903. Griffith, Barton and O'Connor were appointed as the first judges of the Court four weeks later, after Barton had resigned as prime minister and O'Connor had resigned as Senate leader. The court began sitting early in October 1903.

Deakin's perception of the political function that the Court would serve was not generally shared by his parliamentary colleagues. In later years the Court attracted political attention mainly when it made a decision which greatly disturbed politicians from one side of politics or another, and its potential political significance was acknowledged at times when there were vacancies to be filled. Mostly, however, the court operated in a legal cocoon. Until 1980 it was an itinerant court, sitting in all the State capitals as its business required. But its acquisition of a 'home' in the national capital gave it more public exposure. Sir Garfield Barwick, as Chief Justice, persuaded the Whitlam and Fraser governments to build an imposing structure to house the Court within the national capital's parliamentary triangle. He anticipated that with the opening of the new Court building public interest in and awareness of the Court and its activities were likely to change. For one thing, it meant that the Court building joined the list of Canberra's tourist attractions, and the Court's sittings became part of the extravaganza that the tourists could witness. For another, it meant that newspapers could assign permanent correspondents to cover the work of the Court, instead of having to rely on different reporters in different cities to provide occasional reports about its work. Before 1980 it was not uncommon for the Court to hear a case in one city and hand down its judgment in that case in another, making it unlikely that a reporter would have any knowledge of the significance of any particular issues, other than what could be gleaned from the judgments themselves. And public understanding was not assisted by the practice of the Court which permits individual Justices to write separate judgments. There need be no 'majority' judgment and in some cases it may be difficult to work out precisely what the Court has decided. For most of the media, trying to understand what the High Court was doing has been too difficult, or not sufficiently rewarding.

But no matter how abstruse and formidable the legal forms and processes may be or seem, it remains true, as Deakin predicted, that the High Court plays an important political role. The Constitution often requires the High Court, as a court of law, to solve problems which are 'not so much legal as political, social or economic' (as the Privy Council put it in *Bank of NSW v. The Commonwealth* (1949) 79 CLR 497, at 639). Unfortunately the Court rarely acknowledges that it plays such a role.

Part II

Problem areas

2

MABO: THE NATIVE TITLE REVOLUTION

The High Court's decision in the 1992 *Mabo* case can be likened to the imposition of a peace treaty on the winning side in a war that had lasted more than two centuries. In the minds of some critics, what the Court did was suggestive of revolutionary politics rather than the law. Undoubtedly the decision had an enormous political impact, its after-effects dominating political debate even six years later. The High Court achieved for at least some Aboriginal people what the political process would never have given them—the possibility of establishing their native title over some lands. It provided all Aboriginal people with legal recognition of the fact of their prior occupation of Australia, a fact the courts had previously rejected.

Since 1788, when the English colonists took possession of Port Jackson and began to assume sovereignty over the whole Australian continent, any 'rights' possessed by the Aboriginal people whose ancestors had occupied the land for possibly 50 000 years were largely ignored. Although successive British governments urged colonial governors to treat Aboriginal people fairly, invariably they were moved from their lands as the various colonies expanded. Some resisted. But resistance was generally met with wholesale slaughter. Aboriginal people were cleared from Tasmania by force. After 100 years of European settlement the indigenous population was largely restricted to areas of desert and to the tropical north of the country, where many were employed in the pastoral industry. Official government policy looked forward to their assimilation into the Australian community. To this end scores of thousands of 'half-caste' children were taken from their Aboriginal mothers and adopted out to European parents, thousands of kilometres away from their natural parents. It was only in the 1950s that some Aboriginal people—with the active assistance of a relatively small number of politicians and student activists—began campaigning for Aboriginal rights, reflecting on a much smaller scale the civil rights movement in the United States. In that country, civil rights were secured primarily through the courts, beginning with the decision of the US Supreme Court in 1954 in *Brown v. Board of Education* (1954) 347 US 483, which led to the desegregation of schools. In the absence of an Australian Bill of Rights, no similar result could be achieved here. The Australian political campaign's first achievement was federal government approval for a referendum to remove one discriminatory section of the Constitution (which prevented Aborigines from being counted as part of the population) and for an amendment to a section so as to allow the federal parliament to pass 'special' laws for the Aboriginal race. Initially the Menzies government and then the Holt government resisted the second of these proposals. However, it emerged that there was considerable public support for an amendment proposed by a Liberal backbencher, which would have outlawed all racial discrimination. The Holt government decided this went too far, and opted for the 'special' laws race power. That proposed constitutional change was approved by more than 90 per cent of the Australian population at a referendum in 1967.

Little action followed until the election of the Whitlam government at the end of 1972. The Holt, Gorton and McMahon governments were exceedingly reluctant to use the Commonwealth's new powers directly to help the Aboriginal people. The Commonwealth provided increasing amounts of money for Aborigines, both directly through its own programs and by means of grants to the States and the Northern Territory. But it did nothing to interfere with the administration by the States of their Aboriginal reserves and their general administration of Aboriginal policies. It was not until 1974 that the Commonwealth established a special fund to begin to meet the most pressing of Aboriginal demands—for land. It took up the issue of Aboriginal land rights within the territories where it had legislative power (relevantly, the Northern Territory), and introduced legislation to provide for Aboriginal land rights over specified kinds of leasehold and Crown land. The legislation was not passed until 1976, by which time the Fraser government was in power. A second important piece of legislation was the 1975 Racial Discrimination Act (RDA), which gave force as domestic law throughout Australia to the international convention of the elimination of all forms of racial discrimination.

The RDA was tested as a result of a decision by the Bjelke-Petersen government in Queensland to refuse to allow the transfer of a pastoral lease to the Commonwealth Aboriginal Land Fund Commission. The Commission had contracted to buy the land in 1975, but the sale was subject to the transfer of the lease being approved by the relevant minister. He refused to do this, in accordance with a Queensland government policy to view unfavourably proposals to acquire 'large areas of additional freehold or leasehold land for development by Aboriginal people or Aboriginal groups in isolation'. John Koowarta, one of the Aboriginal people who persuaded the Commission to buy the land and who would have been one of those who used it, brought an action to overturn the minister's decision because it breached two provisions of the RDA. Queensland sought to have the RDA declared invalid.

The Court, by a 4–3 majority, decided in *Koowarta v. Bjelke-Petersen* (1982) 153 CLR 168 that the RDA was valid and that the minister's decision breached its provisions. The RDA's validity rested on the Commonwealth's external affairs power (because it put into effect an international treaty). The Court rejected the argument that its validity was also supported by the race power. This was because the RDA applied to people of all races—it was not a special law for a particular race. Nevertheless, the RDA was later to turn out to be of crucial importance to Aboriginal and Torres Strait Islander people in their attempts to obtain land rights.

The Northern Territory Land Rights legislation was a constant source of High Court litigation from the time of its enactment, with the Northern Territory government joining private landowners in resisting the granting of substantial areas of land to Aboriginal people who had established the requisite ties with the land. But the High Court was essentially restricted to interpreting the words of the particular piece of legislation. It did not have the opportunity to rule on any claim to land by Aboriginal people based on the common law.

That issue had arisen in 1971, when Justice Blackburn in the Northern Territory Supreme Court held (in *Milirrpum v. Nabalco Pty Ltd* (1971) 17 FLR 141) that the general law recognised no title in Aboriginal people holding land under traditional tenure. His decision was based on the conclusion that Australia was *terra nullius*, not a settled country, when Britain established its sovereignty. An attempt to challenge this view was rejected by the High Court in a subsequent case (*Coe v. Commonwealth of Australia* (1979) 24 ALR 111) when the Court by a 2–2 statutory majority denied the propriety of a statement of claim which sought to raise this and other issues. The minority thought the Court should have heard a claim that New South Wales was a conquered territory rather than a settled colony of the Crown.

The issue arose directly, however, in a claim brought in the High Court in 1982 by Eddie Mabo and two other members of the Meriam people, who sought declarations that the Meriam people were entitled to the three islands which they had occupied before the islands were annexed to Queensland in 1879. Before the facts in the case could be tried (through remittal to a judge of the Queensland Supreme Court) the Queensland parliament passed the Queensland Coast Islands Declaratory Act, which declared that when these and other islands were annexed all rights were acquired by the Crown in right of Queensland, and any land rights of the inhabitants were extinguished. The legislation was intended to 'deem' that those rights which might otherwise have survived annexation in 1879 did not survive, and for the purposes of 1985 were deemed never to have survived. This attempt at retrospective removal of land rights was considered by the High Court in the first Mabo case, *Mabo v. Queensland [No 1]*

(1988) 166 CLR 186, which by a 4–3 majority held the law invalid because it was inconsistent with the RDA.

In *Mabo v. Queensland [No. 2]* (1991–92) 171 CLR 1, the Court, by a 6–1 majority, found that two of the claimants (but not Mabo himself) had established legitimate claims to land on Murray Island which their families had occupied since before the annexation of the island. The majority decided that native title to land in Australia survived the Crown's acquisition of sovereignty. Native title could be extinguished, however, by the alienation of land through the grant of an interest that was wholly inconsistent with the continuing right to enjoy native title (such as the grant of freehold). A grant which was partly inconsistent would extinguish native title to the extent of the inconsistency. Three members of the Court would have held that Aboriginal people were entitled to compensation for the past and any future extinguishment of native title. The long and complex judgments were summarised in a statement agreed to by the Court, which appeared in the brief joint judgment of Chief Justice Mason and Justice McHugh where they said in part, 'the common law of this country recognises a form of native title which, in the cases where it has not been extinguished, reflects the entitlement of the indigenous inhabitants, in accordance with their laws or customs, to their traditional lands . . .'.

Land tenure in Australia is the responsibility of the States and Territories. Although the Commonwealth has the power to interfere with the way Territories use their powers—and did so when it passed the Aboriginal Land Rights (Northern Territory) Act in 1976—it has no direct power over land in the States. The Crown which has sovereignty is the State Crown. This meant that the States could have abolished native title within their boundaries through legislation and executive actions. However, the High Court pointed out that such actions could not be inconsistent with Commonwealth laws—in particular the Racial Discrimination Act, as it had already determined in *Mabo [No 1]*.

The nature of the native title which the Court recognised was not spelt out in any detail. This was because its nature depended on the laws and customs of the particular people. Native title continued to exist only for as long as the people maintained their contact with the land and their traditional laws and customs, and it could not be transferred to anyone else.

The High Court's decision in *Mabo* created comparatively little political comment at the time. Nor did it feature in the campaign for the federal election which was held about nine months later. It was assumed that the Keating government would be defeated at that election, and that the new Coalition government would then act to minimise any significant impact of the decision, perhaps by removing the fetters of the RDA and allowing each of the States to determine what to do about native title.

Keating, however, won the election and then set about drawing up legislation which would ensure that native title was further protected by Commonwealth law and establishing a national system that would allow for the determination of native title claims. The debate at that point became bitter and highly politicised. Miners and pastoralists, supported by the National and Liberal Parties, wanted native title rights to be restricted or even eliminated. The debate in the Senate was the longest on record to that point. And the High Court came in for a great deal of criticism over its decision.

The Court that made the *Mabo* decision could not have been characterised as radical in any sense. Chief Justice Sir Anthony Mason had been a member of the High Court since 1972, when he was appointed by the McMahon Liberal government. He had previously served for three years as a member of the New South Wales Court of Appeal and before that was Commonwealth solicitor-general to a series of federal Liberal governments between 1964 and 1969. He was regarded on his appointment as relatively conservative, though he could better be described as a 'small l liberal' during the period he was Chief Justice, from 1987 to 1995. The principal judgment in the *Mabo* case was written by Sir Gerard Brennan, who later succeeded Sir Anthony as Chief Justice. Justice Brennan was appointed to the Federal Court in 1977 and to the High Court in 1981, by the Fraser Liberal government. He was educated in Queensland, where his father had been a Labor politician before being appointed to the Supreme Court. His son, Father Frank Brennan, was a Jesuit priest who had taken an active part in promoting Aboriginal causes, including land rights.

Justice Brennan's judgment was also approved by Justice Michael McHugh, a Labor appointee to the High Court, whose wife was a member of the federal Labor government. Justice McHugh was, however, one of the more conservative members of the High Court, a black-letter lawyer.

Justice John Toohey was another Labor appointee, who had originally been appointed to the Federal Court by a Liberal government. He had extensive knowledge of Aboriginal peoples and their traditions, having worked as a lawyer for the Aboriginal Legal Service in his home State, Western Australia, and then been the Aboriginal Land Commissioner responsible for determining land claims under the Northern Territory Land Aboriginal Act.

The most radical views in the *Mabo* case were expressed by Justices Deane and Gaudron, who not only believed that native title existed but also considered that Aboriginal people should be compensated for past dispossession. Justice Deane was another Liberal appointee who had previously served on the Federal Court, and again was regarded as having very conservative views. However, in his last few years on the Court he became much more radical, supporting the idealistic views he later expressed when he became Governor-General and adopting a relatively activist approach to his judicial work. Justice Mary Gaudron was a Labor appointee, who had previously been solicitor-general to the New South Wales Labor government and who had been a member of the federal Arbitration Commission.

The dissenting member of the Court was Sir Daryl Dawson, who had been Victorian solicitor-general before being appointed by the Fraser Liberal government to the High Court. He was staunchly conservative and the one consistent states-rights member of the Court in the early 1990s. His view was that native title rights which may have existed were not recognised by the Crown and had been extinguished on annexation.

The Keating government's Native Title Act, which came into effect on 1 January 1994, created a Native Title Tribunal to receive claims and required miners and others whose actions would impact on native title to become involved in a negotiation process with native title claimants. More importantly, it set up a system that prevented the States and Territories using their powers over land tenure to diminish or destroy native title from 1 July 1993. The law was based, in constitutional terms, on the power to make special laws for the people of any race. It was challenged by the Western Australian government which, prior to the passage of the Native Title Act, passed a law which replaced native title in Western Australia with another form of title which was more amenable to ministerial control.

The Court, in a unanimous decision, held that the Western Australian Act was invalid both because it was inconsistent with section 10 of the Racial Discrimination Act and because it was inconsistent with the Native Title Act. It held that the Native Title Act was valid, other than one section which sought to give statutory force to the common law in relation to native title.

The High Court gave that decision in March 1995. In mid-1993, following the *Mabo* decision but before the Native Title legislation came before the parliament, the Wik people lodged a native title claim with the Federal Court, basing their claim on the common law. Eventually, in January 1996, Justice Drummond decided on preliminary questions of law that their claim could not succeed. He held that because the land claimed had at some time been the subject of pastoral leases (though one of those leases had never been taken up and the Wik had never been removed from the land) any native title had been extinguished. His ruling was in accordance with the views of Justice Brennan in *Mabo [No. 2]*, and the opinion of the federal parliament, but not specifically provided for in the Native Title Act. An appeal against Justice Drummond's decision was removed into the High Court and on 23 December 1996 it decided by a 4–3 margin that native title was not necessarily extinguished by the grant of a pastoral lease because those pastoral leases did not grant their holders exclusive possession of the land.

By this time, the membership of the High Court had changed. Sir Anthony Mason had retired on reaching the age of 70, and Sir William Deane had become Governor-General. The new judges were William Gummow, who had been a fairly conservative judge on the Federal Court, and Michael Kirby, who had been appointed by the New South Wales Labor government as president of the New South Wales Court of Appeal and who was regarded as relatively radical. The majority in the *Wik* case comprised Justices Toohey, Gaudron, Gummow and Kirby, with Chief Justice Brennan and Justices Dawson and McHugh dissenting.

The majority made it clear that the rights of pastoral lease holders depend on the terms of their lease and on the relevant State land legislation. Whether native title rights are extinguished has to be determined by looking at the specific circumstances of each lease. But if there is any inconsistency between native title and the rights of the leaseholder, the native title 'must yield'.

This decision caused immediate political uproar. The Court was denounced by conservative politicians, lawyers, pastoralists and miners. It was in this context that deputy prime minister and National Party leader Tim Fischer promised that the next three appointments his government made to the High Court would be 'capital C conservatives'. The States were even more upset by the decision. Queensland, under both Labor and Coalition governments, had, since the passage of the Native Title Act, acted on the presumption that pastoral leases had extinguished native title. More than half the State was now said to be 'up for grabs' (though that claim ignored the fact that there was no Aboriginal access or habitation on most pastoral leases). Of more direct concern was that the State had not complied with the provisions of the Native Title Act in issuing more than 4600 mining tenures between the beginning of 1995 and the time of the *Wik* decision almost two years later and decisions in relation to hundreds of pastoral leases had also been taken. The State could have been subjected to huge damages and compensation, and the various leases could have been invalidated.

John Howard, who had become prime minister early in 1996, promised to 'fix' the *Wik* decision. He proposed a 10-point plan to change the Native Title Act, which would validate all that the States had wrongly done in 1995 and 1996. There were also changes to reduce the ability of Aboriginal people to make claims, and a virtual upgrading of pastoral leases to allow them to be used for agricultural purposes (allowing some future extinguishment).

According to Tim Fischer, the plan would deliver 'bucket loads' of extinguishment. It barely satisfied Queensland's National Party premier, Rob Borbidge, who would have preferred complete extinguishment. But that would have been too costly, financially and politically. It was, nevertheless, the solution touted by the One Nation Party of Pauline Hanson.

But Howard, like Keating before him, did not have control over the Senate. His legislation was amended by the opposition and the parties and independents controlling the balance of power. Despite Howard's threats that he would hold a double dissolution election to resolve the matter, the Australian Democrats were prepared to grant him only about 85 per cent of his 10-point plan. He finally compromised with one of the independents, Senator Brian Harradine, one of whose advisors was Father Frank Brennan. The consequence of the Harradine intervention was that Howard achieved slightly more than 90 per cent of his plan. The compromise was reached after the Queensland State election in June 1998, an election that resulted in a defeat for the Borbidge government and a huge loss of conservative votes to One Nation. Howard recognised that he would probably lose a double dissolution and that native title was not winning him any votes: the abolitionists supported One Nation and those who sympathised with the Aboriginal people were turning from the Liberals to Labor.

The package that finally passed the federal parliament will come before the High Court again, as will dozens of other aspects of native title. Because native title has both legislative and common law aspects, the High Court will be called upon to resolve extremely difficult legal issues which will throw up political problems for whatever governments are in power, nationally and in the States. The High Court's critics complain that it changed the common law when it recognised the existence of native title. That is true, though its decision was in accord with decisions by courts in other common law countries with indigenous populations—Canada, New Zealand and the United States. It is also true that the Court's decision in *Mabo* forced the federal government to take legislative action in a field that it had largely avoided (the Hawke government had wanted to tackle native title but had been persuaded not to do so in the late 1980s by the then Labor government in Western Australia). But the High Court could not sidestep the issue when it was directly raised by Eddie Mabo. The Court, unlike the politicians, had to make a decision, one which would force the issue on to the political agenda. That it was a politically divisive issue was not a consequence of anything the Court did.

The stolen children

Aboriginal people were quite unsuccessful in their attempts to obtain compensation for the 'stolen children' generation either from the courts or from the political process. These were the children who were removed from their parents by officials and fostered out to white parents many thousands of kilometres away and completely out of touch with their true families. The issue was examined in great detail by the Human Rights and Equal Opportunity Commission, which in May 1997 published a report, 'Bringing them home: report by the national inquiry into the separation of Aboriginal and Torres Strait Islander children from their families'. The report concluded that from approximately 1910 until 1970 between one in ten and one in three indigenous children were forcibly removed from their families and communities. Not one indigenous family escaped the effects of forcible removal, and most families had been affected in one or more generations by the removal of one or more children.

The report consisted primarily of stories of individual children who were taken from their families. It generated tears among hardened MPs and a great deal of political heat, not least because the prime minister, John Howard, refused to make an apology on behalf of the Australian people for the policies which had caused such hardship to Aboriginal people.

A legal action by some of the stolen children, and by one of the mothers whose child was taken, was launched in 1995 and a series of preliminary questions of law decided by the High Court in July 1997. The case was argued before the 'Bringing them home' report was published. The Court found that what had happened to the children was legal, though by varying majorities on a range of issues that were raised. It said the Commonwealth did have the power to make the various Ordinances which allowed the children to be taken from their parents. Under the Aboriginals Ordinance of 1918 the Chief Protector of Aboriginals, and later the Director of Native Affairs, was allowed to undertake the care, custody or control of any Aboriginal or 'half-caste' person if it was necessary to do so or was in the interests of that person. The Chief Protector had the power to have any Aboriginal person kept within a reserve or Aboriginal institution, sent to an institution or 'placed in the service of suitable people'. As Chief Justice Brennan observed, 'The practice of enforced separations is now seen to be unacceptable as a general policy. However, the erroneous formation of an opinion by the Chief Protector which purported to enliven the exercise of power conferred by [the regulations] does not deny the validity [of the laws].'

Most members of the Court rejected submissions that the Commonwealth's constitutional power did not allow the law to be made because of various implied rights, guarantees, immunities or freedoms. In particular, the law was not invalid because of an alleged requirement of legal equality, or because of a 'right' to freedom of movement and association, or because of a supposed conflict with the genocide convention, or because of an alleged conflict with the provision in the Constitution guaranteeing freedom of religion.

The Court's consideration of the argument about genocide raised considerable interest because of the use of that word in the Human Rights Commission report. Essentially all the members of the Court agreed that the Ordinance did not authorise the commission of acts which had the intention of bringing about genocide. Justice Toohey, for example, stressed that the Genocide Convention in its definition of genocide refers to a number of acts 'committed with intent to destroy, in whole or in part' various groups. But there was nothing in the Ordinance 'which would justify a conclusion that it authorised acts "with intent to destroy, in whole or in part" the plaintiffs' racial group'.

Secret women's business

The High Court twice became involved in the Hindmarsh Island Bridge affair, a dispute which gained notoriety because of claims by a group of Aboriginal women that the construction of a bridge should be halted under provisions of the Aboriginal and Torres Strait Islander Heritage Protection Act. They refused to detail their claims in public, claiming it involved 'secret women's business'. A Royal Commission in South Australia found that the claims were fraudulent. The Labor Minister for Aboriginal Affairs, in accordance with the provisions of the Act, appointed a 'reporter', Professor Cheryl Saunders, to investigate the claims and make a report to him. The Federal Court, on administrative law grounds, struck down the report. The minister then appointed the president of the Administrative Appeals Tribunal, Justice Jane Mathews, to conduct the investigation. Her appointment was challenged in the High Court, which by a 6–1 majority held that it was invalid, on the ground that the function required of her was constitutionally incompatible with the independence required of a member of the federal judiciary (*Wilson v. Minister for Aboriginal and Torres Strait Islander Affairs* (1997) 189 CLR 1).

The Howard government, which came to office in 1996, was committed to allowing the construction of the bridge to proceed. It introduced legislation to exempt the area where the bridge was to be built from coverage by the Heritage Protection Act. The Bill was passed at a time when the Howard government was having difficulty getting its 10-point plan to change the Native Title Act through the parliament. The Aboriginal women then challenged the validity of the Hindmarsh Island Bridge Act, in part to see if the High Court's decision would indicate whether changes to the Native Title Act which diminished the rights of Aboriginal people would be unconstitutional. On this point—whether a special law for Aboriginal people which was detrimental to their interests could be passed by the parliament—the Court was unhelpful. Two Justices did not decide the constitutional issue at all and the other four split equally over it. But the Court held that the legislation was valid because it was merely a partial repeal of the earlier Heritage Protection Act.

The decision in the *Hindmarsh Island Bridge* case, *Kartinyeri v. The Commonwealth* (1998) 72 ALJR 722, meant that any changes made by the Howard government to the Native Title Act would be challenged. The challenge would be based on two points: on the constitutional issue of whether the power, under the special law provision in the Constitution, could be used in a manner that removed rights under the common law, and on whether some of the provisions in the legislation were invalid because they conflicted with provisions of the Racial Discrimination Act which was preserved by the changes made in the Senate to the 10-point plan.

3

Rights, implied and otherwise

Those who criticised the High Court's decision in the *Mabo* and *Wik* cases were equally vociferous in denouncing the High Court's decision in the series of cases in which it decided that a constitutional right to political free speech was to be implied from various provisions of the Constitution establishing representative government. The highwater mark of these decisions was reached in *Theophanous v. Herald & Weekly Times Ltd* (1994) 182 CLR 104 and *Stephens v. West Australian Newspapers Ltd* (1994) 182 CLR 211, where the Court held that the common law and statutory law in the States and Territories was to be supplanted by new rules (which the majority decision detailed) in defamation actions involving State as well as federal politicians. The Court in *Lange v. the Australian Broadcasting Corporation* (1997) 189 CLR 520 subsequently modified its views somewhat, but, in a unanimous judgment of the whole Court, confirmed the existence of the implied right and of the need for the common law and statutory defamation laws in the States and Territories to conform with the minimum requirements of the constitutional freedom.

The Court in *Lange* said that 'freedom of communication on matters of government and politics is an indispensable incident of that system of representative government which the Constitution creates by directing that the members of the House of

Representatives and the Senate shall be "directly chosen by the people" of the Commonwealth and the States, respectively'.

The Court said that sections 7 and 24 (which use the phrase 'directly chosen') and related sections of the Constitution 'necessarily protect that freedom of communication between the people concerning political or government matters which enables the people to exercise a free and informed choice as electors. Those sections do not confer personal rights on individuals. Rather they preclude the curtailment of the protected freedom by the exercise of legislative or executive power.' The Court made it clear that the implied freedom was not limited to election periods, and extended to cover all actions by government, public servants and other authorities for which ministers were responsible. It also covered the discussion of government or politics at the State, Territory and local government level as well as at the Commonwealth level. However, the freedom was not absolute. It did not prevent laws being made which were compatible with the maintenance of the prescribed system of representative and responsible government, provided also that the laws were reasonably appropriate and adapted to achieving that legitimate object.

The Court drew a distinction between the freedom of communication it was discussing and the right of freedom of speech contained in the first amendment to the United States Constitution. The Court said, 'Unlike the First Amendment . . . which has been interpreted to confer private rights, our Constitution contains no express right of freedom of communication or expression.' The Court expanded the defence of qualified privilege under the common law, holding that a person could not get damages for the publication of material where the publisher establishes that it was unaware of the falsity of the matter, did not behave recklessly in publishing, and the publication was reasonable in the circumstances.

This is, very deliberately, a far cry from the American freedom of speech position, but it is likely to free up the discussion of political issues in Australia and reduce the damages which politicians collect from errant newspapers and broadcasters. In the past, defamation actions have been a notorious way for some politicians to supplement their incomes with a tax-free capital gain—some have named holiday homes, swimming pools or tennis courts after the particular newspaper or proprietor who funded the acquisition through a careless (or perhaps deliberate) defamation. This may help to explain why politicians have been among the severest critics of the Court's decisions in the *Nationwide News* and *Australian Capital Television* cases where the new freedom of political communication was first enunciated, and in the later cases where it was developed.

In *Nationwide News Pty Ltd v. Wills* (1992) 177 CLR 1, the Court unanimously decided that a section of the Industrial Relations Act which created an offence of contempt of the Industrial Relations Commission was invalid. A journalist had been prosecuted for an article headlined 'Advance Australia Fascist' in which he indulged in a virulent attack on the integrity and independence of the Arbitration Commission and its members. A section of the Industrial Relations Act purported to provide the Commission with the same kind of protection as 'contempt of court' laws provide for true courts. However, it went a good deal further by making it an offence to insult a member of the Commission or bring a member into disrepute.

Several members of the High Court decided the case on the basis that such a law was beyond the power of the Commonwealth, because the Commonwealth power to make laws for 'conciliation and arbitration' did not provide power to make a law infringing freedom of speech. Others relied on what they said was the doctrine of representative government contained in the Constitution to imply a freedom of communication about the performance of political functions, which limited the scope of the conciliation and arbitration power.

Australian Capital Television Pty Ltd v. The Commonwealth (1992) 177 CLR 106, which was handed down at the same time as the *Nationwide News* case, concerned legislation which was intended to restrict the broadcasting of political advertising during federal, State and local government elections. One aim of the law was to limit the cost—to political parties—of election campaigns. Four members of the Court—Chief Justice Mason and Justices Deane, Toohey and Gaudron—based their judgments invalidating the advertising ban legislation on an implied freedom of communication in relation to political matters arising from the principles of representative government which were enshrined in the Constitution. Justice McHugh thought the freedom arose directly from the provisions in the Constitution (sections 7 and 24) concerning elections. He did not accept the need to imply a general right of political communication. Justice Brennan thought there was such an implied right, but it was not offended by this law. Justice Dawson thought there was no such implication and that the law was valid.

The politicians had drafted the law in ignorance of the fact that the Commonwealth Constitution was about to be interpreted by the High Court as containing an implied protection of political free speech. Yet the existence of that implied freedom would not have necessarily meant that this law was invalid, and certainly did not prevent the development of a law which largely achieved the objective the politicians had in mind. The object of the law in prohibiting political advertising, as Justice Dawson noted, was not to withold information or to stifle discussion, but to reduce the burden otherwise imposed on the politicial parties of raising large sums in order to wage election campaigns by using the electronic media. The object was to reduce the possibility of corruption (brought about by the need to raise very large quantities of campaign finance) and, in Justice Dawson's view, to enhance rather than impair the democratic process. He referred briefly to the fact that television political advertising is more concerned with image than content. Perhaps a more significant criticism is that it is almost entirely negative—aiming to detroy opponents rather than promote policies. Justice Brennan took a similar view, saying it was both simplistic and erroneous to regard any limitation on political advertising as offensive to the Constitution.

Politicians were particularly annoyed at the decision in the *Australian Capital Television* case. They considered that the business of how elections should be conducted was of purely political concern—it was a patch solely reserved for politicians, on which judges should not tread (though the High Court may be involved in the aftermath of the electoral process, as the Court of Disputed Returns).

But although the political attack centred on the effect of the decisions, conservative lawyers were equally outraged because of the method adopted by the Court in reaching those decisions. They did not believe it was right for the Court to establish new rights by drawing implications from the Constitution. As Professor Greg Craven, the Dean of Law at the University of Notre Dame Australia, wrote (1997b, p. 9):

> . . . the Court simply has begun the process of inventing appropriate rights, and purporting to 'imply' them from the Constitution . . . the rights thus created by the Court owe nothing to any genuine process of implication, not indeed to any process of interpretation, properly understood. Instead, they have as their true basis merely the belief of the Court that they should be part of the Constitution, rather than any interpretative conviction that they indeed are.

Justice Roddy Meagher (1998), a member of the New South Wales Court of Appeal, put it bluntly:

> 'Civil rights' do not exist except to the extent that they are manufactured out of thin air by the High Court, which acts like a sort of legal Doctor Coppelius, fashioning delicate and novel toys—and, one hopes, ephemeral toys at that.

The question of the way the Court should approach its task of interpreting statutes and the Constitution is discussed later, in chapter 13. The discussion here is more concerned with the decisions the Court has made about what rights Australians have as a consequence of living in a society governed according to a Constitution.

Chief Justice Mason said in the *Australian Capital Television* case (at 136):

> . . . it is difficult, if not impossible, to establish a foundation for the implication of general guarantees of fundamental rights and freedoms. To make such an implication would run counter to the prevailing sentiment of the framers [of the Constitution] that there was no need to incorporate a comprehensive Bill of Rights in order to protect the rights and freedoms of citizens.

> That sentiment was one of the unexpressed assumptions on which the Constitution was drafted.

He repeated the comments of earlier judges and commentators that the rights of individuals were secured through political power, not by putting them into the Constitution. Yet this traditional view does not do full justice to what actually happened at the Constitutional Conventions. The 1898 Convention considered a proposal by the Tasmanian Legislative Assembly which would have included as part of section 117 of the Constitution a provision identical to the 14th amendment of the United States Constitution, which prevents a State from depriving a person of life, liberty or property without due process of law, and would have given everyone within a State the equal protection of the law. Delegates debated the way this amendment in the United States had been intended to prevent discrimination against blacks after the American Civil War, and how in Australia it would affect discriminatory legislation against Chinese and others. Nevertheless, it was only narrowly defeated, in a vote of 23–19.

Despite Sir Anthony Mason's rejection of the implication of 'general guarantees of fundamental rights and freedoms' he concluded that freedom of communication was of vital importance. He said (at 140):

> The fundamental importance, indeed the essentiality, of freedom of communication, including freedom to criticise government action, in the system of modern representative government has been recognised by courts in many jurisdictions. They include Australia, England, the United States, Canada and the European Court of Human Rights.
>
> Freedom of communication in the sense just discussed is so indispensable to the efficacy of the system of representative government for which the Constitution makes provision that it is necessarily implied in the making of that provision.

The notion that implications about individual rights could be drawn from the Constitution had been pressed, unsuccessfully, by Justice Lionel Murphy. In *Miller v. TCN Channel Nine Pty Ltd* (1986) 161 CLR 556, Justice Murphy said, 'The Australian

Constitution must be interpreted against a background of responsible government and democratic principles generally. Implications should be made which would promote such principles, rather than those of arbitrary government and tyranny.' He catalogued a series of such rights (by reference to earlier cases), including the rule of law, a prohibition on slavery or serfdom, a prohibition on the infliction of cruel and unusual punishments, a prohibition on persons being tried and found guilty of criminal offences by a non-judicial body, and guarantees of free speech and other communications and freedom of movement.

Another way of reading rights into the Constitution is to see the Constitution as embodying basic common law rights. Justice Toohey, in a speech given in Darwin shortly after the *Nationwide News* decision, suggested that at some future time the Court might consider that fundamental common law liberties could be construed as part of the Constitution. A few months earlier he joined with Justice Deane in a judgment in *Leeth v. The Commonwealth* (1992) 174 CLR 455, where they said a 'doctrine of legal equality' was to be implied in the Constitution and they commented that it was 'the ordinary approach of the Constitution not to spell out the fundamental common law principles upon which it is structured'.

This approach was ridiculed by the then Minister for Justice, Senator Michael Tate, who in answer to a question without notice said he found it 'quite remarkable—breathtaking in fact—that a High Court Justice should speak of fundamental common law liberties as though they were the foundation for the judgment the other day' (he was referring to the *Nationwide News* and *Australian Capital Television* cases). He said that representative government was never conferred by the common law judges, who did not even give people the right to vote. Nor did the common law protect religious dissenters, conscientious objectors or the right to privacy—all of which were rights created by parliament.

Senator Tate's comments were accurate enough, though two further observations are necessary to round out the relationship between the common law, parliament and civil rights. The first is that the common law is not static. It is forever changing, and is currently doing so quite quickly, influenced in part by the development of international law. It now recognises rights which it did not recognise a century or even a decade ago. Australia's common law, for example, now recognises native title. The second point is that such common law rights as do exist can be overturned by parliament. The only rights which parliament cannot destroy or ignore are those which are imbedded in the Constitution, directly or by implication.

Constitutional rights

Such rights as the Constitution does protect are scattered through the document. They are concerned with judicial process, discrimination based on residence (federal rights), freedom of trade and property rights, voting rights, and freedom of religion.

Judicial process

The most important of the rights, according to Justice Deane in *Street v. Queensland Bar Association* (1989) 168 CLR 461, is the guarantee that the citizen can be subjected to the exercise of Commonwealth judicial power only by courts established under the requirements of Chapter III of the Constitution. This means that people cannot be tried before administrative tribunals, but only before courts whose judges are appointed (originally for life, now until age 70) in such a way as to try to ensure their independence from government. Recent decisions of the High Court have applied this rule to defence personnel, who otherwise could have been tried by courts-martial. The High Court has now restricted the military courts to disciplinary matters, at least in time of peace. In *Polyukhovich v. The Commonwealth* (1991) 172 CLR 501, the *War Crimes* case, a majority of the Court ruled that parliament cannot usurp the judicial power of the Commonwealth by exercising that power in the form of legislation—a law would be invalid if it inflicted punishment on a specified person without a judicial trial.

The doctrine of the separation of powers also applies to the States, but only indirectly, because the State Constitutions do not have as rigid a separation of powers as that which the High Court has read into Chapter III of the Commonwealth Constitution. Nevertheless, the High Court, in *Kable v. Director of Public Prosecutions (NSW)* (1996) 189 CLR 51, ruled that the State Supreme Courts could not act in a way that was incompatible with the way a federal court under Chapter III had to act. This was because the Supreme Courts were invested with federal jurisdiction, and this affected their activities even when they were not exercising that jurisdiction. The case in which that issue arose involved legislation by New South Wales empowering the Supreme Court to make an order for the detention of a prisoner if it was satisfied that the person was more likely than not to commit a serious act of violence. The legislation was confined to the named person, Kable, but a similar law had previously been passed in Victoria, also providing for what was in effect preventive detention. Whether States can pass such laws in general remains an open question. What the High Court decided in Kable was that Supreme Courts could not be a party to such incarceration.

Of more general importance was a series of cases in which the High Court set out some requirements for a fair trial. In one sense, this right flows from an implication in the Constitution, a right to 'due process'. But the Court has taken a different route to establish the various 'fair trial' rights. The High Court is the ultimate court of appeal in criminal as well as civil matters in Australia. As such it has to decide whether a person's conviction is in accordance with law. It has always insisted that it has the power to overturn a conviction which is not 'fair', though what constitutes 'fairness' may vary over time.

In 1992 the Court, by a 5–2 majority, decided in *Dietrich v. The Queen* (1992) 177 CLR 292 that it was unfair to make a person charged with a serious criminal offence stand trial without legal representation. It decided that where an accused was poor, and did not have legal representation through no fault of his or her own, then except in exceptional circumstances the trial should be adjourned until legal representation is provided. The Court's view about what constituted fairness had changed in thirteen years. In *McInnis v. The Queen* (1979) 143 CLR 575, the Court by a 4–1 majority (Justice Murphy dissenting) held that it was not unfair in that case to refuse an adjournment to a person whose representation was withdrawn by a Legal Aid Commission on the day before the trial was to begin.

The Court's decision in *Dietrich* has resulted in it being strongly attacked by both federal and State politicians, particularly after 1996 when the federal government began slashing legal aid funds. Some of the States, particularly Victoria and South Australia, accepted the thrust of the High Court's decision, particularly when it decided in later cases that the ruling did not affect committal proceedings. However, the Commonwealth attorney-general, Daryl Williams QC, frequently criticised the decision, saying it 'lacked logic'. He said legal aid decisions were for the political branches of government, not for the courts. In 1998 he foreshadowed federal and State legislation to restrict the effect of the *Dietrich* principle.

Another important decision about the fair-trial process, which also had funding implications, was received less critically. In *McKinney & Judge v. The Queen* (1991) 171 CLR 468, the Court effectively attacked the practice of police verballing of suspects. It said that trial judges should warn juries that careful consideration should be given to the dangers involved in convicting an accused where substantially the only basis for finding that guilt had been established was an uncorroborated confession made to the police. In effect the Court required that police interviews with suspects should be videotaped or sound recorded. Some States and Territories had already adopted this procedure as a matter of law. The remainder quickly followed.

A decision in a criminal case which was less acceptable to the politicians was *Ridgeway v. The Queen* (1995) 184 CLR 19, where a majority of the Court decided that a trial judge could exclude evidence of an official who had acted illegally in order to trap the accused. In this case the illegality involved the importation of heroin, imported by police as part of an arrangement with officials in Malaysia. The Court rejected arguments that a defence of entrapment was available in Australia. It also ruled that it was not an abuse of process to bring proceedings against a person whose conviction would result from illegal conduct by officials. However, it said a trial judge had a discretion to reject evidence that was unlawfully procured. Following this decision, the Commonwealth parliament passed a law which allowed officials carrying out an entrapment to import prohibited drugs without breaking the law, thereby permitting their evidence to be used in prosecutions.

Although the High Court has been unable to detect many substantial rights of judicial process in the words of the Constitution, it has used the common law to erect some other barriers against the destruction of those rights associated in the United States with due process rights. Australian courts generally have the power to stay proceedings that are an abuse of process, whether such abuse results from excessive delay or otherwise. While endorsing this power, the Court has declined to say that there is a right to a 'speedy' trial, whether based on the common law or on the provisions of Magna Carta (see *Jago v. District Court (NSW)* (1989) 168 CLR 23). Essentially the test to be applied is one of fairness, and this is intended to take into account not only the interests of an accused person, but also the interests of the community generally. Similarly, the Court has also upheld the privileges of an accused person against self-incrimination (see *Hammond v. Commonwealth of Australia* (1982) 152 CLR 188) and legal professional privilege (*Baker v. Campbell* (1983) 153 CLR 52). But in all these cases the 'rights' which the courts have established can be overturned by Commonwealth or State legislation, so long as the legislation is clearly expressed in terms which the courts cannot overcome.

A right that has not been expanded by the High Court is the right to trial by jury, which is specifically included in the Constitution in section 80 which states, 'The trial on indictment of any offence against any law of the Commonwealth shall be by jury, and every such trial shall be held in the State where the offence was committed . . .' But this says far less than a quick reading might suggest. It does not guarantee trial by jury. It requires trial by jury only if there is an indictment. But there is nothing to stop the parliament providing for summary trials, that is, trials which are not by indictment and therefore not by a jury. And the parliament has created offences where trials would be summary and where people have been sentenced to gaol for twelve months, without the benefit of a jury trial, and has made laws providing for penalties up to life imprisonment where the accused are not to be tried by a jury. The High Court, with some notable dissenters along the way (Dr Evatt, Sir Owen Dixon, Lionel Murphy and Sir William Deane foremost among them), has stuck to its literal reading of the section. The restrictive construction of section 80, by ignoring substance in favour of form, made the prescription of trial by jury 'a hollow mockery which could be avoided by the stratagem of subjecting persons accused of even the most serious offences to summary trial by a magistrate', as Justice Deane said in *Street v. Queensland Bar Association*. Or, as Sir Garfield Barwick wrote in *Spratt v. Hermes* (1965) 111 CLR 226, 'whereas s. 80 might have been thought to be a great constitutional guarantee, it has been discovered to be a mere procedural provision'. Yet this mere procedural provision also prevents a person who is being tried by indictment from opting to be tried by judge alone, according to the High Court in *Brown v. The Queen* (1986) 64 ALR 161.

FEDERAL RIGHTS

A series of provisions in the Constitution prevents the Commonwealth from discriminating between people in different parts of the country when it imposes taxation, section 51(ii), offers bounties, section 51(iii), or levies customs and excise duties, sections 88 and 90. But the most important of these rights is contained in section 117, which says: 'A subject of the Queen, resident in any State, shall not be subject in any other State to any disability or discrimination which would not be equally applicable to him if he were a subject of the Queen resident in such other State.'

This too proved to be worthless, at least until 1989. The High Court in two decisions (in 1904 and 1973) allowed the section to be avoided in one case by the use of 'domicile' rather than residence as the means of imposing discrimination, and in the other by approving legislation which required a citizen of another State to have 'temporary' residence before benefiting from provisions of the State's legal system. The Court ruling in both those cases was concerned with the form of the legislation it was considering, rather than its substantive effect. The Court's decisions, inter alia, allowed Queensland to protect its barristers and solicitors from interstate competition. But in *Street v. Queensland Bar Association* the Court reversed those decisions. It decided that the States would no longer be able to pass laws or engage in administrative practices which gave preference to its own citizens over those from other States, or which discriminated against people from out of the State (except to require proper residential qualifications, for example, for voters in State elections).

Trade and property

The freedom of trade, commerce and intercourse guaranteed by section 92 was extended by the High Court to prevent the nationalisation by the Commonwealth of any interstate trader (for example the privately-owned banks) and had the effect of giving interstate traders advantages over those trading in a purely intrastate market. The guarantee in section 51(xxxi) that the Commonwealth could only acquire property 'on just terms' failed to prevent State or Territory governments from acquiring property on other than just terms: a State could, for example, nationalise all the coal fields within its boundaries without offering compensation to their owners. Nor could the guarantee be used to prevent the Commonwealth imposing taxes or penalties, and thus 'acquiring property'.

The High Court gave section 92 and section 51(xxxi) a very special position in the galaxy of Commonwealth powers. All other Commonwealth powers were made subject to them. Property could not be acquired by the Commonwealth using some other head of power which avoided the 'just terms' provision; nor could use of the trade and commerce power permit the Commonwealth to escape the 'free trade' requirement of section 92. The Court's decision in *Cole v. Whitfield* (1988) 165 CLR 360 disposed of the special protection afforded to the property of interstate traders. But in relation to section 51(xxxi) the Court still has to determine conclusively what constitutes 'acquisition'. Tasmania argued in the *Dams* case that the freeze on land use imposed by the legislation amounted to acquisition. Only one judge (Justice Deane) accepted the thrust of this argument, though only in relation to those areas where the 'race' power was used to prohibit use. The compensation terms provided in the legislation did not satisfy the 'just terms' requirement, he considered, because it did not provide an immediate right to compensation, but forced a long and uncertain procedure to be followed.

VOTING RIGHTS

Two sections of the Constitution might be thought to confer important voting rights on Australians. The first, in section 41, seems to be written in emphatic terms: 'No adult person who has or acquires a right to vote at elections for the more numerous House of the Parliament of a State shall, while the right continues, be prevented by any law of the Commonwealth from voting at elections for either House of the Parliament of the Commonwealth.' But according to the High Court there are two substantial limitations on the 'right' conveyed. The first is that the prospective voter has to be an adult, and in *King v. Jones* (1972) 128 CLR 221 the Court ruled that 18-year-olds who had acquired the right to vote in South Australia on turning 18 were not able to insist on a vote in the 1972 federal elections because they were not 'adult', meaning 21 years of age. The second limitation is even more devastating. In a 1983 case (*R v. Pearson; ex parte Sipka* (1983) 152 CLR 254) the Court held that the section only controlled the terms of the first Commonwealth law made under section 30 of the Constitution, and the only limitation in that section is that each elector has only one vote in each election. In other words, section 41 is a completely 'dead' provision.

The other constitutional provision that might have affected voting rights is section 24, which says that 'The House of Representatives shall be composed of members directly chosen by the people.' In 1975 in the *McKinlay* case (*Attorney-General (Cwlth), ex rel McKinlay v. Commonwealth* (1975) 135 CLR 1), it was argued that the phrase 'directly chosen by the people' implied that there should be one vote, one value (that is, that all electorates should contain equal numbers of electors). The High Court rejected this proposition (Justice Murphy dissenting) despite the fact that the same phrase in the United States Constitution had been taken by the US Supreme Court to require one vote, one value. Some members of the majority thought that in cases of gross inequality, or where there was anything less than universal adult suffrage, the election would not be 'by the people'. But that was not the case on the facts presented to the Court.

The case was in effect reargued in *McGinty v. Western Australia* (1996) 186 CLR 140. By a 4–2 majority, the Court rejected the argument that what it had said in the political free speech cases about the underlying concept of representative democracy could be used to imply other political rights. Chief Justice Brennan explained (at 169):

> It is logically impermissible to treat 'representative democracy' as though it were contained in the Constitution, to attribute to the term a meaning or content derived from sources extrinsic to the Constitution and then to invalidate a law for inconsistency with the meaning of content so attributed.
>
> The decision meant that the reasoning for the decision in the *Nationwide News* and other cases could not be used to extend the right of political free speech to other political rights.

Freedom of religion

Section 116 of the Constitution provides that:

> The Commonwealth shall not make any law for establishing any religion, or for imposing any religious observance, or for prohibiting the free exercise of any religion, and no religious test shall be required as a qualification for any office or public trust under the Commonwealth.

The Commonwealth (once again, this is a clause which is not directed to the States, even though it is placed in the chapter of the Constitution dealing with 'The States') cannot establish a religion, which means it cannot, for example, follow Great Britain in making the Church of England the 'established' church of the nation. Nor can it prevent any religion from being followed by Australians. This does not mean that the Commonwealth cannot recognise the existence of religions, and it is not prohibited from using them for its own purposes, or providing them with such assistance as it determines. A religious organisation may be given tax exemptions. The officials of a religious organisation may be authorised to perform the civil (non-religious) requirements of a marriage.

In *Church of the New Faith v. Commissioner of Pay-Roll Tax (Vic)* (1982–83) 154 CLR 120, the Court decided that the word 'religion' should be given a wide meaning, and for the purposes of Victorian legislation the church established by the practitioners of Scientology was exempt from pay-roll tax. Members of the Court gave a wide range of the criteria which might be considered to determine whether a religion should be recognised, including (1) belief in a supernatural being, thing or principle, and (2) the acceptance of canons of conduct to give effect to that belief. It was specifically said in relation to the second criterion that canons of conduct which offended against the ordinary laws were outside the area of any immunity, privilege or right conferred on grounds of religion. This took up some of the principles stated in American decisions based on a similar (though not identical) constitutional provision, and also the findings of the Court in *Adelaide Company of Jehovah's Witnesses Incorporated v. The Commonwealth* (1943) 67 CLR 116, where the Court held that the Constitution did not prevent the Commonwealth from making laws prohibiting the advocacy of doctrines or principles by a religious order which were prejudicial to the conduct of a war in which the Commonwealth was engaged. In *Black v. The Commonwealth* (1980–81) 146 CLR 559, the Court (Justice Murphy dissenting) held that a law providing financial aid to church schools was not a law for the 'establishment' of a religion.

Other Civil and Political Rights

The High Court's foremost decision on political rights was its invalidation of the Menzies government legislation to outlaw the

Communist Party—a decision which in a sense achieved popular support when the voters (narrowly) rejected a referendum designed to change the Constitution to give force to the proposed law. The Communist Party Dissolution Act 1950 purported to dissolve and declare unlawful the Australian Communist Party and other associations which the government declared were affiliated with it or were prejudicial to the security and defence of the Commonwealth. It also disqualified communists from holding office in trade unions. The legislation was enacted at the beginning of the 'cold war' but at a time when Australia was not engaged officially in war. The Court, in *Australian Communist Party v. The Commonwealth* (1951) 83 CLR 1, said the law was not valid under the defence power, or under any implied power to make laws for the preservation of the Commonwealth from internal attack or subversion. The major problem with the law was that it did not prohibit subversive conduct, but rather outlawed an organisation and people because the government itself had determined that they were guilty of subversion. This was an infringement of the Court's responsibility to make findings about 'constitutional facts' upon which the decision about whether a law was constitutional or not might be determined.

Important though the High Court's decision was, it did not establish any particular political or civil rights for Australians. What it said was that the Commonwealth did not have the power to pass a particular piece of legislation. It certainly did not establish that there was any constitutional bar to State legislation banning political or other social organisations, nor did it put any limits on legislation to limit freedom of association or freedom of speech.

Also, it did not establish that even under Commonwealth law all citizens were entitled to all the attributes of citizenship. The issuing of a passport, for example, was said by the Menzies government to be at the discretion of the executive government. That was the excuse it gave for not issuing a passport to Wilfred Burchett, a journalist who worked (for western newspapers) on the communist side of the line in the Korean and Indo-China wars. The absence of a passport did not prevent Burchett from travelling (other governments were prepared to give him identity papers sufficient for that purpose), but it did prevent him from returning to Australia, because airlines and shipping companies would not carry him without proof that he could land in Australia. The problem was finally settled by the High Court in *Air Caledonie International v. The Commonwealth* (1988) 165 CLR 462, where the whole Court noted at one point, 'The right of the Australian citizen to enter the country is not qualified by any law imposing a licence or "clearance" from the Executive.'

A BILL OF RIGHTS?

The courts, particularly the High Court, have been adept at developing the common law to provide an increasing range of rights and liberties, particularly in the field of criminal justice. The problem is that in another time the courts may decide that these rights and freedoms are less important than the rights of the state. More importantly, the parliaments at both the State and Commonwealth level are free to override these rights, without even acknowledging the significance of their actions. The fact that a law negates or overrules a common law rule does not allow the courts to declare it invalid. Such a law replaces the common law and has to be observed and enforced by the courts.

But lawyers and judges who are conscious of this underlying weakness of the common law to preserve rights in the face of a legislative attack have led the resistance to the development of a bill of rights becoming part of the Australian Constitution. The major fear, it seems, is that in interpreting such a law the courts would be engaged in a political rather than a legal exercise. As former Chief Justice Sir Garfield Barwick put it (quoted by David Marr 1980, p. 227):

> With a bill of rights you make political decisions, you don't make legal decisions, and how long of course a populace is prepared to allow an unelected body to decide political questions is itself a question . . . The slant of a man's mind undoubtedly must enter into judgment. If he is a wise man he is watchful. I think some of us are—watchful—that this or that shouldn't happen. But so far as the decisions are concerned,

having no bill of rights, we are able to decide them by legal means, as legal propositions—and we do.

While the judges appear to have been concerned primarily about the nature of the decision they might be called on to make, the person whose 'rights' have been trampled on by government is concerned only with having those 'rights' upheld. The issue should not be about whether the Court has to make a political decision, but whether the citizen has real 'rights' which the Court will protect.

In the past decade or so there has been a change in the legal climate. In 1988 Sir Anthony Mason, in a speech to the Australian Bar Association, acknowledged that his initial reaction to the idea of a bill of rights—an adverse reaction, the 'very idea seemed alien to our traditions'—had by then changed. He did not enthusiastically embrace the idea, but he recognised that it had more virtue than he perceived initially. He surveyed the arguments for and against a bill of rights. The arguments against included: judicial review is undemocratic; a bill of rights turns judges into law makers; the issues to be determined are essentially political and not legal; a bill of rights gives too much power to judges; a bill of rights would politicise the judges; and a bill of rights is not needed. The advantages he saw were: there would be more protection for the individual from the exercise of power by institutions and pressure groups; it offered principled and reasoned decision-making on fundamental issues; it enhanced the role of law; it ensured that the power of the majority could not override the rights of minorities and individuals; it deterred parliament from abrogating the rule of law; and it would have a major educative role in promoting greater awareness of and respect for human rights.

At a constitutional convention in Sydney in April 1991, lawyers and judges actually led the way in advocating the adoption in the Constitution of a bill of rights. The change of attitude in the legal profession in half a generation has been very great. Later the Law Council of Australia joined in sponsoring a conference intended to promote the idea of a bill of rights. In

1993 a Federal Court judge, Murray Wilcox, published a book, *An Australian Charter of Rights?*

In England the most senior judges have moved further and faster to accept the inevitability and desirability of a bill of rights. Most of the Law Lords have spoken (and indeed voted) in favour of Britain incorporating the European Convention on Human Rights as part of its domestic law. That legislation failed through lack of time to pass in 1995, but it is likely to be passed with the support of the Blair government. Nevertheless, there are critics. Professor John Griffith, author of *The Politics of the Judiciary* (1997), is opposed to giving the judges more power, considering them to be too conservative. In the latest (fifth) edition of his book, he wrote:

> In the societies of our world today judges do not stand out as protectors of liberty, of the rights of man, of the unprivileged, nor have they insisted that holders of great economic power, private and public, should use it with moderation. Their view of the public interest, when it has gone beyond the interest of governments, has not been wide enough to embrace the interests of political, ethnic, social or other minorities . . . In both democratic and totalitarian societies, the judiciary has naturally served the prevailing political and economic forces.

In Australia Frank Brennan, the Jesuit whose father was Chief Justice of the High Court, has a different reason for opposing a constitutional bill of rights. In his latest book, *Legislating Liberty: A Bill of Rights for Australia?* (1998), Father Brennan is less concerned with the conservatism of the judges than with the fact that a bill of rights would require them to make decisions about such subjects as abortion and free speech. His answer is for a constitutional guarantee of a few rights—banning capital punishment, racial discrimination, and discrimination based on gender or sexual orientation—a legislatively based bill of rights, which could be overruled by the parliament, and a Senate committee to report on possible legislative abuses of rights and freedoms.

But the most important opponents of bills of rights are in the parliaments. Politicians are more opposed to Australia having a bill of rights than are judges or lawyers. Politicians have shown relatively little interest in the subject, particularly when confronted with the High Court's decisions on implied Constitutional rights. Most do not want to concede more power to the courts, particularly the High Court, to place limits on the powers of the parliament. However, public opinion polls show a significant majority of voters do want Australia to have a bill of rights. Almost every other western democratic country has a bill of rights, and by the turn of the century Australia may be the only such country without one. But it will only get one if a political party decides to harness the underlying view of the community that judges are more to be trusted than politicians when it comes to guarding such rights as Australians may lay claim to.

4

DESTRUCTION OF THE STATES

The High Court has delivered so many blows against the States that it is difficult to decide which might have been the ultimate mortal blow to their independence. The history of Commonwealth–State relations is replete with decisions by the Court which helped make them the inferior partners in the Australian federation. Almost all of them involved decisions about the way the Commonwealth Constitution should be interpreted. Probably the most important concerned financial matters—in particular, taxes and who could levy them. Others involved the extent of the legislative powers of the Commonwealth in section 51 of the Constitution, and the way the Court has applied section 109, which provides that where the Commonwealth and the States make laws that are inconsistent, the Commonwealth shall 'prevail' and the States' laws are invalid.

The inevitable decline of the States was predicted only a year or so after the Commonwealth came into being. Federal Attorney-General Alfred Deakin, writing anonymously as the Australian correspondent for an English magazine, predicted that the 'independence of our States is doomed'. He based this claim on the fact that the States were utterly dependent for most of their revenues on receipts from customs duties, but following the inauguration of the Commonwealth these receipts were now paid into the Commonwealth's coffers. For just ten years they would be entitled to three-quarters of those receipts. 'After the decade they will be able to claim nothing as of right, and must be content with any amount the Federal Parliament chooses to spare them.' Later in the article the writer used a phrase which caught the imagination of subsequent observers of the Australian scene, for its succinct and vivid statement of what would transpire: the Constitution, he said, had left the States 'legally free, but financially bound to the chariot wheels of the central Government'. The article continued, 'Our Constitution may remain unaltered, but a vital change will have taken place in the relations between the States and the Commonwealth. The Commonwealth will have acquired a general control over the States, while every extension of political power will be made by its means and go to increase its relative superiority.'

While it is possible to cavil somewhat with the notion that the Constitution had left the States 'legally free' (after all, they were made subject to its provisions, and it was those provisions which gave the Commonwealth predominance when the Commonwealth and the States shared any particular power), Australia's subsequent political history has followed the path Deakin forecast.

This has occurred because the determination by Commonwealth governments of all political persuasions to achieve this financial dominance has been supported, and in some cases prompted or provoked, by the High Court.

The first legislative and legal steps to establish that dominance occurred when Deakin was prime minister, in 1908. The constitution-makers had given the Commonwealth and the States a series of directions about the way their financial affairs were to be organised in the early years of federation. The States were to be paid all the revenues from customs duties (less expenses) until such time as the Commonwealth imposed uniform customs duties (Constitution, s. 89). Those uniform duties came into effect on 8 October 1901. For the first five years after federation, and until such time as the parliament otherwise provided, the Commonwealth had to pay its unexpended balances of revenue to the States (s. 93). And for the first ten years after federation, and until the parliament determined otherwise, the Commonwealth had to pay three-quarters of its net revenue from customs and excise to the States, plus any of the remaining quarter of that revenue which it did not utilise for its own expenditures. The policy of the Convention was clearly pro-State; but the wording of the Constitution did not guarantee a pro-State outcome.

In 1908 Deakin's government, with the approval of the High Court, showed how the Commonwealth could ignore the intentions expressed in the Constitution and establish its own priorities. Faced with the need to begin financing both a new navy and an old-age pension scheme, the government decided to begin setting aside money to meet these future commitments. In March 1908 the attorney-general, Littleton Groom, gave an opinion in which he expressed a fairly tentative view that the Commonwealth could appropriate money from its so-called surplus revenue into trust accounts, provided those accounts were for defined purposes (such as naval defence). The parliament enacted the Surplus Revenue Act in mid-year and in October the same year the High Court held the procedure valid despite the inclination of the majority of the Court in other judgments at this time to adhere to the doctrine of reserved powers. On this occasion there was no attempt by the Commonwealth to make a law in an area 'reserved' for the States, whatever the financial implications might be. Chief Justice Griffith said that 'if a sum of money is lawfully appropriated out of the Consolidated Revenue for a specific purpose, that sum cannot be regarded as forming part of a surplus until the expenditure of it is no longer lawful or no longer thought necessary by the Government' (*New South Wales v. The Commonwealth* (1908) 7 CLR 179, at 191). Justice Barton said that 'to become "surplus revenue" so as to be claimable [by the States] they [i.e. the moneys] must have been either wholly unappropriated for any purpose of the Commonwealth, or appropriated for something which is not such a purpose—that is, illegally' (at 193). Those judgments made it comparatively simple for the Commonwealth to ensure from then on that it could reserve all or most of what otherwise would have been surplus revenue for its own future purposes.

The Commonwealth, armed with the High Court decision, was able to negotiate with the States in 1909 an agreement as to what the Commonwealth would do after the expiry of the ten-year term of section 87 of the Constitution, the section giving the States three-quarters of the customs and excise revenue of the Commonwealth. In future the States would be paid each year an amount equivalent to 25 shillings per head of population. The States insisted that this be written into the Constitution. The Bill passed the parliament (by the narrowest of margins, and over the opposition of the Labor Party), but it failed to get the approval of the people at a referendum in 1910. Subsequently a Labor government gave legislative effect to the agreement in 1910, but the legislation gave the States no guarantees that their relative funding position would be maintained.

During World War I the relative importance of the States was further diminished, and the Commonwealth entered the income tax field as well as introducing a wide range of other taxes, primarily to finance expenditure on the war. The High Court agreed that the defence of the Commonwealth was paramount, and that the financial needs of the Commonwealth took precedence over those of the States.

Section 96 grants

It was not until the mid-1920s that the High Court provided the next shackle to bind the States to the chariot wheels of the Commonwealth. This was a remarkable judgment in a case called *Victoria v. The Commonwealth* (1926) 38 CLR 399. What was remarkable about the case was the brevity of the judgment, as well as its extraordinary impact on federal–State relations. The case involved a challenge by Victoria and South Australia (supported by New South Wales) against the validity of grants made by the Commonwealth to the States for road construction purposes. The validity of the Commonwealth Aid Roads Act 1926 was based primarily on section 96 of the Constitution, though the Commonwealth also pleaded that it was valid because the Commonwealth could spend money on State roads for defence purposes and immigration and other (unspecified) Commonwealth purposes. Section 96 says: 'During a period of ten years after the establishment of the Commonwealth and thereafter until the Parliament otherwise provides, the Parliament may grant financial assistance to any state on such terms and conditions as the Parliament thinks fit.'

The claim for invalidity was argued by a young Victorian barrister, Robert Menzies, who had achieved extraordinary success in an appearance before the High Court in 1920. The case he then argued had provided the Court with the vehicle needed to overthrow the reserved powers doctrine which had prevented the Commonwealth from utilising to the full those powers which the Constitution had granted it. In this case, however, Menzies was to take a position which did not sit well with the argument he had advanced in the *Engineers* case (*Amalgamated Society of Engineers v. Adelaide Steamship Co. Ltd.* (1920) 28 CLR 129). He argued here that the legislation was invalid because it was a law relating to road-making and not a law for granting financial aid to the States. He also argued that the grants did not comply with section 96. Parliament, he argued, could not attach as conditions to its grants under section 96 any conditions which amounted in substance to the exercise of any legislative power which was not within section 51 of the Constitution.

The argument received short shrift. Indeed, the Commonwealth was not even allowed to give its full argument in reply to the States. One day after the Court heard the argument it produced a written judgment of which the full text was:

> The Court is of the opinion that the Federal Aid Roads Act no. 46 of 1926 is a valid enactment.
>
> It is plainly warranted by the provisions of sec. 96 of the Constitution, and not affected by sec. 99 or any other provisions of the Constitution, so that exposition is unnecessary.
>
> The action is dismissed.

The decision was, despite its brevity, one of the most crucial in the history of Commonwealth–State relations. It meant that the Commonwealth could use its power to make grants to the States under section 96 of the Constitution for any purpose, not just a purpose within those heads of power given to the Commonwealth parliament.

In 1939 and 1940 the High Court and the Privy Council

added further weight to the grants power. They held in *Moran's* case (*W.R. Moran Pty Ltd v. Deputy Federal Commissioner of Taxation* (1939) 61 CLR 735 and (1940) 63 CLR 338) that the grants to the States could be discriminatory, and the fact that they appeared to run counter to the non-discriminatory requirements of the Commonwealth's tax powers in section 51(ii) and section 99 did not matter so long as discrimination was not a real object of the Commonwealth's scheme.

It required only one more step to secure Commonwealth dominance—the use of the grants power to impose a condition which in a sense involved the surrender by the States to the Commonwealth. This occurred when the Commonwealth decided it was time that Australia should have a uniform taxation system (at least for income tax) and when the High Court approved of the arrangement. What the Commonwealth did was initially to use its war powers to get a monopoly of income tax powers, and to use its grants power under section 96 to persuade the States to accept the Commonwealth's supremacy.

Uniform taxation

The High Court was asked twice by the States to save them from the Commonwealth's takeover of income and company taxation, in 1942 and in 1958. The first was a war-time case, and because Australia was then at war and the Commonwealth needed access to as much money as it could raise for defence purposes, the States stood comparatively little chance of success. The case concerned the validity of four Commonwealth Acts: the States Grants (Income Tax Reimbursement) Act 1942, the Income Tax (War-time Arrangements) Act 1942, the Income Tax Assessment Act 1942 and the Income Tax Act 1942 (*South Australia v. The Commonwealth*—the *First Uniform Tax* case—(1942) 65 CLR 373). The first law provided for grants to the States each financial year of amounts approximately equivalent to what they were currently collecting from income taxes, the grants not being payable unless the Commonwealth Treasurer was satisfied that in that year a State had not collected income tax. The second provided for a complete takeover of the State tax-collecting offices (all the States except Western Australia had, until this time, collected their own income taxes plus the income taxes levied by the Commonwealth). The third gave the Commonwealth priority in the collection of income tax over any State income tax. And the fourth imposed very high rates of income tax, rising to 90 per cent on income over four thousand pounds a year. The States claimed (rightly!) that the whole scheme was a dastardly Commonwealth plot, designed to implement uniform taxation and prevent the States from ever re-entering the field. The Court refused to admit evidence in the form of reports and speeches by the Treasurer in parliament which would have proved the point (such evidence would have been admissible from the mid-1980s), but, as Chief Justice Latham pointed out (at 411), the absence of the evidence was irrelevant:

> The intention to get rid of State income tax and of State income tax departments is clear in the case of the three first-mentioned Acts, and if such an intention is fatal to the validity of Commonwealth legislation it is not necessary to allege or prove any 'scheme' . . . The defendants do not seek to conceal the scheme: they assert it and justify it.

Only one judge was sufficiently disconcerted by the threat to the States to suggest that two of the Acts were invalid. That was Justice Starke, who was concerned at the use of section 96 grants to disable the States, and at the scheme which the Commonwealth had devised. But the scheme did not matter unless the legislation was 'connected together and the provisions of the legislative Acts are dependent the one upon the other, which is not, as I think, the case here' (at 448). But he objected strongly to the way the Commonwealth used section 96 to try to disable the States' ability to have their own income taxes. He said (at 443) that the object of the Grants Act:

> . . . is not merely to grant financial assistance to the States, but there is linked up in it an object and an end that is inconsistent with the limited grant of power given by sec. 96 to the Commonwealth, namely, making the Commonwealth the sole effective taxing authority in respect of incomes and compensating the States

> for the resulting loss in income tax. The argument that the States Grants Act leaves a choice to the States, offers them an inducement but deprives them of and interferes with no constitutional power, is specious and unreal.

He also held that the Commonwealth could not use the defence power to take over the State tax offices.

The Chief Justice agreed with Justice Starke about the tax office takeovers, but otherwise the Court held that all four Acts were valid, though for somewhat differing reasons. What was important for the future, however, was that only one member of the Court, Justice McTiernan, relied primarily on the defence power to reach that conclusion.

This meant that when the war ended, the Commonwealth was able to continue the uniform tax scheme. It had by then absorbed the States' taxation offices, and needed to keep in place its higher tax rates and its tax reimbursement grants under section 92. Although the Liberal Party campaigned on a promise to do away with uniform taxation, it did not change the system when it came to power at the end of 1949. Despite frequent complaints from the States, it was not until 1956 that several of the States decided once again, in a peace-time environment, to try to overturn what was by then a well-established system. In fact it was so well-established that two judges, Justices Williams and Fullagar, thought that it was too late for the two States, New South Wales and Victoria, to challenge the scheme. Although they said the legislation was somewhat different from that which had been approved by the Court in the first *Uniform Tax* case, the laws which were being challenged had assumed their 'present permanent character in 1946'. And now only two of the States were challenging them. In the circumstances, what the Court had decided in 1942 should not be reconsidered (*Victoria v. The Commonwealth*—the *Second Uniform Tax* case (1957) 99 CLR 575 at 655).

The other members of the Court did reconsider the issues raised by the States, but upheld the validity of the scheme, with one insignificant exception. Four of the seven members of the Court held that the Commonwealth could not (in peace-time) insist on priority in payment for its tax bills. But given that the States were being bribed not to impose income taxes, this made not a scrap of difference to the uniform scheme. This was because, apart from anything else, the States succumbed to the bribe: they did not impose their own taxes even though, in theory at least, they were legally able to do so. Indeed, they would not do so even when Prime Minister Malcolm Fraser later agreed to change the rules somewhat to allow the States to impose a small additional tax.

Other State taxes

Throughout the next three decades various State premiers tried desperately to find a way either to persuade or to force the Commonwealth to concede them more financial independence, or to evade the Commonwealth's grip by devising new taxes. All failed, because of the political determination of successive Commonwealth governments, supported by successive High Courts and the way they applied sections 90 and 96 of the Constitution.

The way in which the Court had blessed the Commonwealth's use of section 96 in the two uniform tax cases gave the Commonwealth its strongest weapon. And that weapon was used in its bluntest fashion by the Gorton and McMahon Liberal governments in the late 1960s and early 1970s. When Gorton became prime minister in 1968 he was faced with a situation in which the Victorian government, headed by Sir Henry Bolte, was actively exploring ways of increasing that State's financial resources. Western Australia had begun imposing a receipt duty on 'moneys received', and in 1966 this was copied by Victoria, and then extended to include a requirement that the duty be paid on wage and salary payments received. Gorton claimed that this aspect of the tax breached an agreement between the Commonwealth and the States and warned that unless the tax was removed in two years the Commonwealth would reduce the payments it made to that State under the section 96 tax reimbursement grants. Any attempt to increase the rate of tax would result in immediate Commonwealth action, the Victorians were told. But the Commonwealth told all of the States that they could copy the Western

Australian stamp duties or 'turnover' tax, so long as they did not exceed a set rate of $10 specified by the Commonwealth.

The States, particularly Victoria and New South Wales, protested that the Commonwealth was taking upon itself the right to determine what taxes the States might or might not impose. They argued that the States were not obliged to consult anyone before they imposed taxes that were within their own constitutional powers. To which Prime Minister Gorton replied, 'I think you have the legal and constitutional right to do what you have said you will do; but I think it can only be helpful if, in deciding whether to exercise that legal and constitutional right and how far to exercise it, you know the Commonwealth Government's attitude.' Sir Henry Bolte conceded that the rights his State might have were of no value 'if the Commonwealth Government then decides to deduct revenue raised by that tax from the tax reimbursement grant. If the Commonwealth Government assesses the amount and says: "We will deduct this or else", what is the use of having the legal and constitutional right? It no longer counts.' (See this author's account of the wrangle in his chapter on Commonwealth–State relations in Harris & Dutton 1971, and an account by Professor Geoffrey Sawer in the *Current Affairs Bulletin*, January 1971.)

The Commonwealth's intransigent line was continued by Gorton's successor, McMahon, despite the latter's desperation to appease the (Liberal) States. Faced with a Victorian challenge to Commonwealth legislation imposing payroll tax on the State governments, the parliament passed legislation to deduct from the section 96 grants due to Victoria any shortfall in the Commonwealth's revenue caused by a successful action by Victoria in the High Court. In fact the law did not have to be invoked, the High Court deciding unanimously that the Commonwealth's payroll tax was validly imposed. Later the McMahon government agreed to move out of the payroll tax field and leave it to the States, who promptly increased its incidence by a 40 per cent margin. Although this might be counted as a minor victory for the States, it demonstrated once again that the States were free to do only what the Commonwealth was prepared to let them do.

More accurately perhaps, it should be said that the States

could do what the Commonwealth politically and the High Court judicially were jointly prepared to let them do. Gorton was prepared to let the States impose a turnover tax so long as it did not exceed $10. When the States tried to implement this scheme it was held invalid by the High Court. Although Gorton was prepared to legislate to have the Commonwealth government impose the turnover tax and collect it on behalf of the States, the scheme came unstuck when the Senate rejected the legislation. The High Court's decision in this matter was based on its interpretation of section 90 of the Constitution, and what the Court has determined in this area has proved as devastating to the States as its decisions on section 96.

THE SECTION 90 POWER

Section 90 provides that: 'On the imposition of uniform duties of customs the power of the Parliament to impose duties of customs and of excise, and to grant bounties on the production or export of goods, shall become exclusive . . .' The key provision is that which gives the Commonwealth exclusive power over the imposition of duties of excise, and this has been vital because of the broad definition of excise which the High Court has gradually adopted.

The Court invalidated the turnover taxes of Western Australia and Victoria in 1970 because a bare 4–3 majority held that duties imposed on receipts of payments from sales, at any stage from manufacture to consumption, of goods manufactured in Australia were duties of excise within the meaning of section 90. The States argued that the tax was imposed on the receipt of money, and that there was no necessary relationship between the amount of the tax and the value or price of the goods. In that case (*Western Australia v. Chamberlain Industries Pty Ltd* (1969–70) 121 CLR 1), Chief Justice Barwick said that 'it should be regarded now as acceptable and settled doctrine that the tax will be a duty of excise if it is upon or in respect of goods at any point including the point of manufacture or production, as they pass to consumption' (at 13). And he concluded (at 17), 'I have no doubt that to tax the receipt of the purchase price or any part of the purchase price of the sale of goods is to tax a step in the movement of goods into consumption. It is . . . a tax upon the transaction of sale itself and, to my mind, is clearly of the essential nature of a duty of excise.'

This is a very different interpretation of what constitutes duties of excise from that adopted by the first High Court and maintained by successive Courts for some decades. The first Commonwealth government acted on an opinion by its attorney-general, Alfred Deakin, to the effect that 'excise is a duty upon goods manufactured or produced within a country. It is the product that is taxed—not the process of production' (Brazil and Mitchell 1981, p. 32; quoted also by Justice McHugh in his dissenting judgment in *Philip Morris Ltd & ors v. Commissioner of Business Franchises & anr* (1989) 167 CLR 399). The High Court agreed when in 1904 it heard its first section 90 case, *Peterswald v. Bartley* (1904) 1 CLR 497. The term excise, the Court said, was 'intended to mean a duty analogous to a customs duty imposed upon goods either in relation to quantity or value when produced or manufactured, and not in the sense of a direct tax or personal tax' (at 509). This was a limited and very Australian view—a fact which the Court acknowledged. But here was a case where the Justices of the High Court knew the intentions of their fellow constitution-makers, and their views were not clouded by the reserved powers doctrine.

Their views on excise were overturned for different reasons and in an accumulation of cases which left the meaning of 'excise' in section 90 as uncertain as was 'freedom of trade and commerce' in section 92 until 1988. The narrow definition of excise was gradually broadened: manufacture and production became manufacture, production, distribution, and then sale. Any sales tax, and possibly any consumption tax, could be classified as an excise tax.

This was important only because section 90 barred the States from excise taxes—the wider the definition of excise, the wider the restriction on the kind of taxes which the States might impose and the revenues which they might raise for their own needs.

In 1960 the Court made a decision which, as it turned out, ameliorated the effect of those earlier decisions for some 37 years. In *Dennis Hotels Pty Ltd v. Victoria* (1960) 104 CLR 529, the

Court decided that a provision of the Victorian Licensing Act, which calculated licence fees according to sales in a prior period, was not an excise and was therefore valid. (The licence was an annual licence, and the sales period was the year that ended six months before the new licence period began.) The Court split badly: three judges said the tax was an excise, and it didn't matter that the fee was calculated by reference to past sales; three said it was not an excise because (among other reasons) it was not calculated by reference to current sales; the remaining judge (the one whose decision determined the result) decided that the fee was not an excise because he said excise was a tax on production or manufacture, not on sale or distribution. That idiosyncratic view of Justice Fullagar was rejected by all the other judges and by all the later Justices on the Court, other than Justice Murphy, who was later to suggest an even narrower interpretation of excise.

The Court endorsed the result it reached in *Dennis Hotels* in two subsequent cases: *Dickenson's Arcade Pty Ltd v. Tasmania* (1974) 130 CLR 177, and *H. C. Sleigh Ltd v. South Australia* (1977) 136 CLR 475. Those cases concerned the licensing of tobacco and petrol sellers, with fees determined again according to levels of sales in a prior period. The Court in those and subsequent decisions signalled that it was extremely unhappy with the outcome of these cases—they were something of an embarrassment.

Yet for political reasons the Court felt unable to review their correctness. Those reasons were explained in *Philip Morris*, which was argued in March 1989 and determined the following August. Chief Justice Mason and Justice Deane said in their joint judgment (at 438):

> There are powerful considerations against overruling the actual decisions in those cases. Financial arrangements which are of great importance to the governments of the States and perhaps to the economy of the nation have been made for a long time past on the faith of these decisions. The power of this Court to overrule its previous decisions would not be properly exercised to disturb those arrangements unless, in the light of later insights into the true meaning of the Constitution, obedience to its terms or the

> interests of certainty in those arrangements clearly demanded that those decisions be reconsidered.

They then added:

> That cannot presently be said of at least the first two of the trilogy of cases. *Dennis Hotels* and *Dickenson's Arcade* can be rationalised by reference to traditional considerations relating to the licensing of dealings in alcohol and tobacco and to the particular characteristics of those items of personal consumption.

That last comment demonstrates that high-sounding principle may play little real part in some of the Court's more political decision-making. The 'traditional considerations' concerning tobacco and alcohol licensing was an argument which was not accepted by other members of the Court. It was a minority view (though these two Justices formed part of the majority in this case). The way they determined the case amounted to an invitation to anyone opposed to petrol licensing by the States to try their hand at overturning that particular exception to the ban on State sales taxes (if other Justices held to their own individual views, there would be a 4–3 majority which would hold that petrol licensing did amount to an excise). Yet how would this review be justified given the dependence of the States on this form of revenue, the main argument they referred to earlier?

Material produced to the Court demonstrated how reliant the States were on these three varieties of sales tax. Between 1974 and 1988 tobacco licence fees increased in Victoria from 5 per cent to 30 per cent, and licence fees as a percentage of total State taxation from 5.5 per cent to over 11 per cent. Total State revenues from tobacco, alcohol and petrol licensing in 1988–89 were more than $1.5 billion. Three of the States gained about 20 per cent of their taxation revenues from these three types of licence fees.

Justice Murphy took the view that the duties of excise which any State was forbidden to raise by section 90 were taxes on goods produced or manufactured in that State. That interpretation would probably fit very easily with the Court's current views on section 92, and would not deny the States access to a wide range of sales and consumption taxes, so long as they did not discriminate in favour of State-produced goods. The Commonwealth, through its general power over taxation, and its powers under section 96, would still be able to regulate the use by States of these taxes, and the Commonwealth's ability to control the national economy would not be diminished.

If the Court were to have adopted the *Peterswald* approach there would be no threat to the revenue of the States—the position of the States would be markedly improved. This was the attitude taken during the argument of *Philip Morris* by the South Australian solicitor-general, John Doyle QC, who proposed the reopening of the licensing cases so that he could argue that the Court should adopt a view of excise like that of the Court in *Peterswald*, or like that proposed by Justice Murphy. He made it clear, however, that he would rely on the licensing cases to support the validity of the licences challenged in *Philip Morris* if the Court would not conduct such a fundamental review.

These arguments resurfaced in *Ha v. New South Wales* (1997) 189 CLR 465, where the Court, by a 4–3 majority, rejected the submissions of the States that the Court should adopt a narrower definition of excise to allow them to tax goods. More significantly, the majority also decided to rid itself of the *Dennis Hotels* line of cases which allowed for hefty sales taxes poorly disguised as licences on alcohol, tobacco and petrol. The majority pointed out that New South Wales tobacco taxes had raised $157 million in 1986/87, and ten years later were estimated to have raised $852 million. Chief Justice Brennan and Justices McHugh, Gummow and Kirby said that the States had overreached their entitlement to raise business licence fees.

The majority said they recognised that the judgment had the 'most serious consequences' for State finances. In fact, the financial consequences in the short term were negligible. The federal government recognised that it had to take over and impose the same level of taxes which the States had imposed, and recompense the States for their lost revenue. In the medium term, the judgment meant that the States lost the ability to continue to increase the revenue they could get from these taxes—any further increases in tobacco, alcohol and petrol taxes would be solely determined by federal government policies and would be unlikely to be passed on to the States.

More important, however, was that the decision further reduced the capacity of the States to fund their own services and programs, and increased their reliance on federal handouts, so reducing their independence. The inability of the States to raise taxes on incomes or goods has severely limited their ability to raise their own revenue. Before the decision in *Ha*, they could raise only about 60 per cent of the money they spent; afterwards, the amount was slightly over 50 per cent. The remainder came from the Commonwealth, much of it in tied grants. This vertical fiscal imbalance (as the economists call it) between the resources of the Commonwealth and the States is in the long run the consequence of High Court decisions which have allowed the Commonwealth government to make decisions allowing it to dominate governmental revenue raising.

One other development in the excise field which has political significance for the States was the Court's decision in *Harper v. Minister for Sea Fisheries* (1989) 168 CLR 314. In that case the Court held that a licence on the taking of abalone in Tasmania was not a tax, and therefore not an excise. It was a licence on the exploitation of a limited public natural resource, a kind of property right for a conservationist purpose. That decision possibly could clear the way for State environmental taxes so long as they were not discriminatory. More significantly perhaps, it shows that public policy considerations, whether acknowledged or not, may play a significant role in the Court's determination of purely legal concepts such as what constitutes a tax.

INDIRECT POWER

The High Court's interpretation of section 96 of the Constitution 'added greatly to the financial (and therefore political) predominance of the Commonwealth'. But, Sir Robert Menzies believed, the overall results had 'some good elements'. One of those results was the way in which the Commonwealth was able to make grants to the States for State universities, saving them from financial disaster and allowing new universities to be established (Menzies 1968, p. 88).

Menzies was responsible for that particular development. It was one of the two major achievements of his sixteen-year period as prime minister, he said at his retirement press conference. (The other was the impetus he gave to the growth of Canberra as the national capital.) It is noteworthy that the growth in Commonwealth power which this represented came under the auspices of a prime minister from the conservative side of Australian politics, whose party proclaimed the virtues of States' rights and the return of taxing power to the States. Sir Robert later wrote (Menzies 1968, pp. 88–9):

> The whole matter is a very good illustration of how something which was not anticipated in the Constitution when it was first enacted can come into existence by judicial interpretation and the inexorable demands of new circumstances.
>
> . . . Section 96 has been used to enable the Commonwealth to assist States in carrying out developmental works, such as roads and ports and railways outside the limits of Loan Council programs.
>
> Since then, what has been called uniform tax . . . has continued to be a feature of the relations between the Commonwealth and States in the financial field.
>
> I say this in no gloating Commonwealth fashion. I am a Federalist. I subscribe to the sound political principle that governments exercising independent powers should, if possible, have the responsibility for raising the revenues needed for such exercise. Uniform taxation . . . cuts across this principle.
>
> But historic events have a certain inexorable logic of their own . . .

Historic events don't just happen, however. They have to be made to happen. And Sir Robert Menzies played a very real part in translating the power made available by the High Court's decision in the section 96 cases into Commonwealth dominance of the States. And this despite the fact that he tried to persuade the High Court in 1926 that section 96 did not authorise Commonwealth grants to the States for roads.

Grants for roads, for example, have been used recently by

the Commonwealth to persuade the States to introduce new uniform traffic laws concerning various limits on permissible alcohol drink-driving offences, the regulation of the driving and loading of trucks and buses, and other matters considered important in reducing road accidents. The availability of the Commonwealth money was made conditional on the States making changes to their laws.

In education, the Commonwealth's interest under Menzies in funding universities and non-government schools has expanded to take in every sector. Policies are now determined by the Commonwealth and implemented by the States. University funding is varied to take account of whether individual institutions, set up under State laws, have enrolled the number of students determined by the federal bureaucracy. Resistance is possible, but it brings with it financial pain. The federal government, which under Whitlam introduced free tertiary education, under Hawke brought in what amounted to a tax on students, and under Howard, by reducing funding, forced the universities to cut their staffs while increasing student intakes and forcing the introduction of course fees.

Section 96 grants have allowed the Commonwealth to move when it chooses into any area of governmental policy—national, State or local. And despite the 'new Federalism' of the 1990s, it is clear that most ministers and their departments are more than reluctant to surrender the powers to dictate policy to the States through the provision by the Commonwealth of section 96 grants. It has all been possible because of a judgment that the High Court made in 1926, which at the time seemed somewhat inconsequential.

The federal balance

The States have long since stopped looking to the High Court for help. Although some of them dream that the appointment of the 'right' judges could result in a recognition by the Court of State rights, they know that the appointment of judges is firmly controlled by Canberra, and that all Canberra politicians, whatever their party, support the centralisation of power in their own hands. The only hope for the States is the way they mobilise such political power as they still have. The States have been angered by the way the High Court, in decisions such as the *Ha* case, has destroyed their business licence fees. But they have yet to demonstrate any ability to use the political process to roll back the High Court's decisions.

One of the problems for the States is that they can never be sure which way most High Court judges are going to jump on federal issues. There was a time when the Court's decisions were much more predictable. When Sir Harry Gibbs was Chief Justice in the mid-1980s, there was a group of three judges (Sir Harry, Sir Daryl Dawson and Sir Ronald Wilson) who almost invariably took a States-rights view. But of course three did not constitute a majority. Another problem is that the attitude of a judge towards federal issues is not always indicated by his or her presumed political leanings. The Labor Party, for example, has generally been regarded as a more centralist party than the Liberal Party, but Sir Garfield Barwick, a former Liberal attorney-general, frequently as Chief Justice supported the extension of the legislative powers of the Commonwealth at the expense of the States. On the question of section 90, the Commonwealth exclusive power to impose excises, Chief Justice Barwick favoured bringing more taxes into the Commonwealth's net, whereas Justice Lionel Murphy, a former Labor attorney-general, favoured reducing the range of taxes that fell within its ambit. However, on some centralist issues, for example the right of the Commonwealth to control the sea and natural resources beyond the low-water mark, Barwick and Murphy were in agreement.

The Constitution specifies which legislative powers the Commonwealth may use. Some of these powers are exclusive to the Commonwealth (e.g. tariffs and excise, and control over Commonwealth public servants and places), and some may be exercised by both the Commonwealth and the States, though in any clash the Commonwealth was intended to prevail (section 109). Where it mattered (to the founders) State interests were directly protected: their constitutions were preserved (subject to the provisions of the Commonwealth Constitution) (s. 106); and their railways were given special protection (s. 51(xxxiii and xxxiv)), as were their banks (s. 51(xiii)) and their insurance operations (s. 51(xiv)).

The nature of the legislative powers given to the Commonwealth was an indication that the Commonwealth would play an increasingly important role in the lives of ordinary citizens as it determined to pick up and explore the different heads of its legislative power. For example, it took more than half a century for the Commonwealth to get around to considering the creation of uniform marriage and divorce laws. The fact that most of the leading politicians at the time of federation immediately headed into the Commonwealth arena was an indication of where the founding fathers themselves thought the more important powers had been allocated.

Federalism involves the division of powers between a central government and provincial interests. In the United States and in Australia this was done by allocating specific powers to the national legislature and leaving what remained to the States. In Canada the provinces were given specific enumerated powers and the national parliament had whatever was left.

One of the functions of the High Court is to ensure that the provisions of the Constitution are not ignored. It is not a function of the Court to preserve any sort of balance between the powers and influence of the Commonwealth and the States, perhaps not even to ensure that the States are not discriminated against by the Commonwealth (except in extreme circumstances). Maintaining the federal balance is a job for politicians rather than judges. The problem for the States is that Commonwealth politicians, who largely hold the initiative, more often than not want to explore and expand the limits of their own powers rather than to share those powers with the States. The High Court can only rule on whether what they do is consistent with the Constitution.

5

Environmental invasion

As political issues, conservation and protection of the environment are of comparatively recent origins. This is not to say they have been ignored by governments until recently. The contrary is true. The Australian colonial governments were at the forefront of the national parks movement. Sydney's Royal National Park was the world's second official national park. But political controversy did not envelop the conservation movement until the 1960s and 1970s. When Sir Garfield Barwick, Chief Justice of the High Court, was appointed as the inaugural president of the Australian Conservation Foundation in 1964, no-one suggested that this might involve him in any activities that might compromise the way he exercised his judicial office. For one thing, conservation was not a federal issue. The control of natural resources and land management were quintessential State functions. The States managed Crown land, leased it and sold it. They were responsible for land use planning and development control, though some of these functions they might delegate to local governments which were subject to State laws and administration. Minerals were owned by the (State) Crown and could only be exploited with the approval of, and subject to the controls imposed by, the States. The growth and development and preservation of the urban environment were again a matter for the States and their delegates in local government. Wildlife conservation was also a State matter: the States determined which animals could be hunted and licensed many of the hunters. They also passed laws to control the sale of animal skins as a conservation measure. The Commonwealth's role was limited to the areas where it functioned in effect as a State government, that is, in its mainland and overseas territories and (though the matter was not determined conclusively by the High Court until 1975) in coastal areas beyond the low-water mark and all offshore areas within Australia's jurisdiction.

The situation changed in the 1970s. During the late 1960s there had been a marked increase in public awareness of conservation issues. Sydney's development was jolted by a series of 'green bans' imposed by the Builders Labourers' Federation to protect old buildings or patches of bush. In Tasmania conservationists fought and lost the battle to save Lake Pedder. In Queensland and New South Wales sandmining for exotic minerals such as rutile led to protests, as did suggestions that the Great Barrier Reef might be mined or drilled for oil deposits. There was some reaction in the States to public pressure, and to the example provided by American legislators, with Victoria, Western Australia, Queensland, South Australia and Tasmania all passing environmental protection legislation between 1970 and 1973. The Commonwealth had signalled its awareness of some of the problems when the Senate held inquiries into air and water pollution in the late 1960s, but it was not until the Whitlam government came to power at the end of 1972 that the Commonwealth was ready to provide a substantial legislative framework to highlight national involvement in the issue.

In three years the Whitlam government passed a series of measures which were to set a pattern for future legislation by the Commonwealth. In 1974 the Commonwealth passed the Environment Protection (Impact of Proposals) Act and several States Grants Acts which were intended to encourage State action in relation to nature conservation and soil conservation. In 1975 it passed the National Parks and Wildlife Conservation Act, the Australian Heritage Commission Act and the Great Barrier Reef Marine Park Act. These reflected an interest in conservation, and even a willingness to play a leading role, by way of example.

But, with the exception of the law establishing the Great Barrier Reef Marine Park, the laws were constitutionally unadventurous. They were concerned with the way Commonwealth ministers and instrumentalities should behave towards conservation and environmental problems, and with providing some financial assistance for the States. Except in relation to the Great Barrier Reef, they did not try to displace the States or dictate to them. The Environment Protection Act laid down procedures for Environmental Impact Statements (EIS) for Commonwealth projects. The Heritage Commission Act created a means of drawing up a register of the 'national estate' (a term Whitlam borrowed from United States President John F. Kennedy, and introduced into Australian politics in 1969). However, the legislation provided no special protection for places marked down as part of the national estate, other than the fact that they had been named as such. The only consequence of being placed on the register was that such a 'place' (and listing was available only for places, not, for example, for moveable pieces of the national estate like works of art) could not be interfered with by the Commonwealth without the relevant authority making a decision based on balancing conservation against other policy concerns. The laws were acceptable to the opposition parties, and when the Liberal and National parties were in power in the second half of the 1970s and the early 1980s, they continued their operation, with some legislative amendment.

Some of the limits of other Commonwealth powers were in fact tested by the Fraser government rather than the Whitlam government, though the legislation in issue was the 1974 Environment Protection (Impact of Proposals) Act. The *Murphyores* case, (*Murphyores Inc. Pty Ltd v. The Commonwealth* (1976) 136 CLR 1), concerned a dispute over sandmining on Fraser Island in Queensland. The Commonwealth in effect prevented mining by indicating that it would not grant a permit for the export of the minerals recovered from the mining. There was no interstate or intrastate buyer available, so mining would have been a costly and financially unrewarding exercise that would have resulted in the stockpiling of the minerals. The High Court held that the Commonwealth could decide—solely on environmental grounds—

whether to grant an export permit. This decision was not unexpected. The Court in 1966 had ruled that, when the Commonwealth was making laws about a subject where it had constitutional power, it could lay down conditions which were not directly relevant to the subject matter: a law providing for the licensing of television stations could impose conditions on the licensees which had nothing to do with television (*Herald and Weekly Times Ltd v. Commonwealth of Australia* (1966) 115 CLR 418). Though the principle was clear enough, in the television case there was at least a possible connection between the conditions that might be imposed about who might hold a licence and what the licensee might broadcast. There was no such connection here. The purpose of the exercise of the power to prohibit a particular item had nothing whatsoever to do with exports. The export power was a means of enforcing a Commonwealth policy about conservation and the environment, thereby overruling the State government which had approved the project. The Court said that the Commonwealth Minister for Minerals and Energy was entitled to require an environmental impact inquiry to be held before he approved an export permit, and he was entitled to rely on environmental considerations exclusively in making his decision. The decision clearly left it open for the Commonwealth to take environmental and conservation considerations into account in exercising any of its other powers under the trade and commerce power, such as the power to refuse to allow foreign investment in any particular project.

Applying the principle of the *Murphyores* case, it was clear there were other constitutional powers where the Commonwealth government might take account of environmental concerns. Those that might relevantly be useful were quite extensive. They included:

- Taxation, bounties, customs and excise (ss. 51(ii), 51(iii), 90 and 99 of the Constitution), so that concessions and financial incentives could be provided for activities in accord with Commonwealth policies;
- Special purpose grants (s. 96) to finance State projects, policies and legislation approved by the Commonwealth;

- Territories (s. 122) through which the Commonwealth could use legislation directly to establish an environmental regime in the mainland and overseas territories;
- The 'race' power (s. 51(xxvi)), to protect or conserve sites of significance to Aboriginal and Torres Strait Islander people;
- The corporations power (s. 51(xx)), to require all foreign corporations and all trading and financial corporations to follow environmental policies;
- The external affairs power (s. 51(xxix)), to legislate in relation to all areas beyond the low-water mark, and to implement international treaties and agreements in relation to environmental matters;
- The defence power (s. 51(vi)), particularly in relation to nuclear issues;
- The fisheries power (s. 51(x)), in relation to conservation and environmental issues;
- The 'national implied' power, a power implied from the existence of Australia as a nation, which might be particularly relevant to conservation issues.

Relying on some of these powers, the Fraser government promoted a series of laws to protect the environment in such areas as air and water pollution, uranium mining, historic shipwrecks, wildlife protection and specific measures to regulate Northern Territory areas. But the full measure of the Commonwealth's powers was not explored until the Hawke government came to power with an election promise to prevent the damming of the Gordon River in Tasmania and the implementation of the Gordon below Franklin hydro-electric scheme.

THE *DAMS* CASE

The World Heritage Properties Conservation Act relied on four sources of Commonwealth power—external affairs, corporations, race and the implied national power. The High Court's decision (the legislation was immediately challenged by the Tasmanian government) made it clear that appropriate legislation relying on any of the three specific powers (external affairs, corporations and race) could be used to prevent the dam being built, and that this particular law, as framed, was a valid exercise of the external affairs and corporations power. The Court split 4–3 to uphold the law. Subsequent decisions by later, differently constituted, Courts have confirmed and expanded the Commonwealth's ability to exercise these powers.

The external affairs power could be invoked because the site for the dam and the area that subsequent flooding would affect were within an area which was included (in December 1982) on the World Heritage List, a list prepared in accordance with a convention drawn up under the auspices of UNESCO (the United Nations Educational, Scientific and Cultural Organization). Australia adopted the Convention in 1974 and ratified it in 1975. The Tasmanian government had asked the Commonwealth to nominate the area for consideration as part of the 'world's heritage' in 1981. The 1983 World Heritage Properties Conservation Act included the Convention as a schedule so as to make it part of Australian domestic law. It allowed the Commonwealth government to make regulations to give effect to the Convention and to protect areas that had been made part of the world heritage (that is, they had been included on the official World Heritage List). The previous year the High Court had decided in the *Koowarta* case (*Koowarta v. Bjelke-Petersen* (1982) 153 CLR 168) that a 1975 Commonwealth law (the Racial Discrimination Act), which made a UN convention on racial discrimination part of Australian domestic law, could validly prohibit State government conduct that was illegal or improper under that convention. The *Koowarta* case also had been a split 4–3 decision by the High Court, which had undergone one change (Justice Dawson replacing Justice Stephen who had retired to become Governor-General) in the intervening period. The change in personnel did not directly affect the result. But the majority was somewhat more decisive in their reasoning in *The Commonwealth v. Tasmania* (1983) 158 CLR 1 (the *Dams* case), and the implications of their developing views about the breadth of the external affairs power were to be explored and realised in later environmental cases considered by the High Court.

For the moment, what mattered in the *Dams* case was that

Justices Mason, Murphy, Brennan and Deane considered that the external affairs power allowed the Commonwealth to make laws to implement any genuine international treaty, irrespective of its subject matter. The treaty did not have to be concerned with international affairs as such—the fact that Australia and other countries had thought it necessary and desirable to draw up the treaty was a sufficient indication of the relevance to the external affairs power. The external affairs power was activated because implementation or non-implementation of the treaty might affect Australia's relations with other countries. In fact, there was no necessity for a formal treaty to be concluded before the external affairs power could be invoked. It was enough if the subject matter to which the legislation was directed was related to a matter of real international concern.

The effect of the *Dams* case decision was considered by the Court in the *Lemonthyme and Southern Forests* case (*Richardson v. Forestry Commission* (1987–88) 164 CLR 261). That case involved a challenge to Commonwealth legislation which established a Commission of Inquiry into whether some or all of a large section of forest land in Tasmania should be nominated for World Heritage listing. The law imposed a freeze on all forestry operations in the area (which comprised almost 5 per cent of the Tasmanian land mass) and prevented any other development or destruction in the area without the permission of the Commonwealth minister, until such time as the inquiry was concluded. Although a 5–2 majority upheld the validity of the Commonwealth law and in effect extended the powers available to the Commonwealth, the decision did not provide the Commonwealth with a completely free hand. A majority of the Court thought that any measures must be reasonably considered to be appropriate to give effect to the (external affairs) object, and that this legislation satisfied that test. Chief Justice Mason and Justice Brennan said that the external affairs power supported not only Australia's known international obligations but also its 'reasonably apprehended obligations'. They said (at 295–6):

> In making provision for the establishment of the Commission of Inquiry and for the regime of interim protection of the

> protected area, Parliament has made a legislative judgment about the situation and the Convention obligation that may be proved to exist. It is not for us to impugn the bona fides of that judgment. It is enough that the legislative judgment could reasonably be made or that there is a reasonable basis for making it . . . Of course, if the legislative judgment cannot reasonably be supported, the Court will not hesitate to declare that it is invalid as an excess or abuse of power.

The external affairs power

All this is a long way from the tentative position adopted by the High Court in the *Koowarta* case in 1982, which in accordance with decisions of the 1930s appeared to confine the Commonwealth's power to implement treaties to those treaties which were international in character—that is, those dealing with matters the Court would accept as having an international flavour. In *Koowarta* the Commonwealth solicitor-general, Sir Maurice Byers QC, put a great deal of effort into persuading the Court that the treaty in issue, the International Convention for the Elimination of all Forms of Racial Discrimination, could be traced back to immediate postwar concerns about the racist policies of Hitler. It was a convention based on 1940s European concerns, not 1980s third-world pressures. Not that this should have mattered, but it certainly added weight to the Commonwealth's argument that this was a matter of genuine international concern of long-standing. The argument seemed required by the decision in the *Burgess* case (*R. v. Burgess; ex parte Henry* (1936) 55 CLR 608) in 1936. That case decided that the external affairs power did allow the Commonwealth to make laws to regulate conduct in Australia—it was not limited merely to what Australia might do overseas in relation to its external relations with other countries. Nor was the power limited to the areas where the Commonwealth already had legislative power—this was a new and separate power, though it was limited by (in those days) section 92 and other implied limitations on Commonwealth power. But the power was restricted to implementing the specific terms of treaties. A treaty about civil aviation did not give the Commonwealth power over civil aviation. The Commonwealth's power was limited to implementing the contents of the treaty, its provisions concerning safety or the licensing of pilots and aircraft, and did not extend to making rules about civil aviation issues not agreed to in the treaty.

In a sense, the High Court's decisions of the 1980s have widened the external affairs power only as a matter of degree. The Commonwealth still is not given free rein if it signs a treaty. Any legislation must be directed to implementing Australia's obligations under the treaty. But what has happened since the 1930s is that the subject matter of international treaties has expanded to cover almost every imaginable topic. Nations are more ready now to recognise their interdependence, and do so across a range of subject matters quite inconceivable half a century ago. For example, pollution and the greenhouse effect are now recognised as national and international problems which can only be combated through international co-operation. There seem few limits to the issues on which treaties—multilateral or bilateral—might be agreed. And if there is no treaty in existence, because general multilateral agreement is not (yet) possible, the likelihood is that there will nevertheless be evidence (say, that there are negotiations for a treaty under way) sufficient to satisfy the High Court that the matter is one of genuine international concern, sufficient to justify the Commonwealth making laws under its external affairs power.

Those who protest that these decisions by the High Court have enabled the Commonwealth to invade the exclusive domain of the States can reasonably argue that those who wrote the Constitution could not possibly have envisaged such a development. It can be argued that the words 'external affairs' did not even mean, at the time of federation, that the Commonwealth could control Australia's relations with the rest of the world. The conduct of foreign relations was in British hands prior to federation and nationhood was not going to alter that position. Australia would remain part of the British Empire, and its relations with other countries would be managed by Britain. Insofar as Australia wanted or needed to have contact with other countries, it would use British resources to do so. Direct contact with other nations was, at least until World War I, frowned upon. When Britain entered the world wars in 1914 and 1939 it was assumed, not least by the Australian governments of the time, that Britain spoke for the whole Empire and that, as a consequence, Australia was also at war. (For a further discussion of the development of Australia's position in the world see chapter 10.)

The restricted nature of the 'external affairs' reference in the Constitution can be understood further by looking at the very next power listed in the Constitution, 'The relations of the Commonwealth with the islands of the Pacific.' Logically this makes no sense. Or rather, it makes no sense as a separate power. External relations must surely include relations with this particular group of countries. That argument was indeed considered during the Convention debates. What emerges from an examination of the very brief debate on this particular section is that it was supposed to allow Australia to administer some of the Pacific Islands on behalf of Britain. As Mr Barton told the Convention, 'there are a very large number of people who look forward with interest to the Commonwealth undertaking, as far as it can as part of the British Empire, the regulation of the Pacific Islands'.

What, then, was 'external affairs' supposed to mean? Significantly, it was listed among the legislative powers of the new nation. The actual conduct of foreign relations, from the business of exchanging ambassadors and diplomatic staff and of conducting negotiations, to the ultimate question of foreign relations—declaring war—is a responsibility of the executive government, and does not need to be supported by a power to make laws. In Britain it was the King, and subsequently his Cabinet, who was responsible for the conduct of foreign relations. In the United States it was the President. In Australia, if foreign relations was to be the responsibility of the new nation, it would be the prerogative of Cabinet, acting through the Governor-General. But this 'external affairs' power was different. This was a power which was to be given to the parliament, not to the executive. So what was it? According to the 1901 commentary by Quick and Garran, the external affairs power was intended to give to the Commonwealth parliament the power to implement treaties that had been negotiated and entered into by Britain. It meant that these treaties could be made part of the domestic law of

Australia. The example they gave was the extradition of fugitive offenders. A provision of this kind was necessary because, under the British legal system, international treaties do not normally have the force of domestic law. To have legal effect under domestic law it is necessary for the treaty to be specifically enacted as part of the domestic law. To take the Quick and Garran example, fugitives from justice from outside Australia could only be handed over to that other country if Australia passed a law adopting the terms of the particular international convention or bilateral treaty. Such a law would require magistrates and judges to deal with people brought before them for extradition as fugitives in accordance with the terms of the law and the treaty. In the absence of such a law, an offender would have to be dealt with in accordance with the normal procedures of, say, the Migration Act, and might be entitled to resist deportation to the specific country that was seeking him or her.

This example is not as helpful as it might be. Although there might be limits on the power available under the immigration power to deport some criminals (in particular, the power does not extend to people who are not migrants), there is a separate power over the 'influx of criminals'. The question remains though, whether the external affairs power gives the Commonwealth power to make laws in areas where (external affairs commitments aside) no other constitutional powers are present to support the legislation. Logically, there would be no point in the existence of the external affairs power if it did not provide a separate and independent source of power for the Commonwealth parliament (though, as has been suggested above, in relation to the power to deal with 'the islands of the Pacific' logic is not an impeccable guide to constitutional meaning).

The Convention debates suggest that the power was meant to be extremely limited. The original draft constitution had proposed that this power should take the form 'External affairs and treaties'. The words 'and treaties' were dropped by the Convention when similar words were removed from one of the clauses in the legislation which precedes the Constitution, a clause that states the general jurisdiction of the Commonwealth ('This Act, and all laws made by the Parliament of the Commonwealth under the Constitution, shall be binding on the courts, judges and people'). The New South Wales Legislative Council moved successfully to remove from this covering clause the additional requirement that 'all treaties made by the Commonwealth' would be binding. The reason for both deletions was again explained by Mr Barton: 'The treaty-making power will be in the Imperial Government.' While the new Commonwealth might conduct trade negotiations, even these would have force only if ratified by the Imperial government. 'The sole treaty-making power is in the Crown of the United Kingdom.'

It was almost two decades before that ceased to be true. At the end of World War I Australia took part in the Versailles Peace Treaty negotiations and signed the treaty. In the 1920s Imperial conferences leading to the Statute of Westminster in effect recognised the right of the Dominions to conduct their own external relations. But this acquisition of independence in the foreign affairs field was a gradual matter, which in turn expanded the meaning of the simple phrase 'external affairs' in a constitutional sense.

The High Court had some doubts when it first had to determine whether the power allowed the Commonwealth to make laws enforcing in Australia the provisions of a treaty entered into by Australia. In *R v. Burgess; ex parte Henry* (1936) 55 CLR 608, the Court validated legislation that enacted the terms of the Paris Convention of 1919 on 'aerial navigation', though it invalidated regulations that did not conform sufficiently to the terms of the treaty. However, the power could not be used to permit people holding a licence under the Commonwealth legislation to operate if they did not hold a State licence, according to the Court's decision in *Airlines of NSW v. NSW (No. 2)* (1965) 113 CLR 54. These doubts over the extent to which the use of the external affairs power would enable the Commonwealth to override State powers (along with a natural inclination of federal Liberal governments not to interfere with the States) were sufficient for many years to prevent the Commonwealth from trying to enforce such powers as it might gain under some treaties against the States. In practice, successive Commonwealth governments showed considerable reluctance to enter into treaties that required them to take any actions to impose laws where the States would normally have legislative competence. An apparent need for State approval where State legislation would normally have been necessary to enforce particular obligations (e.g. in relation to employment conditions) inhibited Commonwealth endorsement of many treaties. In some treaties, the Commonwealth took advantage of 'federal' clauses which other countries also sought and which limited the national government's responsibilities where a nation's power was divided under a federal constitution.

The doubts were set aside in the 1980s with the *Koowarta*, *Dams* and *Lemonthyme* decisions, while the fears of the States over their ability to manage their own territories without Commonwealth interference magnified. At the 1989 Australian Legal Convention, lawyers debated the hypothetical problem of whether the external affairs power would, under the current High Court's interpretation, allow the Commonwealth to agree with Liechtenstein to widen Sydney's Pitt Street. The answer was an equivocal 'yes'—it would depend on the reasons for the treaty: but proper, environmental, reasons might be found to justify such an action.

Aspects of the corporations power

The external affairs power is only one of the 'new' powers now available to the Commonwealth to protect the environment. The second is the corporations power, section 51(xx). It was tested and validated in the *Dams* case, though it was available to the Commonwealth primarily because the Hydro-Electric Corporation (HEC), the dam projects proposer, was a corporation within the reach of section 51(xx). The power would not have been relevant had the dam been a direct undertaking by the Tasmanian government, though the law would have stopped government and private corporations from helping in the construction of the dams.

What the High Court decided in the *Dams* case about the corporations power was not 'new'. Just as its decision on 'external affairs' followed logically from its decision in *Koowarta*, so the decision on the corporations power was a proper consequence of its 1971 decision in the *Concrete Pipes* case (*Strickland v. Rocla Concrete Pipes Ltd & ors* (1971) 124 CLR 468) and subsequent decisions in the late 1970s and early 1980s. The decision meant that the Commonwealth could pass a law directed at those corporations covered by its constitutional powers (foreign corporations, and trading and financial corporations incorporated in Australia) to prevent them from specific activities. The Commonwealth's Trade Practices Act took up that legislative challenge, successfully. The *Dams* case proved that the Commonwealth could also direct legislation to a specific objective, even though the legislation might seem to be aimed at just one statutory corporation (in this case) or a few corporations. So the Commonwealth could make laws to prevent constitutionally relevant (i.e foreign, and trading or financial corporations) from engaging in particular environmentally damaging activities, setting whatever criteria (for example approval by a federal minister, following an independent environmental impact statement) it wished to establish. The subject matter of the law would not matter so long as it was directed to the relevant corporations.

One issue not completely resolved by the *Dams* decision was the extent to which the Commonwealth could now make laws directed to trading corporations which did not directly concern their trading activities. It was not necessary for the Court to reach a conclusion on that question because a majority held that the business of knocking down trees and building roads to construct a dam were for the purposes of the trading activities of the HEC, which was in the business of supplying electricity to customers. But three members of the Court held that the Commonwealth was not limited to just dealing with the trading activities of corporations, and another left the question open for resolution at a later time. More significantly, a majority held that the HEC was a trading corporation, a decision contrary to the decision reached by the Court ten years earlier when it had decided that the St George County Council, a local government supplier of electricity, was not a trading corporation. The trend of decisions since the *St George County Council* case (*R. v. Trade Practices Tribunal; ex parte St George County Council* (1974) 130 CLR 533) had been clearly to favour a wider compass for the notion of trading corporations, so the *Dams* decision on this issue was not surprising. There was also the important difference here that the HEC was in the business of manufacturing the electricity as well as being a supplier. The fact that the corporations power does not extend to the direct activities of State governments or individuals is not of great significance in terms of Commonwealth control of environmental issues in relation to major developmental projects. The position was summarised by the then president of the Australian Conservation Foundation, Murray Wilcox QC (later a Federal Court judge), in these terms:

> Almost all significant development in this country is carried out by trading corporations, either on their own account or on behalf of natural persons or governments. If, as now seems clear, the Commonwealth may regulate their activities, in so far as they are 'for the purposes of' trade, then it has a wide scope for environmental control. It would, for example, be possible for the Commonwealth to enact endangered species legislation in which it regulated the activities of corporations in relation to habitat. It would be possible to impose pollution controls upon corporations carrying on trading activities. It would be possible to prohibit trading corporations adversely affecting items on the Register of the National Estate. It would be possible to regulate the conduct of corporations in relation to the supply in the course of trade of no-deposit beverage containers. The list is almost endless.

STANDING TO SUE

Power is one thing; politics another. The High Court's various decisions increasing the potential ability of the Commonwealth to control or influence various environmental decisions and policies of the States and of corporations and individuals do not necessarily mean that the Commonwealth will develop such environmental and conservationist policies and attempt to enforce them. That is a question of political will. The Commonwealth would have to be prepared to introduce legislation if necessary or adopt administrative policies to require adherence to the relevant environmental policies, and a particular government may decide that such a course of action is not desirable or proper. In the absence of Commonwealth action, it is not always possible for other groups or individuals to utilise the laws passed by the Commonwealth or to make use of other developments in environmental law. There is nothing to be gained from the knowledge that you are right and the developer of a particular project is wrong, unless you are able to do something to stop the development. You must be able to get access to the Court, and be heard by the Court. The problem is one of 'standing'. Not everyone can approach the Court to obtain a declaration that what is happening is illegal, or to force governmental action to protect the environment or uphold an environmental law.

In this area of the law, the High Court has moved more slowly. In the *ACF* case (*Australian Conservation Foundation v. The Commonwealth* (1978) 146 CLR 493) the High Court upheld the basic English common law approach to standing: in order for a person to obtain standing he or she needs to establish either that a private right is being interfered with (as well as the public right) or that the person would suffer damage peculiar to himself or herself. The Court (in a 3–1 decision, affirming the earlier decision of another Justice) refused to review the law, and would not allow the ACF to challenge the validity of a decision by Commonwealth ministers to grant foreign exchange approval to the development of a tourist resort by the Iwasaki group in Queensland, despite the fact that the ACF had participated in administrative procedures under the Environmental Protection (Impact of Proposals) Act concerning the development. Despite the ACF's well-known interest in the matters raised in the case and its submission to the inquiry, it had no 'special interest' over and above that enjoyed by the public generally. One member of the majority, Justice Mason, said at the conclusion of his judgment (at 552):

> The Court would exceed its function if it accepted the invitation issued by the appellant's counsel to jettison the settled principle of law relating to locus standi and substitute for it a new rule recognising a mere belief as an adequate special interest on the part of the plaintiff. There are limits to what the courts can and should do by way of altering the law. The court is not a legislature and has no general charter to reform or

> change existing law. This is an evolutionary and continuing process . . .

Justice Mason pointed out that this question of standing had been referred by the government to the Australian Law Reform Commission (ALRC) for investigation and report.

More than a decade later, after the ALRC has reported and recommended changes, and after several attorneys-general have promised that the law would be reformed, there has been no legislative action. But there has been a minute movement in the courts, of the evolutionary type. It occurred in the next standing case, *Onus v. Alcoa of Australia Ltd* (1981) 149 CLR 27. The action concerned Victorian legislation, the Archeological and Aboriginal Relics Preservation Act. Aboriginal people from the area where Alcoa wanted to build an aluminium smelter applied to the courts to prevent any interference with Aboriginal relics. But first they had to establish that they had standing. The Court held that they did, particularly in view of their claim to be the guardians of the particular relics. As for the law, most members of the Court saw no need for any review, though Justices Stephen and Brennan could see the need for development in the future. In fact, Justice Brennan spelt out a new approach to the question of special interest in environmental issues, saying (at 73):

> A special interest in the subject matter of an action being neither a legal nor equitable right, nor a proprietary or pecuniary interest, will ordinarily be found to arise from modern legislation enacted to protect or enhance non-material interests—interests in the environment, in historical heritage, in culture. Where such a statute imposes a public duty to protect or enhance a non-material interest, a breach of the duty is apt to affect a non-material interest, and it would be vain to search for a proprietary or pecuniary damage suffered by a plaintiff. A plaintiff in such a case, though he may be able to show a special interest in what the statute seeks to protect or enhance, would be unable to show a private right or to prove that he has suffered proprietary or pecuniary damage. To deny standing would deny to an important category of modern public statutory duties an effective procedure for curial enforcement.

Justice Murphy, who had dissented in the *ACF* case, ridiculed the search for new ways of measuring special interest. 'Standing,' he said, 'is a judicial invention', and he pointed out that in practice questions of standing were often brushed aside if a court considered that in the public interest the issue of substance should be settled. In this area he thought the test should be broad, and that a cultural or other interest might be sufficient.

A later addition to the Court, Justice Toohey, gave a paper in 1989 to an international environmental law conference in Sydney, where he discussed a number of reform measures. He made it clear he favoured a different approach to standing in environmental issues. There was a 'certain unreality' in applying the conventional standing tests where legislation existed to protect some aspect of the environment, he said. 'It is the community as a whole or in part that will suffer where there has been a breach of some public duty imposed by legislation . . . There are good reasons why an organisation, formed to protect the environment, should be permitted to proceed in such a case.'

Until the High Court overturns its decision in the *ACF* case, the focus for environmentalists is likely to remain on the political arena. It is governments which have to decide whether to enter into treaties, whether to seek listing to protect sensitive areas, whether to introduce legislation, and whether to use and enforce the laws. But decisions of the High Court have created a climate of opinion favouring Commonwealth intervention in environmental issues. The Commonwealth is now expected to 'do something' to protect national estate forests, even though the original legislation envisaged no more than a grand list of places meriting national attention. That expectation would not have arisen but for the way the Court gave its approval to various laws and actions taken by the Commonwealth to protect the Tasmanian and Queensland forests.

6

TAXATION: WHO PAYS?

It is obvious enough that decisions by the High Court about the Constitution, and particularly about the constitutional division of power between the Commonwealth and the States, should have political consequences, and to that extent at least, the Court is an active participant in the political arena. It is less apparent that the Court may also become involved in the political process through its interpretation of legislation. Yet in the 1970s and 1980s, the High Court's various interpretations of key sections of the Income Tax Assessment Act were an important element in the political brawls which led to a major recasting of the national tax system. The Court was accused of giving aid and comfort to people avoiding and evading tax, by refusing to implement the clear legislative policy of the government and the parliament. Its perceived attitude forced governments to legislate in extraordinary detail to fix the gaps that the Courts allowed tax practitioners to explore. There was increasing resort to retrospective legislation to prevent too great a drain on government revenue. A whole range of new taxes was introduced, to try to provide more equity in a system whose progressive nature had been partly destroyed through what was called by (then) Treasurer Paul Keating, the 'rorting' of the system.

The High Court was not necessarily guilty of all the charges made against it. But the fact is that its judgments were an important element in the tax scandals of the 1970s and 1980s, and its public and political standing probably suffered as a result.

Judges are not required to reflect the changing trends of public opinion. As Chief Justice Gibbs retorted, when told by counsel for the Commissioner of Taxation in one special leave application that there had been a 'general hardening of public attitude against tax avoidance', 'We are not concerned with public attitudes, we are concerned with trying legal principles' (*Commissioner of Taxation v. Insomnia Pty Ltd*, 13 May 1983, transcript, p. 4). Nevertheless, judicial attitudes did change over a twenty-year period, and in the same direction as political and public opinion. That they did so reflected at least in part changes in legislation and in the intentions of the parliament—intentions the parliament told the Court that it should have regard to. It also reflected changes in the composition of the Court, the attitudes of newer Justices allowing them to assess differently the 'legal principles' to which Chief Justice Gibbs referred.

This is best exemplified in the history of the Curran scheme, which gave the tax avoidance industry in the 1970s its beginnings and, for some years to come, a measure of legitimacy. Charles Curran was a Sydney stockbroker. The scheme to which his name became attached involved the issue of bonus shares to create a paper loss which was then used to eliminate or reduce profits. Shares were bought in a company which, at the time of purchase, had substantial capital profits. Those profits were, after the purchase, credited in payment of bonus shares issued to the shareholders. A majority of the High Court said that when the taxpayer sold his [or her] shareholding later he [or she] suffered a deductible loss, the taxpayer having paid for the shares by means of credit given to him [or her] by the company—that is, the bonus shares were paid for by the company, though the 'cost' of those shares could be claimed by the taxpayer as a deductible outgoing, or taken into account in determining profit or loss.

It was a perfect 'paper' scheme. The taxpayer had only to find an appropriate accountant or lawyer to carry out transactions that would provide the taxpayer with the deductions needed to reduce his or her assessable income to zero, or as close to zero as the taxpayer thought right and proper. Its costs were comparatively low (in commissions, fees and so on) and the High Court made it risk-free when it handed down its judgment in 1974. It was 'legal' and, according to some High Court Justices, if it was legal there was nothing morally questionable about it.

Thousands of people decided to take advantage of Curran schemes, particularly when the Whitlam government did nothing to close the loophole, other than to say that it would introduce legislation which would have that effect. After the Whitlam government was defeated, the new treasurer, Philip Lynch, took almost two years to give the same undertaking, but it wasn't until April 1978 that another new treasurer, John Howard, brought forward proposals to put these promises into effect. Howard had his legislation backdated to the time of Lynch's announcement, saving hundreds of millions of dollars of deductions from schemes intended to squeeze the last taxation advantages out of the High Court's interpretation of the legislation in the *Curran* case (*Curran v. Federal Commissioner of Taxation* (1974) 131 CLR 409).

The initial government inaction, and its belated reaction, to the High Court's decision in *Curran*, was a measure of public opinion about tax avoidance at the time. By 1990 the Curran scheme had been well and truly legislated out of existence, but the Taxation Commissioner was still dealing with some of the challenges against rulings he made in the 1970s disallowing deductions for Curran schemes. The High Court then took the opportunity to review its earlier decision, though it had no need to do so, as the Commissioner had won in the full Federal Court. But only the High Court could critically assess the correctness of the actual decision in *Curran*, rather than trying to distinguish it (i.e. show that the facts were quite different) as lower courts had to do if they were to avoid following the High Court's decision.

For the purposes of the appeal in *John v. Commissioner of Taxation* (1989) 166 CLR 417, the law the Court had to deal with was exactly the same as the law when *Curran* was decided. But the Court, only six members of which sat on the case, was unanimous in deciding that the decision in *Curran* was wrong and needed to be reversed. Essentially the Court adopted the reasoning of the lone dissenting judge in *Curran*, Justice Stephen.

The 1990 Court decided that where the majority in the 1974 Court had gone wrong was in not properly assessing the cost of the relevant shares. Cost is not just expenditure, it is also 'that which is forgone in exchange for that which is acquired'. The cost of acquiring the original shares included the right to participate in any distribution of the company's surplus assets. Nothing John had was forgone for something else. The joint majority judgment in *John* (Chief Justice Mason and Justices Wilson, Dawson, Toohey and Gaudron—Justice Brennan wrote a separate concurring judgment) said (at 436), 'we are unable to accept that, merely by reason of an amount being credited in payment of bonus shares, the amount so credited is or is properly to be regarded as the cost of the same' and is not to be regarded as a section 51(1) deduction under the Income Tax Assessment Act. The Court concluded that 'the reasoning adopted by the majority in Curran was defective' (at 438).

OVERRULING

But should *Curran* be overruled? The Court has evolved a series of criteria which it often (though not invariably) applies when it considers whether it should overrule any of its previous decisions. The most significant reason for not disturbing the decision in *Curran* was that it had been acted and relied upon, first by taxpayers wanting to take advantage of it, and second by the parliament, to deal with the way in which bonus shares should be treated by the Commissioner. These were, the majority judgment said, 'powerful reasons for following *Curran* in the present case'. (After all, if the High Court had not decided *Curran* in the way it did, the taxpayers awaiting the outcome of the 1990 case would not have made those particular tax avoidance arrangements in 1977.) But the majority approved a statement by Justice Mason in an earlier case, which said (at 439–40):

> The fundamental responsibility of a court when it interprets a statute is to give effect to the legislative intention as it is expressed in the statute. If an appellate court, particularly an ultimate appellate court, is convinced that a previous interpretation is plainly

> erroneous then it cannot allow previous error to stand in the way of declaring the true intent of the statute . . . It is no part of a court's function to perpetuate error and to insist on an interpretation which, it is convinced, does not give effect to the legislative intention.

The majority said that 'in the end the justification for not following an earlier decision construing a statute must be that in the view of the court that earlier decision was wrong, that it was wrong in a significant respect, and that the Court should give effect to the intention of the Parliament'. This applied with equal force to the application of a statutory provision (as was the case here) rather than statutory construction in the strict sense.

That was the end of *Curran*. It was almost as though it had never existed. The mistake had been corrected. Why the Court got it wrong in the first place does not matter. Nor do events in the interim. The Court in 1990 was only making a decision about the 'legal principles' that were applicable and was not affected by public or political opinion or anything else. The same can be said for the 1974 Court.

There had in fact been one change to the legal environment (putting aside personnel changes which meant that a wholly new Court was considering the case). This was the change introduced in 1981, at the same time the parliament had to deal with the replacement of the catch-all anti-evasion section of the Income Tax Assessment Act (of which, more later). By section 15 AA of the Acts Interpretation Act, the parliament required the Court to have regard to the purpose or object of an Act. The section says, 'In the interpretation of a provision of an Act, a construction that would promote the purpose or object underlying the Act (whether that purpose or object is expressly stated in the Act or not) shall be preferred to a construction that would not promote that purpose or object.'

Literal or purposive

There was nothing really revolutionary about the concept of the primacy of the purpose or object underlying an Act involved in this reminder to the Court. It did indeed represent one of the standard approaches normally adopted by courts in their task of construing legislation. However, in August 1980 the High Court had rejected the application of this principle to the Income Tax Assessment Act. In *Commissioner of Taxation v. Westraders Pty Ltd* (1980) 144 CLR 55, Chief Justice Barwick and Justice Murphy had staked out opposite positions on whether the Tax Act should be interpreted literally, and Justice Murphy's purposive approach had lost out. Chief Justice Barwick said (at 59–61) that the case:

> . . . affords an occasion to point out the respective functions of the Parliament and of the courts in relation to the imposition of taxation. It is for the Parliament to specify, and to do so, in my opinion, as far as language will permit, with unambiguous clarity, the circumstances which will attract an obligation on the part of the citizen to pay tax. The function of the Court is to interpret and apply the language in which the Parliament has specified those circumstances. The Court is to do so by determining the meaning of the words employed by the Parliament according to the intention of the Parliament which is discoverable from the language used by Parliament. It is not for the Court to mould or to attempt to mould the language of the statute so as to produce some result which it might be thought the Parliament may have intended to achieve, though not expressed in the actual language employed . . .
>
> Parliament having prescribed the circumstances which will attract tax, or provide occasion for its reduction, the citizen has every right to mould the transaction into which he is about to enter into a form which satisfies the requirements of the statute . . .
>
> [T]he freedom to choose the form of transaction into which he shall enter is basic to the maintenance of a free society.

Justice Murphy, dealing with what he said was acknowledged to be a major tax avoidance scheme, said it was a mistake to hold that any circumstances, no matter how artificial and contrived, that literally fit the words in the relevant section of the Act therefore complied with them (at 78–80):

> The history of interpretation shows the existence of two schools, the literalists who insist that only the words of an Act should be looked at, and those who insist that the judicial duty is to interpret Acts in the way Parliament must have intended even if this means a departure from the strict literal meaning . . . It is an error to think that the only acceptable method of interpretation is strict literalism. On the contrary, legal history suggests that strict literal interpretation is an extreme, which has generally been rejected as unworkable and a less than ideal performance of the judicial function.
>
> It is universally accepted that in the general language it is wrong to take a sentence or statement out of context and treat it literally so that it has a meaning not intended by the author. It is just as wrong to take a section of a tax Act out of context, treat it literally and apply it in a way which Parliament could not have intended . . .
>
> It has been suggested, in the present case, that insistence on a strict literal interpretation is basic to the maintenance of a free society. In tax cases, the prevailing trend in Australia is now so absolutely literalistic that it has become a disquieting phenomenon. Because of it, scorn for tax decisions is being expressed constantly, not only by legislators who consider that their Acts are being mocked, but even by those who benefit. In my opinion, strictly literal interpretation of a tax Act is an open invitation to artificial and contrived tax avoidance. Progress towards a free society will not be advanced by attributing to Parliament meanings which no one believes it intended so that income tax becomes optional for the rich while remaining compulsory for most income earners.

In that case, the view of Chief Justice Barwick prevailed by a 3–2 majority, but the retirement of the Chief Justice soon after was to lead to a fairly rapid change in the Court's approach to the tax legislation and to tax cases. At the very time parliament was changing the Acts Interpretation Act to emphasise the need for courts to pay more heed to parliamentary intention, the Court was demonstrating that it was capable of adjusting its attitude. In *Cooper Brookes (Wollongong) Pty Ltd v. Commissioner of Taxation* (1981) 147 CLR 297, the Court, by a 4–1 majority, rejected a strictly literal reading of several sections of the Act. Chief Justice Gibbs said that if the language of a statutory provision was clear and unambiguous, and was consistent and harmonious with other provisions of the enactment, it must be given its ordinary and grammatical meaning, even if it led to a result that might seem inconvenient or unjust (at 305):

> To say this is not to insist on too literal an interpretation, or to deny that the court should seek the real intention of the legislature . . .
>
> [I]f two constructions are open, the court will obviously prefer that which will avoid what it considers to be inconvenience or injustice. Since language, read in its context, very often proves to be ambiguous, this last mentioned rule is one that not infrequently fails to be applied.

Justice Stephen declined to follow the literal interpretation in this case because it was clear to him that there had been an error by the legislative draftsman, which had resulted in the section becoming an anachronism. But Justices Mason and Wilson (in a joint judgment) thought that the literal construction rule had been expressed more absolutely in the past, and applied too rigidly. They said, 'The fundamental object of statutory construction in every case is to ascertain the legislative intention by reference to the language of the instrument viewed as a whole.' They said the propriety of departing from the literal interpretation extended 'to any situation in which for good reason the operation of the statute on a literal reading does not conform to the legislative intent as ascertained from the provisions of the statute, including the policy which may be discerned from those provisions'. That last phrase came quite close to the object which the parliament wanted to stress in section 15AA of the Acts Interpretation Act, which came into force exactly a week after this judgment was published.

In *Westraders* and in *Cooper Brookes* there was room for argument about the meaning of the relevant sections. But in *Gauci v. Federal Commissioner of Taxation* (1975) 135 CLR 81, it is difficult to understand how the Court could possibly have reached the conclusion it did. In that case the Court was considering the effect of section 190(b) of the Tax Act which says that on an appeal 'the burden of proving that the assessment is excessive shall lie on the taxpayer'. Chief Justice Barwick said that no doubt this required the taxpayer to show that the assessment was excessive, but the section did not raise any presumption about the taxpayer's purpose in acquiring a particular property. Justice Jacobs agreed with the Chief Justice that all the facts were known apart from the state of mind of the taxpayers, and for section 190 to operate there had to be something in the evidence from which an inference could be drawn about their states of mind. Justice Mason dissented (the case was heard by only three members of the High Court). He said he was:

> unable to discern any basis for declining to give effect to s. 190(b), according to its terms . . . There is nothing inherently unfair in a provision which places the onus on a taxpayer to prove his case when the purpose for which an asset was acquired depends so much on his intentions and on circumstances of which he, rather than the Commissioner, has comprehensive knowledge.

Justice Mason was to be vindicated four years later in two cases (*McCormack v. Federal Commissioner of Taxation* (1978–79) 143 CLR 284 and *Macmine Pty Ltd v. Commissioner of Taxation* (1978–79) 53 ALJR 362) in which three other members of the Court made it clear that they approved Justice Mason's dissenting views in *Gauci*. Chief Justice Barwick and Justice Jacobs maintained their views, but they were outvoted. Justice Mason was not a member of either of the Courts which upheld his view in *Gauci*. Indeed it appears that he was assigned to comparatively few cases of any significance in the tax area by Chief Justice Barwick after he published the *Gauci* dissent. (As to how and why the High Court sat as a bench of 3, 4, 5, 6 or 7 on these cases, see the discussion in chapter 11.)

Parliamentary action

The tax avoidance industry explored many of the provisions of the Tax Act in the 1970s and rarely came to grief when challenges reached the High Court. For the Commissioner and for the government, it was, until 1980, a question of plugging loopholes as they were exposed and exploited. The annual reports of the Commissioner detailed the battles as they worked their way through the court system, often to the High Court, and the legislative reaction to them. In his 1978–79 report, for example, the Taxation Commissioner told parliament (page 7 of the report) that the number of people participating in tax avoidance schemes, though a small percentage of the taxpayer population, had 'increased substantially, and the schemes had had a significant effect on tax collections'. He said some $433 million attributable to tax avoidance schemes remained uncollected at the end of that financial year. (The amount had increased to $700 million a year later, and $973 million two years later.)

The Commissioner told parliament that in 1978–79 'there was a perceptible increase in publicity' urging taxpayers not to comply with the basic requirements of the taxation laws. He said that numerous schemes to avoid payment of tax had come to notice, most of them highly artificial and none of them easy to define in all their ramifications because of the difficulty in obtaining concrete information about the mechanics and procedures employed. The Commissioner reported on all the legislation parliament had passed to deal with some of the schemes: amendments, for example, to deal with Curran schemes, with current year loss schemes, with pre-paid interest, pre-paid rent and similar schemes, with trust stripping arrangements, with modified versions of the Curran scheme, with commodity trading schemes, with share trading loss schemes and with expenditure recoupment schemes. Legislation had at that stage been promised also to deal with the carrying forward of losses created by tax avoidance schemes and depreciation schemes.

The following year the Commissioner complained (page 7 of his report) that an 'alarming tactic much in evidence during 1979–80 is stripping companies or trusts of their tangible assets without making provision for payment of tax assessed or to be assessed. This use of legal forms and procedures would be regarded by most as pure tax evasion not really capable of passing under the euphemism of "avoidance".' A year later he said (page 12) that these tactics had continued in 1980–81 and 'frantic activity' was in evidence immediately before 4 December 1980 when the Crimes (Taxation Offences) Act 1980 came into operation to counter them.

That legislation was important because it signalled that the government was no longer prepared to adopt just a catch-up approach to the tax avoiders. The legislation provided for criminal sanctions against those engaged in the asset stripping of companies to avoid income tax. Legislation in 1982 strengthened that initial response by imposing a vendors recoupment tax on shareholders who sold shares in the stripped companies, and a promoters recoupment tax on those who had promoted the schemes.

At the same time the government was acting to replace the key anti-avoidance provision of the Income Tax Assessment Act, section 260, with a more comprehensive provision, Part IVA, which came into effect from 27 May 1981. The government felt bound to take this action because of the way in which the High Court had effectively destroyed section 260 as an important anti-tax-avoidance tool.

SECTION 260

Section 260 had a long history, and it had mostly achieved its purpose until the late 1960s. It was (as s. 53) part of the original (Commonwealth) Income Tax Assessment Act in 1915. It was applied in an important case (*Jaques v. Federal Commissioner of Taxation* (1924) 34 CLR 328) by the High Court to overrule a scheme which Justice Isaacs explained was 'to manufacture a situation to get the better of the Income Tax Act . . . It was in no true sense a business operation' (at 360). That type of approach was echoed by the Privy Council when it was able to evaluate section 260 in *Newton v. Federal Commissioner of Taxation* (1958) 98 CLR 1. There, Lord Denning, speaking for the Privy Council, provided the following test (at 8):

> In order to bring the arrangement within the section you must be able to predicate—by looking at the overt acts by which it was implemented—that it was implemented in that particular way so as to avoid tax. If you cannot so predicate, but have to acknowledge that the transactions are capable of explanation by

> reference to ordinary business or family dealing, without necessarily being labelled as a means to avoid tax, then the arrangement does not come within the section.

This came to be known as the 'predication' test, but it was no sooner proposed than it was disposed of by a High Court which showed an unusual (for the time) and rapid reluctance to follow the dictates of the Privy Council.

Lord Denning had rejected a series of arguments put by Sir Garfield Barwick QC, counsel for the taxpayer, one of which Lord Denning said, if accepted, 'would deprive the words of any effect'. But within a few years Chief Justice Barwick was in a position where he could lead the Court into judgments which did indeed effect that result. In 1971 the Court brought down a decision in *Commissioner of Taxation v. Casuarina Pty Ltd* (1970–71) 127 CLR 62, which effectively ignored the Privy Council's decision in *Newton*, and instead gave effect to the High Court's decision in *W. P. Keighery Pty Ltd v. Federal Commissioner of Taxation* (1957) 100 CLR 66, a case which had been discussed and not approved by the Privy Council in the *Newton* case. In *Keighery*, the successful counsel for the taxpayer was Sir Garfield Barwick QC. He had argued that what was done by the taxpayer was within the contemplation of the statute, and not an attempt at circumventing the statute—what had been done was what the Act allowed to be done (at 82). The Court in *Keighery* had agreed, saying that section 260 could not be relied on to deny 'the appellant company the benefit arising from an exercise which was made of a choice offered by the Act itself' (at 93).

In *Casuarina*, the 'choice principle' adopted in *Keighery* was reasserted and the majority of the Court said it had not been affected by subsequent legislation or decisions, and that *Newton* had not disposed of it (at 101–2). The majority judgment in *Casuarina* was written by Justice Walsh, but Chief Justice Barwick added an important indication that the 'predication' test in *Newton* should be considered to have no application when the 'choice' principle could be invoked (at 81). That approach prevailed in subsequent cases in the 1970s, which finally convinced the Taxation Commissioner that he should cease even to bother arguing that section 260 should be applied by the courts. The cases involved were *Mullens v. Federal Commissioner of Taxation* (1976) 135 CLR 290, *Slutzkin v. Federal Commissioner of Taxation* (1977) 140 CLR 314, and *Cridland v. Federal Commissioner of Taxation* (1977) 140 CLR 330.

The *Mullens* case was decided by a court of three (Chief Justice Barwick and Justice Stephen, Justice McTiernan dissenting). Chief Justice Barwick said (at 298), 'The Court has made it quite plain in several decisions that a taxpayer is entitled to create a situation in which the Act attaches taxation advantages for the taxpayer. Equally, the taxpayer may cast a transaction into which he intends to enter in a form which is financially advantageous to him under the Act . . .' In *Slutzkin*, decided by a unanimous Court (Chief Justice Barwick and Justices Stephen and Aickin), Chief Justice Barwick said (at 319), 'The choice of the form of transaction by which a taxpayer obtains the benefit of his assets is a matter for him.' In *Cridland* a Court of five adopted the judgment of Justice Mason who pointed out (at 339) that Lord Denning's judgment in *Newton* had not been regarded subsequently by the High Court as the expression of a universal or exclusive criterion of operation of section 260.

Section 260 was dead. It was buried by the parliament in 1981, to be replaced by Part IVA. But then in 1985 it was suddenly brought to life in a series of cases involving doctors—*Commissioner of Taxation v. Watson and Gulland, Pincus v. Commissioner of Taxation* (1985) 160 CLR 55—by a High Court which was very differently constituted from the benches that considered the section when Sir Garfield Barwick presided. And yet, typifying the somewhat shell-shocked approach of the Tax Office to section 260 following its disasters in the 1970s, the resurrection was not as complete as it might have been, because the Commissioner did not seek directly to overturn the Barwick Court's decisions. Theoretically, *Slutzkin*, *Cridland*, *Casuarina* and *Keighery* were still good law after the *Watson* decision and *Newton* was not. The section 260 slate was not wiped clean in as thorough a way as happened with *Curran*. Perhaps it really did not matter, given that section 260 applied only to a diminishing number of disputes concerning pre-1981 tax liability.

The choice principle

What was interesting in the *Watson* and *Pincus* cases was the way in which the High Court dealt with the 'choice principle' which the Barwick Court had used to supplant the predication test. Chief Justice Gibbs, who had been a member of the Barwick Court, thought the two tests were not inconsistent. He said that the test from *Newton* had been applied in the *Peate* case (*Peate v. Federal Commissioner of Taxation* (1966) 116 CLR 38 and (1967) 1 AC 308 (in the Privy Council)), which involved the tax affairs of a doctor, as did the present case. The similarities were such as to persuade the Chief Justice that the decision in the *Peate* case was applicable here. He rejected argument that *Mullens, Slutzkin* and *Cridland* had effectively overturned *Peate*, saying that *Peate* was not mentioned in those later cases.

As for the choice principle, the Act did not allow a taxpayer the opportunity to have his or her own income from personal exertion taxed as though it were income derived by a trust and held for the benefit of a number of beneficiaries (at 70). Justice Brennan said that the choice principle was inapplicable when the arrangement, as in the present case, sought to divert income from one taxpayer to another (at 79). He said an arrangment that had the effect of avoiding tax was not within section 260 unless the avoidance of tax was 'a purpose for which the arrangement was made'. He said the 'true reconciliation between the choice principle and the *Newton* test of purpose is to limit the former to cases depending upon a specific provision of the Act' (at 81). Justice Dawson, with whom Justice Brennan said he otherwise agreed, said that an extreme view of the *Keighery, Casuarina* etc. cases would tend to deprive section 260 of any practical effect. The problem, he said, was to reconcile section 260 with the rest of the Act. That was a matter of construction, and was the basis of the decision in *Newton* (at 107). Justice Dawson said that the choice or choices available to a taxpayer may be limited because of the presence of section 260 in the Act, however much they might have been available in the absence of that section. Justice Wilson agreed with the reasoning of both the Chief Justice and Justice Dawson, which makes it somewhat difficult to discover the true reconcilation between the choice and *Newton* principles which the majority arrived at.

The dissenting judgment of Justice Deane, who provided an excruciating analysis of the way the High Court had destroyed the effectiveness of section 260, perhaps showed that reconciliation was not possible. He pointed out that *Casuarina* made plain that the predication test was incapable of being applied at all to a case coming within the choice principle (at 88). He said the cases made it clear that the choice theory 'has nothing to do with a legislative intent to give a choice between specific alternatives' (at 91). The effect of *Mullens* and *Slutzkin*, he said, 'was to deprive s. 260 of much of what one would have thought was its intended operation'. The Barwick approach 'unjustifiably divorced the provisions of s. 260 itself from the other provisions of the Act' (at 93). Then came something of a *cri de coeur* (at 94):

> It should be apparent from the foregoing that I have difficulty with the emphasis upon legal form and the disregard of substance which *Mullens* and *Slutzkin* require in the application of s. 260. Uninstructed by authority, I should have thought that the legislative intent to be discerned in s. 260 was that identified by Isaacs J in *Jaques* and by the Privy Council in *Newton*, namely, that if it can be objectively predicated that either form or substance must be explained as—to use the vernacular—a 'tax dodge', it should be disregarded.

But *Cridland* had settled the construction of section 260 and the Court had not been asked to overturn it here (at 94):

> The reason for that was, no doubt, that the calls by this Court for legislative reform have, after a quarter of a century of inaction by Governments of differing political persuasions, finally evoked some response. Section 260 has now, at long last, been amended so as not to apply to contracts, agreements or arrangements made or entered into after 27 May 1981 and replaced by the new Part IVA of the Act as regards any 'scheme' entered into after that date . . .

A MORAL CHOICE

At the height of the tax evasion crisis, one of the loose-leaf services (Butterworths) which provided lawyers and accountants with references to all the legislation and case law they needed for their day-to-day practices included in its outline of section 260 a note on 'The morality of tax avoidance'. It said:

> The following comments of Barwick CJ in a pay-roll tax case, *Brambles Holdings Ltd v. Federal Commissioner of Taxation* (1977) 8 ATR 108, are relevant in considering the question of whether a taxpayer is entitled to consider the method most advantageous to him in determining his policies:
>
> > *In the administration of taxation laws it is, in my opinion, fundamental that the citizen is entitled to take advantage of the provisions of the statute, even if the result is not something contemplated by the draftsman. If that result is not acceptable to the Parliament, no doubt Parliament will amend the statute, an exercise which occurs with frequency and seemingly without difficulty. Provisions such as s. 16T of the Pay-roll Tax Assessment Act, 1941, as amended (Com) and s. 260 of the Income Tax Assessment Act 1936, as amended (Com) ought not to be construed as denying such a right to the citizen, even where he deliberately chooses the form of a transaction into which he contemplates entering so as to attract the benefit of the statute, the transaction of course not being a sham or pretence . . .*

It is hardly surprising that accountants and lawyers who were in the market place selling and advising on avoidance schemes felt that they had been badly done by when the parliament passed laws which resulted in many of them paying large fines and some of them being sent to gaol. A different view of the morality of tax avoidance was given by Justice Murphy (who never sat on a s. 260 appeal) during a National Press Club speech in 1983:

> The Court no longer encourages the tax avoidance industry—it is no longer regarded as the tax avoider's temple. The Court used to read Acts of Parliament absolutely literally—the words were all important—the spirit was often ignored. This made it easy for any competent lawyer or accountant to devise schemes to turn profits into tax losses. Because of this many of the rich

> ceased to pay tax and the burden fell on the workers and the scrupulous. This literal approach has now been abandoned by the Court, which now adopts the correct judicial approach that Acts of Parliament should not be interpreted in a way which Parliament could never have intended.

But the tax fiasco which the High Court oversaw became a political issue of such significance that a change by the Court in its approach to the tax laws was not the complete answer. The problem had to have a political solution, whatever turnabouts might subsequently be undertaken by the High Court. Investigations such as those undertaken by McCabe and Lafranchi in Victoria, and by Frank Costigan QC as a Royal Commissioner, produced reports about the misuse of the tax laws by white-collar criminals so startling as to demand political intervention. Legislation having retrospective effect was demanded rather than frowned upon. And a total revision of the tax system seemed to be required. A tax summit was followed by the introduction of fringe benefit taxes, capital gains taxes and other devices which were intended to ensure that the tax laws could not be used for large-scale evasion, whatever attitude was adopted by the High Court.

The High Court was re-evaluating its own role at the beginning of the 1980s, but by then it was too late. The politicians knew that they had to come up with a better tax system, with laws which could not be distorted by clever accountants and lawyers. In political terms the government of the day did not react quickly enough or strongly enough, and it was left to a new government to implement really substantive reforms through the mid-1980s. The High Court's rewriting of its own decisions on the tax laws through the same period was of legal rather than political interest. Needless to say, the High Court upheld the drastic penalties which the parliament introduced to deal with bottom-of-the-harbour operators (*MacCormick v. Commissioner of Taxation* (1984) 158 CLR 622) and to apply the new taxes even to State governments (*Queensland v. The Commonwealth* (1986–87) 162 CLR 74).

7

CORPORATIONS: AN ACQUIRED POWER

On 8 February 1990 the High Court handed down a decision that stunned the Commonwealth government's principal legal advisors and its policy-makers in the area of corporate law. By a 6–1 majority, the Court rejected the central, basic provisions of the massive (998-page) Corporations Act 1989. The Court ruled that the Commonwealth did not have the constitutional power to regulate and control the incorporation of companies in Australia. Without this power, the new legislative package to establish a single national law controlling trading and financial corporations in Australia would have no force. Indeed the Commonwealth, at an early stage in proceedings inaugurated to test the validity of the Corporations Act, gave an undertaking that it would not proclaim the less contentious parts of the law if it were to be held by the Court that it did not have the specific power to control incorporation.

That promise was easily given, because the Commonwealth had no doubts about the outcome of any challenge. For a decade and a half its principal advisors had given formal advice to the effect that it had the power to legislate for a national companies code, including all the main areas covered by the 'cooperative' national scheme enacted by the States and Territories in the 1970s. It had pressed ahead, over the opposition of many of the States, with the development of its new laws, with plans to replace the National Companies and Securities Commission with a new Australian Securities Commission and to take over (or make redundant) the apparatus the States had built up to regulate and collect fees from local companies. It had bludgeoned some of the States into accepting its proposals, doing deals about the amount of revenue that would be returned to those States, the number of employees who would be taken over, and the location of the headquarters and operational centres of the new national bureaucracy. It had even managed to buy off one of the three States challenging the new scheme on the eve (literally) of the challenge being argued in the High Court.

The High Court, which had been expected to give its approval to the scheme which was scheduled to become fully operational on 1 July 1990, instead knocked away its foundations. For the government it was a severe blow. The damage might be controllable, though the timetable would have to be changed. For the Court, normally immune from and rarely affected by criticism, it brought forth many comments that made it clear that the Court's judgments were not always held in great awe, comments like those made by Trevor Sykes, editor of *Australian Business*: 'The decision will delight pedants, lawyers and zealots for States' rights. But to anyone who has to live in the real commercial world it looks stupid' (*Australian Business*, 21 February 1990, p. 6).

It took the Commonwealth government five months to negotiate a way out of the mess in which its own intransigence and the Court's decision had left it. But in June the Commonwealth and the States (and the Territories, whose views did not really matter because the Commonwealth did have the constitutional power to make its legislation apply directly to them) did reach agreement on the need for the Commonwealth to bring its scheme into existence, and on the mechanism that would give the States some small say in its operation. The negotiations were more fruitful than those which preceded the Court's decision because the Commonwealth no longer saw itself as operating from a position of strength and superiority. It had to get the States to agree, or face the prospect of introducing a quite different kind of legislative scheme which would leave the States with the power to control the incorporation of companies. The States, despite the superiority of their constitutional position, were conscious of the fact that the regulatory regime they had been in control of had failed to detect and prosecute the company and financial abuses that marked the end of the 1980s or to prevent the host of corporate crashes of that period. The major States, New South Wales and Victoria, were agreed that the Commonwealth should be running a national scheme, but Victoria in particular did not want to refer its constitutional powers to the Commonwealth. After several months they agreed on the means they would adopt—an application of laws regime, in which the States would apply within their own boundaries the law made by the Commonwealth for itself and for the Australian Capital Territory.

Strangely enough, the outcome of the High Court's decision and the negotiated settlement by the various governments may have produced a scheme which is stronger and more secure from constitutional attack. Such an attack would be mounted not by the States, but by a corporation which fell foul of the new national regulatory scheme. However, future decisions by the Court may further enhance the Commonwealth's powers to deal with corporations and with trade and commerce. That suggestion is based on the way the Court reached its decision in this and previous cases dealing with the relevant constitutional powers, and the attitude of the Court to the Constitution and the functioning of government. Nevertheless, there are problems for the Commonwealth in the enforcement area which are yet to be resolved.

THE FIRST LAW

The corporations power is contained within section 51(xx) of the Constitution, which gives the Commonwealth parliament the power to make laws with respect to: 'Foreign corporations, and trading or financial corporations formed within the limits of the Commonwealth.'

In 1906 the newly established Commonwealth parliament decided to utilise this power to create an Australian version of the United States Sherman Act, the anti-trust law passed by the United States Congress in 1890 to outlaw monopolisation and restraint of trade. The local version was called the Australian Industries Preservation Act. But the law was emasculated by the High Court two years later in *Huddart, Parker & Co. Pty Ltd v. Moorehead* (1908) 8 CLR 330. More significantly, the High Court's reading down of the corporations power was so severe that for another half a century and more the Commonwealth did not consider that it could re-enter the field unless it could change the Constitution. On four occasions different governments sought to broaden the corporations power, but on each occasion the referendum to change the Constitution was defeated.

Huddart, Parker was a company formed under Victorian law which refused to answer questions in relation to offences which the Comptroller-General of Customs believed had been committed against sections 5 and 8 of the Australian Industries Preservation Act. The company and its manager were each fined five pounds for having refused to answer the questions, and those fines were then challenged on the grounds that the relevant sections of the Act were unconstitutional.

Section 5(1)(a) made it an offence for any foreign corporation, or trading or financial corporation formed within the Commonwealth, to make a contract or engage in any combination 'with intent to restrain trade or commerce within the Commonwealth to the detriment of the public'. Section 8 made it an offence for any of those corporations to monopolise any part of the trade or commerce within Australia 'with intent to control, to the detriment of the public, the supply or price of any service, merchandise or commodity'.

The High Court held by a 4–1 majority that the provisions were invalid. Chief Justice Griffith and Justice Barton held that the corporations power allowed the Commonwealth parliament to make a law prohibiting the relevant corporations (that is, foreign corporations and trading or financial corporations formed within the limits of the Commonwealth) from engaging in trade or commerce within a State, or to impose conditions subject to which they could engage in such trade or commerce, but it could not control the operations of those corporations which lawfully engaged in that trade and commerce. Their reasoning was based on the fact that section 51(i) of the Constitution gives the Commonwealth the power to make laws with respect to '[t]rade and commerce with other countries, and among the States'. They believed that the fact that the trade and commerce power did not include power over intrastate trade and commerce meant such powers were 'reserved' to the States. It was not possible to use the corporations power to get around this 'reservation' of power to the States. The Constitution had to be construed as if it contained an express declaration that power to make laws with respect to trade and commerce within a State was reserved to the States except so far as the exercise of power by the Commonwealth was necessary for or incidental to the execution of some other power conferred on the Commonwealth. Here the contracts and combinations which the Commonwealth sought to ban were governed by State law, and the Commonwealth could not invade that area of State powers either (*Huddart, Parker*, particularly at 352, 354).

Justice O'Connor held that the Commonwealth could not make laws regulating and controlling the business of corporations, while Justice Higgins thought that the Commonwealth could regulate the conditions under which they might carry on business, but not the contracts into which they might enter. The sole dissenter was Justice Isaacs. However, all the members of the Court agreed that the Commonwealth's power (such as it might be) was limited to foreign corporations and trading or financial corporations created by State law.

The notion of 'reserved powers' was to continue to dominate the High Court's determination of the powers of the Commonwealth parliament until the *Engineers* case (*Amalgamated Society of Engineers v. Adelaide Steamship Co. Ltd* (1920) 28 CLR 129) when the Court, following the departure of its three original Justices, decided that there was no true basis for such an approach. From then on, the Commonwealth's powers were to be interpreted without preconceived notions about particular areas being reserved for the States. As Justice Isaacs had pointed out in *Huddart, Parker* (though he couldn't muster a majority for his view until 1920), the issue was whether there was a grant of power to the Commonwealth. 'It is always a question of *grant*, not of prohibition, unless that is express' (at 391, the emphasis provided by Justice Isaacs).

A SECOND ATTEMPT

It was not until the 1960s that the Commonwealth decided to see what legislation it could pass to control unsociable corporate behaviour. The Australian Industries Preservation Act of 1906 had been based on the political culture of the United States at the time, and the legislation broadly followed the American model. This time it was Britain that would provide the impetus for Commonwealth regulatory activity. Britain had introduced a Monopolies law in 1948, which was followed in 1956 by a Restrictive Trade Practices Act. Various restrictive trading practices had to be registered, but might be approved after it was demonstrated to the Restrictive Practices Court that they were in the public interest. Australia was prompted to look at restrictive trading practices and their regulation in a similar way and in 1963 the attorney-general, Garfield Barwick, published proposals for Australian legislation along British lines.

It was left, however, to his successor, Billy Snedden, to have the new law drafted and to get it approved by Cabinet and by the backbench. Despite the fact that it was a watered-down version of the Barwick proposals (Barwick had wanted to outlaw various practices, to make it an offence not to register a restrictive practice, and to make it punishable if the practice were followed, while Snedden favoured administrative control mechanisms), Snedden had extraordinary difficulty in getting the proposals through Cabinet. According to Snedden's memoirs, the detailed debate was carried on through 27 Cabinet meetings and occupied more than 200 hours. For Snedden what was important was that '[i]t was a commencement. It turned around the philosophy [of the Government] from one of no trade practices legislation into one of acceptance of trade practices legislation. The Government was committed to it' (Snedden and Schedvin 1990, p. 65).

So too, was Sir Garfield Barwick, who was Chief Justice of the High Court by the time the Trade Practices Act of 1965 was challenged. Barwick had thought it within the Commonwealth's power to legislate about restrictive trade practices, and now he was able to make a judicial pronouncement to that effect.

The Snedden legislation came before the High Court in the form of a challenge against a decision by the Commonwealth Industrial Court to dismiss charges against three companies which had made an agreement restricting the sale and supply of concrete pipes by them in Queensland (*Strickland v. Rocla Concrete Pipes Ltd & ors* (1971) 124 CLR 468). The Industrial Court had dismissed the prosecutions because it considered (and necessarily so, given that lower courts must follow the decisions of courts superior to themselves in the judicial hierarchy) that the outcome of the case was governed by the High Court's decision in the *Huddart, Parker* case to hold the relevant sections of the new legislation invalid. The Industrial Court's decision turned out to be right, but for the wrong reasons.

The High Court in 1961 was unanimously of the view that *Huddart, Parker* had been wrongly decided by the High Court in 1909 because of the way in which the majority in that case had relied on what Sir Garfield Barwick now referred to as 'the so-called reserved powers doctrine which was exploded and unambiguously rejected by this Court in the year 1920' in the *Engineers* case (at 485). That doctrine, he explained, had meant that the earlier Court 'was driven to emasculate the legislative power given by s. 51(xx) and to confine it in substance to the statutory recognition of corporations falling within the terms of the paragraph and the fixing of conditions upon which they might enter trade in Australia: for the rest, their trading activities in intra-State trade was a matter for the State legislation exclusively' (at 488). But he considered that the relevant parts of the Australian Industries Preservation Act 'dealt with the very heart of the purpose for which the corporation was formed, for whether a trading or financial corporation, by assumption, its purpose is to trade . . .' (at 489). The law controlling such trading activities was clearly a law with respect to section 51(xx), and *Huddart, Parker* should be overruled.

And everyone agreed, at least on this point. The Court was less sure about the terms of the newer legislation they were actually considering. The then attorney-general, Tom Hughes QC, conceded that the drafting of the legislation was too general, because the Commonwealth had hoped for a reference of powers from the States to validate it. This had not happened. But he thought it could be saved by the Acts Interpretation Act (at 472). But five of the Justices, including Barwick, thought not, though in striking down the legislation Barwick made it fairly clear how it might be recast by the Commonwealth to ensure that it would survive a future challenge.

The Commonwealth government reacted quickly and within three months the parliament had passed the Restrictive Trade Practices Act 1971, to replace the former law. That in turn was replaced after the Whitlam Labor government came to power by the Trade Practices Act of 1974, a law which returned to the original 1906 model by outlawing various kinds of anti-competitive corporate activities. It also contained a formidable, modern consumer protection code.

Companies legislation

The Whitlam government had far broader designs on corporate law, however. Before it came to office, the collapse of a mining boom had prompted an extensive inquiry by a Senate Committee (headed first by Sir Magnus Cormack and then by Senator Peter Rae) into securities and exchange. When that committee reported in 1974, the Commonwealth tabled a Companies and Securities Industries Bill, which proposed to regulate stock markets and stock exchanges and people dealing with securities. It also proposed to require the registration of public companies and to require their compliance with auditing, disclosure, takeover and prospectus matters. But the Bill was not enacted, and companion legislation had not been introduced when the parliament was dissolved in November 1975.

The Fraser government decided to adopt a cooperative route to national companies regulation. In the early 1980s a series of Companies Acts were introduced in the Commonwealth, States and Territories, designed to implement a cooperative scheme. A Ministerial Council presided over the scheme and over the

National Companies and Securities Commission. But it was not answerable to any parliament, and the scheme in effect prevented any parliament from amending any Companies legislation brought before it. The scheme avoided the constitutional difficulties which may have plagued the 1974–75 proposals, but it was unwieldy and unable to cope with the corporate crises of 1985–90.

In 1988 the Commonwealth committed itself to a new national scheme, based on Commonwealth legislation under the corporations power. It was passed by parliament in 1989, but challenged by three States, one of which withdrew immediately before the hearing of the *Corporations* case *New South Wales v. The Commonwealth* (1989–90) 169 CLR 482. In the High Court the States based their arguments mainly on the use in the Constitution of the word 'formed', saying that this meant 'already formed'. They relied on the acceptance of this proposition by the Court in the *Huddart, Parker* case.

The Commonwealth argued that the problem words, 'formed within the limits of the Commonwealth', were used in the Constitution simply to make the distinction between those corporations and 'foreign' corporations. Faced with the challenge from the Court, 'How did all the members of *Huddart, Parker* who were at the Convention, and Quick and Garran who were at the Convention, get it so wrong?', the Commonwealth was forced to say that perhaps they acted too precipitately, and in any event most of the Court relied on the 'reserved powers' doctrine. The solicitor-general used a sea-going analogy (befitting the Huddart, Parker company's activities as a shipping company) to say that the *Concrete Pipes* case not only disabled the good ship *Huddart, Parker* but it left it sunk with all hands. The States were seeking to attach themselves to single pieces of flotsam which they saw as still afloat 81 years later. But their efforts were misplaced, because it was really jetsam. *Huddart, Parker* should be regarded by the Court as sunk, having been wholly overruled in the *Concrete Pipes* case.

The Court (or to be more precise, six of its members: Justice Deane dissented) thought otherwise. It held that while a majority of the Court in *Huddart, Parker* relied on the doctrine of reserved powers when they considered the Australian Industries Preservation

Act, all the members of the Court had relied on 'purely textual considerations' when they decided that the Commonwealth did not have power under section 51(xx) to legislate for the creation of corporations. And the rejection of *Huddart, Parker* by the Court in the *Concrete Pipes* case did not extend to a rejection of the views in *Huddart, Parker* concerning the power of the Commonwealth to provide for the creation of corporations. Chief Justice Mason was later to say that, whatever its fundamental structural (and doctrinal) faults, the good ship *Huddart, Parker*, though later sunk with all hands, would never be lost without trace (Mason 1990, p. 2).

The Court said the history of the section confirmed that the language of the paragraph was not directed towards the subject of incorporation. It referred to the successive drafts of the section and the Convention debates, and the contemporary opinion of commentators. Finally, it expressed doubts about the complexity of the legislation, which, it suggested, stemmed from construing section 51(xx) so as to include a power to legislate for the creation of corporations within the confines otherwise imposed by that paragraph. That construction, the majority said, 'is supported by neither the language of the provision, nor its history nor authority'.

The case was argued before the Court over three days in early October 1989, and the Commonwealth made it clear it wanted a decision as quickly as possible, so that it could complete the final negotiations with the States early in the New Year. It was anxious that the Corporations Act should come into effect on 1 July 1990. The decision on 8 February 1990 left it with an entirely different problem: how to resurrect a law which it had undertaken to the Court not to implement at all, following the Court's decision not to recognise the primary basis on which validity was argued. It might have redrafted the law to accept that the States would deal with the incorporation of corporations but insisting that the Commonwealth alone would regulate all trading and financial corporations, holding companies and the like. But instead, once the federal election was out of the way, it decided to try to persuade the States to effectively surrender their powers to allow for national control of almost all Australian companies.

POLITICAL COMPROMISE

Success was announced after a meeting of the relevant ministers in Alice Springs in June 1990, in time (just) to allow the head of the Australian Securities Commission (ASC) to be installed also as head of the soon-to-be-abolished National Companies and Securities Commission. The announcement said that constitutional, legal, administrative and financial issues had all been settled. In anticipation of problems with the Western Australian parliament (particularly its upper house, which was controlled by the opposition) there was a special note that there would be detailed arrangements made for the maintenance of the 'current level of services in the States'.

Just how the scheme would operate was not revealed until the legislation was tabled in November. The 1989 Act was amended and re-enacted as a law for the Australian Capital Territory, while the States and the Northern Territory were to pass laws in effect adopting the Corporations Law as their own, and giving them power to administer the law within their boundaries. State and Territory courts were to be given cross-vesting power to ensure uniform application of the law and 'relatively simple administration and enforcement' of the law. The Commonwealth revealed that the States and the Northern Territory would, as a result of this legislative package, be paid $102 million a year, that amount being indexed to inflation.

Other aspects of the Alice Springs agreement included a restructuring of the Federal–State Ministerial Council and a diminution in its powers. The new ASC would be responsible directly to the Commonwealth attorney-general and the Commonwealth parliament, not to the Ministerial Council. The council would be consulted about all legislative changes to companies and securities laws, but the Commonwealth would have sole responsibility for national markets regulation. On the Ministerial Council the Commonwealth would have four votes and a casting vote—this meant it needed to get the support of only two of the States to win any vote. If its policies and arguments were not adequate to get that level of support, presumably it might have second thoughts in any event about the wisdom of its position. However, the States also agreed that the

Ministerial Council could not force the Commonwealth to introduce legislative changes with which it did not agree.

The results of the 'stupid' High Court decision in the *Corporations* case could be seen in a very different light, some twelve months later. The Commonwealth government, backed by an all-party Senate Committee report in 1987, had decided that the old cooperative Companies Code scheme had to be replaced by a national law, administered by a national agency adequately funded by and responsible to the Commonwealth. Its approach to the States was essentially on a take-it or leave-it basis: either they surrendered their powers and received some financial compensation, or they would be left without anything anyway. The High Court, adopting a thoroughly legalistic approach and relying ultimately on the meaning of the word 'formed', said the Commonwealth's legislative scheme was unconstitutional. The, no doubt, unintended consequence of the Court's decision was that the Commonwealth government was forced into serious negotiations with the States. Those negotiations were possible because the States fully recognised the deficiencies of the old scheme. The problem was to achieve a settlement which gave the States not only monetary compensation but a continuing input into policy formation.

The new legislative regime has some constitutional (and a great many political) advantages over the scheme that the High Court rejected. This is because of the inherent constitutional limitations on the corporations to which Commonwealth law could extend. These were those corporations listed in section 51(xx)—namely, foreign corporations and trading or financial corporations, together with corporations referred to in other parts of section 51, such as banks and insurance companies.

During the hearing of the *Corporations* case, the Court pointed to many possible difficulties which might be faced by the Commonwealth in covering holding companies and other companies not falling directly within the constitutional spread of corporations. The problem was mentioned in the majority judgment, when it was said, 'The fact that the character of a corporation may vary, so that it may be at one time a trading or financial corporation and not at another, makes it less likely at least that s. 51(xx) was intended to confer power upon the Commonwealth to incorporate companies over which its power of regulation might fluctuate, possibly without knowledge upon either side.' That problem would have certainly come before the Court again if the Commonwealth had brought in a scheme where its powers were limited to certain named types of corporations. But under its power to make laws for the Territories, there are no such limitations. The only limitations in the revised legislation are those agreed upon between the Commonwealth and the States which preserved the status quo under the former cooperative scheme as to the reach of the legislation.

So the Commonwealth ended up with a more comprehensive and less constitutionally suspect scheme than it originally proposed, a scheme in which the States were minor, but constitutionally vital, partners.

Although the new venture in State adherence to Commonwealth legislation appears to overcome most constitutional objections to the new Corporations Law, it does not settle all the constitutional problems the Commonwealth may have to face as it uses the corporations power for other policy ends. How far can the Commonwealth go, for example, in regulating particular actions by trading or financial corporations? Can it validly, for example, say that no corporation in trade and commerce, and no foreign corporation, may advertise or promote cigarettes or smoking? Could it forbid corporations trading in tobacco from sponsoring sporting events?

In the *Concrete Pipes* case Sir Garfield Barwick said that it did not follow from the validity of the Australian Industries Preservation Act sections that 'any law which in the range of its command or prohibition includes foreign corporations or trading or financial corporations formed within the limits of the Commonwealth is necessarily a law with respect to the subject matter of s. 51(xx). Nor does it follow that any law which is addressed specifically to such corporations or some of them is such a law' (at 489–90). In *Huddart, Parker*, Justice Higgins said that if the Australian Industries Preservation Act was valid 'the Federal Parliament is in a position to frame a new system of libel laws applicable to newspapers owned by corporations, while the State law of libel would remain applicable to newspapers owned by individuals'. He also gave other examples of how the Commonwealth might make corporations subject to Commonwealth laws about wages, or maximum interest rates, or the Statute of Frauds or Limitations legislation.

Both these statements were considered by the members of the Court in the *Dams* case. All agreed that the power in section 51(xx) is expressed 'as a power with respect to persons, namely, corporations of the classes therein specified'. But they weren't agreed as to what that meant. Justice (later Chief Justice) Mason said the power was not confined to the trading activities of trading corporations. Justice Wilson (no longer on the Court) said he did not find it necessary to decide whether the nature of the power precluded its exercise in a manner which confined its operation to a strictly localised situation and perhaps to one corporation. Justice (later Chief Justice) Brennan said that the law must 'discriminate: that is to say, it must be a law which operates to confer a benefit or impose a burden upon those persons when its operation does not confer a like benefit or impose a like burden on others'. Justice Deane said that the power should not be restricted just to the trading activities of trading corporations, whereas Justice Dawson thought it should. Plainly, the Court has yet to decide on the scope of the power.

In 1998 another potential problem emerged, concerning the enforcement of the new Companies Law. The Federal Court was given prime jurisdiction by the States over the law, through cross-vesting legislation. This survived a challenge by the barest possible margin in *Gould v. Brown* (1998) 72 ALJR 375 (a 3–3 decision, refusing an appeal from the Federal Court). The main issue was whether (as the statutory majority held) the States had the power to invest jurisdiction in a federal court, where the Commonwealth was willing to accept jurisdiction, or whether the Constitution prevented federal jurisdiction being expanded by the States. Two members of the majority retired from the Court shortly after this decision, making a future challenge inevitable, though whether such a challenge would be successful is less clear. However, defeat of the cross-vesting principle would result in a significant challenge for federal and State politicians, and a reshaping of the court system or the respective jurisdictions of the federal and State courts.

8

INDUSTRIAL RELATIONS: ENTER THE JUDGES

The waterfront has always been at the forefront of the political and legal battle over industrial relations, though it is a myth that Australian federation was brought about in part as a reaction to the nationwide strikes in the maritime and pastoral industries of the early 1890s. The Convention debates of the 1890s belie that. In the 1891 Convention, South Australia's Mr Kingston proposed that the Constitution should contain a clause to provide for 'the establishment of courts of conciliation and arbitration, having jurisdiction throughout the commonwealth, for the settlement of industrial disputes'. He introduced his proposal by saying he thought that 'in view of the magnitude of the recent industrial disturbances which have affected Australia and the whole of the civilised world, it is desirable when we are framing this federal constitution, that we should at least consider whether we cannot do something in the way of avoiding difficulties of the character to which I have referred'. The only means which occurred to him, he explained, was the appointment of a tribunal to investigate any dispute, to reconcile the parties if possible, or to make an award 'which will fix what, according to the decision of the court, is right and proper to be done, and will carry with its pronouncement, the means of its enforcement' (Sydney Convention debates, 1891, p. 688). After a brief intervention by Sir Samuel Griffith, the amendment was withdrawn so that it could be considered in the judicature section of the Constitution. When that was reached, Mr Kingston proposed that the courts which the Commonwealth could establish should include 'courts of conciliation and arbitration for the settlement of industrial disputes' (p. 780). Sir Samuel Griffith opposed the amendment, suggesting that it would interfere with the rights of the States, and with property and civil rights. The amendment was soundly defeated. A dozen men voted for it, 25 against.

In the 1897 Convention the proposer of a similar amendment was Henry Bournes Higgins. He originally proposed that the legislative power be in the form 'Industrial disputes extending beyond the limits of any one State.' Given the way the High Court was later to interpret the arbitration power, that original proposal by Higgins would have given the Commonwealth vast powers over industrial relations, and in particular it would have given it the power to make laws directly about any industrial dispute rather than, under the existing Constitution, the power only to make laws to establish conciliation and arbitration procedures. The issue was not discussed in these terms, however, and during the debate Higgins made it clear that what he wanted was a power for the Commonwealth to establish courts of conciliation and arbitration. He finally amended his proposal to read 'Conciliation and arbitration for the prevention and settlement of industrial disputes', and after a little prodding added 'extending beyond the limits of any one State'. His concessions did his cause no good. Again the proposal was defeated, on this occasion by 22 to 12 (Debates of the Adelaide Convention, 1897, pp. 782–93).

Success finally came in the Melbourne Convention, in January 1898, though the margin was quite small—22 to 19, the majority including conservatives such as Sir John Forrest and Sir George Turner. Sir John Forrest explained that he thought the federal parliament would be better able to deal with the subject 'and deal with it more moderately' than the States. 'I think that it will not be so likely to be influenced by party feeling as local Parliaments will be' (Debates of the Melbourne Convention, 1898, p. 210). One delegate who changed his mind between Adelaide and Melbourne was Sir Joseph Abbott, who explained that he had been impressed by the argument of one of the opponents of the proposal, Mr Symon, to the effect that it was either idle words or a mischievous proposal. If they were only idle words, Sir Joseph asked, what harm would be done by putting them in the Constitution, if their insertion had 'the effect of satisfying a sentiment which we know largely prevails throughout a certain class in Australia . . .' (p. 197). He argued that the Commonwealth might not use any power which was given to it, but that if it did not have the power 'in no instance can they interfere in a dispute, although they may be deeply interested in it' (p. 198).

Mr Symon had earlier argued (p. 192) that there was no such thing as an interstate dispute, that, for example, a maritime strike was a strike that involved particular States: 'a maritime strike does not take place on the high seas. A man comes into port and he leaves his ship.' He said the maritime strike of 1890 was, like all other strikes, the outward and visible sign of the real dispute between the parties. In the case of the maritime dispute it was settled by the Victorian law. He feared that giving power to the Commonwealth would be 'an invitation to mischievous men . . . to increase and extend the area of the strike in order to bring about something like civil war' (p. 193). Sir John Downer, another opponent of the proposal, was concerned that the use of compulsory arbitration (what he called 'main force') raised the problem of what you can do when you have exercised your main force (p. 188)?

> What is asked for cannot be done . . . a power of this sort will actually invite the very differences which it is sought to prevent and will deceive unfortunate persons by the supposition that in the event of there being a dispute there is a court of law that can not only decide, but that can compel their masters to concede what they desire.

Mr Symon was concerned also that the introduction of a Commonwealth authority could lead to 'enforcing the same wages all over Australia' (p. 190).

There were many speakers who supported the Higgins proposal, including its originator, Kingston, who told the Convention that the aim of the Constitution was to give the Commonwealth power to legislate for the 'peace, order and good government of the Commonwealth'. He asked the delegates (p. 186):

> By what means are the peace and order of the various colonies most disturbed, and their good government threatened, at the present time? By strikes and lock-outs. Shall we not then be wanting in our duty if we do not give to the Federal Parliament power to legislate in such a way as will prevent strikes and lock-outs, and enable industrial questions of the greatest difficulty to be amicably settled between the parties, upon considerations of right and wrong rather than because of the relative strength of the disputants?

The speeches at the Convention provide little guide to the way in which the Commonwealth was subsequently to exercise its powers over conciliation and arbitration, and to exercise other powers provided for it in the Constitution which enabled it to intervene in industrial disputes and allowed it to influence the course of industrial relations. They do, however, give a fair indication of the political mood at the time—at least of the conservative and liberal parties. The attitude of the labour forces was not presented to the conference, other than through the fears of those who sought to prevent any Commonwealth interest in this area.

The Labor Party did not come into existence as a federal party until the various MPs and Senators who had been elected under Labor banners in the 1901 elections met as a caucus. They adopted a constitution for what they called 'The Commonwealth Labor Party' and a five-point fighting platform, which included 'compulsory arbitration' (Stevens & Weller 1976, pp. 12–16). Barton, the Protectionist first prime minister, did not consider the subject of great importance. A federal system of conciliation and arbitration would be established, he said in his policy speech for the first election, but 'this was a power the necessity for the exercise of which it is to be hoped will seldom arise' (quoted by Sawer 1972, p. 16). (Sawer comments: 'A vain hope, as the rest of this history will show.')

Legislation

When the Barton government did get around to producing legislation to introduce a conciliation and arbitration system, it immediately struck trouble. Kingston resigned from Cabinet when it refused to adopt his proposal that the system should cover all shipping engaged in the Australian coastal trade (Sawer 1972, p. 20). (Sawer then comments: 'Thus industrial arbitration policy began its long career as a wrecker of governments.') The House of Representatives also thought the legislation too restrictive. It voted to amend it to cover industrial disputes in the State railways. The government decided not to proceed with the amended Bill.

After the 1903 elections the Deakin government produced another Bill, which the House again amended, this time to cover State railway workers and other industrial workers employed by the States. The government treated this as a vote of confidence and resigned. A minority Labor government, headed by Watson, took power and when it faced parliament reintroduced the Bill. But it too suffered amendments that it could not approve, and treated a vote on the Bill as a motion of confidence and resigned. Then Reid formed a minority government of his free traders, and finally the parliament was able to approve the compromise Commonwealth Conciliation and Arbitration Act of 1904. The court that was to preside over the new system consisted of a president, chosen from among the Justices of the High Court.

Within two years the High Court became involved. In the *Railways Servants* case (*Federated Amalgamated Government Railway and Tramway Service Association v. NSW Railway Traffic Employees Association* (1906) 4 CLR 488), it held that the provision over which the parliament had fought so long, as to whether the Commonwealth power should be extended to cover workers employed by State railways, was invalid. This was based on the unanimous view of Chief Justice Griffith and Justices Barton and O'Connor that the Commonwealth could not, unless expressly authorised by the Constitution, fetter, control or interfere with the States. (This was later overturned in the *Engineers* case.) Nevertheless, in 1908 and 1909 the Court made a series of decisions which gave a fairly extended meaning to some of the phrases in the Constitutional power. In the *Jumbunna* case (*Jumbunna Coal Mine, No Liability v. Victorian Coal Miners' Association* (1908) 6 CLR 309), the Court held that an organisation of employees in a single State could be registered under the provisions of the Act. In the *BHP* case (*R. v. Commonwealth Court of Conciliation & Arbitration; ex parte Broken Hill Pty Co. Ltd* (1909) 8 CLR 419), it held that an interstate dispute could be constituted by demands by the employees of different branches of the one employer operating in several States; and that a dispute could be created by the making of 'paper claims', but that no award could be made which extended beyond the claims made in the log. In the *Sawmillers* case (*Federated Saw Mill Employees' of Australasia v. James Moore & Son Pty Ltd* (1909) 8 CLR 465), the Court held that an interstate dispute could be created by the concerted demands of workers within an industry and that it did not matter that the employers had not concerted their replies to the demands; and that it did not matter that the Commonwealth Court had the power to make enforceable awards that were inconsistent with an award of a State arbitration court or an industrial agreement made under a State law, but it could not make an enforceable award that was inconsistent with the determination of a State Wages Board. But within a few years the Court began moving away from some of these decisions, and for four or five decades *Jumbunna*, which decided only what preconditions there should be for union registration under the Commonwealth legislation, was regarded as one of the high-water marks of Commonwealth power in this area.

Referendums

Interaction between the Court and the government was already apparent, however. The Court in December 1910 declared invalid the Seamen's Compensation Act 1909, which provided for obtaining security for the payment of compensation for any sailor injured during a coastal voyage in Australian waters. The fact that it dealt with intrastate as well as interstate trade, and in a manner that did not allow the two aspects of trade to be separated, meant that the whole Act was invalid. In 1911 the parliament repealed the earlier Act, and passed it in a form that would be more acceptable to the Court. At the same time the parliament, now controlled by the Labor Party, passed a series of amendments to the Arbitration legislation broadening its scope to include domestic servants and agricultural workers, and to try to exempt the Arbitration Court from supervision by the High Court. The parliament also made the first of six attempts to persuade the Australian people to change the Constitution to broaden the power under section 51(xxxv), 'Conciliation and arbitration for prevention and settlement of industrial disputes extending beyond the limits of any one State.' On that first occasion, in 1911, the proposal gained a majority in only one State (Western Australia) and mustered throughout Australia less than 40 per cent of the vote. In 1913 the second-largest vote for change was recorded (49.33 per cent, with majorities in Queensland, South Australia and Western Australia), while three States also voted for change in 1919 and 1946. On that last occasion a majority of voters (50.30 per cent) wanted the power expanded, but the proposal received majorities in only New South Wales, Victoria and Western Australia.

The referendums reflected continuing frustration by governments of all political persuasions with the limitations of the constitutional power over conciliation and arbitration and of the way in which that power was interpreted by the High Court. This frustration continues today. For example, until recently the High Court had held that the words 'industrial disputes' in section 51(xxxv) meant that the dispute had to involve a dispute about industrial matters, such as terms of employment and conditions of work, and was not confined to disputes in an industry. That last phrase had dominated the Court's thinking from the 1920s, the Court holding, for example, that schoolteachers were not engaged in an industry, and nor were firefighters, though bank officials were able to be covered by a Commonwealth award because banking and insurance were said to be incidental to industry. Reviewing these earlier cases, the whole Court, in the *Social Welfare Union* case (*R. v. Coldham; ex parte Australian Social Welfare Union* (1983) 153 CLR 297), decided that the correct approach was that adopted in dissent by Justice Higgins in

1919—the words had to be given their popular meaning, and they rejected any notion that the use of the word 'industrial' confined disputes to those in productive industry and organised business carried on for the purpose of making profits.

The narrow way in which the earlier Courts were prepared to comprehend Commonwealth power led the parliament into exploring other constitutional heads of power, to avoid the limitations of the arbitration power. Apart from the trade and commerce power, which was unsuccessfully invoked to protect the rights of seamen, parliament also utilised its virtually unfettered power to make laws in relation to territories and the power to control its own public servants to set standards which often had to be followed by other employers in other places throughout Australia. The trade and commerce power had also been used to control working conditions on the waterfront, and in the air (flight crew being provided for some time with a separate tribunal to determine their conditions of work and service).

Other powers

In the 1920s, however, the Commonwealth's alternative sources of power under the Constitution were insufficient to overcome the restricted approach of the Court, and the conservative governments of the day were led into politically disastrous territory by their frustration at the hands of the Court. In 1925 the government was confronted by a seamen's strike, headed by Tom Walsh and Jacob Johnson. The union's tactics had been to bypass the arbitration system as much as possible, and it was deregistered in June 1925. At the same time the government acted to break the union's strike tactics by deporting its leaders and suspending legislative protection for seamen in the coastal trade, allowing foreign shipping to compete without requiring them to pay Australian wages. The legislation caused a furore, but proved an ideal excuse for a federal election, which the government won. (The story is recounted in Sawer 1974, pp. 237–9 and Edwards 1965, pp. 111–20.) The High Court prevented the deportation of Walsh and Johnson (*Re Yates; ex parte Walsh and Johnson* (1925) 37 CLR 36), holding that after residence in Australia of 32 years and 15 respectively they could no longer be treated as migrants. After the election more strikes followed and Bruce brought in legislation to have 'industrial extremists' dealt with under the Crimes Act. He also sought an amendment to the Constitution, to give the Commonwealth more power to settle industrial disputes directly, arguing that it was 'unthinkable', as some people had proposed, that the Commonwealth arbitration system be abolished (Edwards 1965, p. 125). The referendum failed, the strikes continued, and Bruce tried to toughen the provisions of the arbitration legislation and also to bring in laws based on the trade and commerce power to deal with particular problems with waterside workers. On the eve of the 1938 election, the government produced another controversial piece of legislation, allowing the Governor-General to make regulations controlling the way in which waterside workers were hired and fired and had to work. Though this did not provide the main subject of debate in the elections, it did mean that once again industrial relations was an important issue. When the government was returned, it put the regulations into legislative form. (Its opponents called it the Dog-Collar Act, because waterside workers, like dogs, had to have licences.) Within a few months Bruce had decided that the Commonwealth should retire almost completely from the arbitration area. It would retain control over waterside workers and seamen (using the trade and commerce power) and over its own public servants. For the rest, the States would have to determine wages and conditions and establish conciliation and arbitration procedures as they wished. The proposals were contained in a Maritime Industries Bill, the key provision of which was to repeal all the Commonwealth Conciliation and Arbitration Acts. Although it gained a second reading, the Bill failed in committee where government rebels voted for delay. The government treated the vote as a matter of confidence, and resigned. As Sawer commented (1974, p. 312), 'Industrial arbitration had again wrecked a federal government.'

The arbitration system was saved by the voters, who decided on a change of government, and when, three years later, there was another change of government, abolition had ceased to be on the conservative agenda. In 1933, for example, the Victorian attorney-general, R. G. Menzies QC, said that for a 'long time' the repeal of section 51(xxxv) 'recommended itself very strongly to me, but further consideration has satisfied me that it must be rejected' (Menzies, 'The distribution of the industrial and trade and commerce powers', in Portus 1933, p. 70). This was because of the need for some disputes to be dealt with on a uniform basis over two or more States, if justice was to be done. There was also a political reason, 'we cannot put back the clock', and there were large vested interests to be considered. What was necessary was to amend the section to give the Commonwealth power to legislate generally in respect of all industrial matters, he considered (pp. 70–5).

Menzies said that the history 'of the interpretation of the conciliation and arbitration power is a perfect illustration of the way in which the politico-legal philosophy of personally disinterested judges can affect their interpretation of constitutional documents' (p. 58). He was referring particularly to the way in which the Court changed its mind about the reserved powers of the States in the *Engineers* case and overturned the doctrine of the immunity of State instrumentalities. But his complaint was wider than that: he was also concerned about the way in which the Court adopted different notions of what was a 'dispute', what State awards might be overturned, and how far 'industrial' might be extended, to cover, for example, the profitable operations of municipal councils (pp. 58–9).

Almost half a century later a political opponent was echoing his sentiments. Clyde Cameron, who was Minister for Labour between 1972 and 1975, wrote in 1982 in disparaging terms about the effect of High Court interpretations on the arbitration power. For example, he said (1982, pp. 300–1) that when a bench:

> . . . divides so completely as has the High Court on whether a dispute about the manning of one-man buses can be settled by the Arbitration Commission, it is difficult to dismiss from one's mind the fear that judges' opinions may reflect their views that such a dispute is one in which employees *should* have no voice. In other words if one's social and economic philosophy remains in the day of Adam Smith, that is likely to be reflected in opinions about the meaning of words in the Constitution.

Cameron complained about the 'havoc' caused by the High Court interpretations which meant that there was no constitutional way of settling disputes, which meant that the strike was the only weapon available to unions (p. 301).

Some of Cameron's criticisms were to be met by later decisions by the High Court during the 1980s, when it overturned the schoolteachers case, made it clear that it would allow firemen to be covered by the Commonwealth system, and even allowed disputes about management prerogatives to be classified as disputes which could be heard by the Commission.

Splitting the system

The Court has not, to date, had a chance to reconsider one decision which had very great industrial and political effects, namely the decision in the *Boilermakers* case (*R v. Kirby; ex parte Boilermakers' Society of Australia* (1956) 94 CLR 254 (High Court) and *Attorney-General v. R* (1957) 95 CLR 529 (Privy Council)). The Privy Council approved the majority (by 4–3) decision of the High Court that the Court of Conciliation and Arbitration (as the body was then known) was not able to exercise both the power to arbitrate and the power to judicially consider awards made by itself and breaches of those awards—that the Commonwealth, because of the structure of the Constitution (primarily, the fact that the judicature is dealt with in a separate chapter, as are the parliament and the executive), cannot combine judicial and non-judicial powers in the one body. On one earlier occasion the Commonwealth had been forced to reshape the arbitration system by a High Court decision. That followed the *Alexander* case (*Waterside Workers' Federation of Australia v. J. W. Alexander Ltd* (1918) 25 CLR 434) in which the High Court held that the Court of Conciliation and Arbitration was not a proper court because its members did not have life tenure, as seemed to be required by section 72 of the Constitution as it then stood. That problem was overcome by giving the judges life tenure. In a way, the problem caused by the *Boilermakers* decision was even easier to overcome: the old court was split into two bodies, the Conciliation and Arbitration Commission and the Industrial

Court. But there remain problems, not all of which were recognised by Clyde Cameron, who said the *Boilermakers* judgment 'wrecked Australia's laws and procedures for the prevention and settlement of industrial disputes' (1982, p. 309). Cameron's main complaints were that the only body empowered to impose penalties for award breaches had 'absolutely no knowledge of all the circumstances that led to the making of the award. What is more, the Industrial Court repeatedly refused to listen to the details of mitigating circumstances whereas under the old Arbitration Court system, the judges concerned in prosecutions for breach awards would have been fully aware of tensions, conditions and special circumstances peculiar to a particular industry' (pp. 309–10). He was also concerned that the Federal Court (which succeeded the Industrial Court) was the only body with power to interpret awards, though it had nothing to do with the making of them. He thought it was necessary for an award to be interpreted according to the spirit of the proceedings which led to its making (p. 310).

More significant, however, was the impact of *Boilermakers* on the Commission, the body which makes the award, which has to patrol and deal at first instance with most of the skirmishes and battles that occur on the industrial battleground. The government attempted to disguise the fact that the Commission had lost its status as a court by undertaking a further division within the Commission—those who handled conciliation work were to be called commissioners, while those involved in arbitration were to have the title 'Judge'. These titles were no doubt intended to persuade the public (if not the combatants appearing before the arbitrators) that this body was a judicial one. The legislation gave it the same protection as courts have, in terms of dealing with contempt for example, and the presidential members who were called judges were given the same salaries and pension rights as judges who operated within the federal court system. The judges on the Commission were not, however, given lifetime appointments or even, after 1977 when the Constitution was changed to provide for federal judges to be appointed till age 70, appointment to that age. Theoretically the Commission 'judges' could only be dismissed in the way that federal judges could be—by the Governor-General on an address by both Houses of Parliament on the grounds of proved misbehaviour or incapacity.

Government influence

The new Commission was more likely to be amenable to government policy directions, though it could not be given policy directives other than through legislation (e.g. to take economic consequences into account in its decision-making). But the true nature of the Commission was not to be revealed until the Commission's Mr Justice Staples began to act as though he was a true judge who could balance and determine issues independently of policy set by the Commission. He incurred the displeasure of the Fraser government (which unsuccessfully offered him another job to get him off the Commission) and was then sidelined by the then President of the Commission, being removed from all his work except full bench work, where he could be outvoted if necessary. When a new President took over, Staples lost even this opportunity to perform an active role on the Commission. He was unable to obtain an explanation for his treatment. A decade later a parliamentary inquiry was also unable to get an explanation, but it did not press for one. Staples was finally removed when the government brought in new legislation to replace the Commission by the Industrial Relations Commission, a new body almost identical to the old Commission, with almost the same powers and even procedures, but with a new name. Abolition of the old body meant that new personnel had to be appointed to the new body. All the old 'judges' and commissioners were reappointed, with the exception of Staples, who was given an early pension (the legislation deemed him to be old enough to get a pension to which he would not otherwise have been entitled).

The Staples affair demonstrated that the Commission was not an independent judicial body and that any member of it who resisted or rejected government policy could be removed or neutralised. Any hopes the judges and commissioners might have had that their complicity in or silence over the dispatch of Staples would spare them from further interference was removed, however. The government decided, without telling the Commission, that the salaries of its judges were no longer to be the same as proper federal judges, but were to be determined by the Remuneration Tribunal and/or by the parliament. The opposition went along with the government's moves, being equally anxious that when it came to power it could direct or influence the policies adopted by the Commission. (Other implications of the Staples affair are discussed in chapter 11.)

Thus, one of the results of the *Boilermakers* case has been to increase the power of governments to influence the way in which the conciliation and arbitration power is exercised. When that power was put in the hands of a court, it had to be applied according to judicial principles. In the hands of a Commission which is subject to legislative direction and governmental manipulation, no such independence can be guaranteed. Conciliation and arbitration is no longer insulated from governments or unaffected by election results.

This development has coincided with the growing availability to governments of other powers that can be used to effect changes in industrial relations generally and in work conditions and the relationship between employers and employees. In the 1960s Menzies expressed fears that what he called the Evatt doctrine would allow a government to legislate using the external affairs power to deal with any matter that had been dealt with in an agreement with any country. An International Labor Organisation (ILO) convention favouring equal pay would allow that doctrine to be adopted (legislatively) in Australia (Menzies 1968, pp. 132–4). Menzies' fears about what the High Court might do with the Evatt doctrine were realised in the *Koowarta* case, and subsequently in the *Dams* case and the other environmental cases. Menzies' suggestion that the external affairs power be used to regulate conditions of employment was finally taken up by the Keating government in 1993 (see below).

Meanwhile, the Commonwealth for many years had used the trade and commerce power to regulate some industries, particularly industries that have an overseas component. Maritime workers, including waterside workers, have been brought under direct Commonwealth control, as have airline pilots, though the tendency has been for the Commonwealth to use its existing tribunals to determine award conditions, rather than setting them directly through legislation and through regulations. This power could prove far more extensive following the High Court's decision in *Cole v. Whitfield*, which may allow the Commonwealth wider powers to directly control wages and working conditions and prices under its trade and commerce power.

But the most significant alternative power possessed by the Commonwealth is the corporations power. This was employed by the Fraser government in 1977, when it passed an amendment to the Trade Practices Act. The new section 45D of the Act was intended to deal with what it described as 'secondary boycotts'. Effectively, these are strikes organised by a trade union which are intended to damage the economic interests of a corporation. They involve persuading another union (or more than one) to impose a ban on that employer-corporation. Alternatively, a union imposes a ban where it has not been involved in arrangements between the employer-corporation and its workers (as in the Mudginberri dispute). The High Court has held that the central provisions of the legislation are valid.

The Hawke government watered down the secondary boycott laws, while the Keating government strengthened the legal position of unions by introducing the first statutory recognition of a right to strike (in connection with enterprise bargaining). This conferred a limited immunity from civil liability. The 1993 reforms went much further, however, in also giving the Commonwealth the power to make laws affecting the States as well as Commonwealth awards. It did so by using the external affairs power to supplement the conciliation and arbitration power. Relying on a series of ILO conventions to which Australia was a party, the Commonwealth was able to impose on employers standards in relation to minimum wages, equal pay, termination of employment, discrimination in employment and family leave.

The High Court essentially endorsed this further extension of the reach of the Commonwealth's industrial relations power. First, in the *Education Union* case (*Re Australian Education Union; ex parte Victoria* (1995) 184 CLR 188) the Court held that industrial awards made by the Commonwealth could apply to

State public services, including the ordinary administrative services of the States. The States were protected from federal awards only if those awards would interfere with the rights of States to determine the number and identity of its employees and those it might want to dismiss on redundancy grounds. The States were allowed absolute control of the terms and conditions of those employed in the 'higher levels of government'. Then, in the *Industrial Relations Act* case (*Victoria v. The Commonwealth* (1995–96) 187 CLR 416) the Court approved the use of ILO conventions to set minimum standards which should apply in virtually all workplaces throughout the country. It also approved the use of an ILO convention to provide for the proposed limited right to strike in relation to federal unions involved in collective bargaining.

By the time the High Court brought down this endorsement of a legislative approach which would allow the Commonwealth to largely dictate the minimum terms and conditions under which Australians generally would be employed, there had been a change of government in Canberra. The Howard government's approach to industrial relations was fundamentally different from that adopted by its predecessor. It wanted to break down central control and reduce the power of the Industrial Relations Commission, particularly in relation to dispute settlement, but also over the minutiae of awards. Its Workplace Relations Act reduced union power by encouraging individual employees to reach workplace agreements with their employers, excluding unions from the negotiation process. Preference for unions was abolished, and penalties for strike and other actions restored through enhanced secondary boycotts provisions in the Trade Practices Act.

Yet again, the waterfront was to be a battleground between employers, unions and the Commonwealth. In 1997–98 the government began a concerted campaign to destroy the maritime union's dominance of the waterfront, a campaign which the union resisted at first with strikes and then through the courts. Although it appeared at first that the law had been changed to such an extent that defeat of the union was inevitable, just one provision in the Workplace Relations Act—a requirement that there could be no discrimination in dismissing employees because of union membership—enabled the union to get the dispute into the courts, including the High Court. The prospect of huge damages for conspiracy helped persuade the employers to re-engage the workers, while the union agreed to very substantial cuts in the waterfront workforce, to improve efficiency. The final outcome of the industrial and legal disputes was unclear at the time of writing. What is certain, however, is that the High Court's most recent decisions provide the Commonwealth with far more direct power to implement its industrial relations policies, whatever they might be.

9

Section 92: The Nationalisation Bogey

Section 92 of the Constitution has proved to be a political minefield. No other section of the Constitution has so involved the High Court in decisions having a direct political effect. No other section has caused the Court to invalidate so many State and Commonwealth laws. But in the light of the most recent decisions of the High Court, much of what earlier Courts had decided was wrong, and many of the laws that were struck down should have been upheld. If what the High Court now says about section 92 had been applied by all its predecessors, Australia's political history would have been very different.

It is extraordinary that a relatively obscure part of the Constitution should have had the drastic impact which marks the history of section 92. But for almost half a century the High Court found in the words of the section a philosophy of individual rights which they elevated to pre-eminence over almost everything else in the Constitution. Almost all the legislative powers that the Constitution assigned to the Commonwealth parliament were made subject to section 92—by the decisions of the High Court and the Privy Council. And so too were the powers of the States, which the Constitution left untouched, subject only to the Constitution itself. The ways in which the various Justices developed their ideas is beyond the scope of this book—they have been traced in a host of books and articles by legal writers. The concern here is with the effect of the Court's work on the political life of the nation.

Section 92 says:

> On the imposition of uniform duties of customs, trade, commerce, and intercourse among the States, whether by means of internal carriage or ocean navigation, shall be absolutely free.
>
> But notwithstanding anything in this Constitution, goods imported before the imposition of uniform duties of customs into any State, or into any Colony which, whilst the goods remain therein, becomes a State, shall, on thence passing into another State within two years after the imposition of such duties, be liable to any duty chargeable on the importation of such goods into the Commonwealth, less any duty paid in respect of the goods on their importation.

The words of the first paragraph of section 92 are deceptively simple. They appear in Chapter IV of the Constitution, which is headed 'Finance and Trade' (ss. 81–105). Section 86 hands over control of the collection of customs and excise duties and responsibility for bounty payments to the Commonwealth. Section 87 deals with the 'surplus revenue' from customs and excise duties. Section 88 requires the imposition of uniform customs duties by the Commonwealth within two years of federation. Section 89 provides for payments to the States before uniform duties. Section 90 gives the Commonwealth exclusive power over customs, excise and bounties. Section 91 makes some exceptions as to bounties. Section 93 is concerned with payments to the States for five years after uniform tariffs are imposed. Section 94 deals with surplus customs revenue, section 95 with customs duties of Western Australia. In this context, and looking at the second paragraph of section 92, it would not have been surprising if the High Court had regarded section 92 as a statement to the effect simply that there should not be any internal customs duties placed on traffic and goods within the new nation. The creation of a 'common market' was one of the forces which helped bring about the creation of the new federation. But for almost every judge who has had to rule on the meaning of section 92, this notion that it bans border tariffs does not go far enough. The words 'absolutely free' seem to have persuaded them that it was necessary to go further and prevent the States and the Commonwealth from interfering with that freedom, whatever it was.

Just what that freedom was, who was being given the freedom and from what has occupied the High Court and the Privy Council more than any other issue of Australian constitutional interpretation. And it has produced more interference in the political process than any other set of decisions on any other part of the Constitution. There were no hints of what was to come in the first few cases involving section 92. In 1909, in *Fox v. Robbins* (1909) 8 CLR 115, the Court invalidated a Western Australian law which imposed a licence fee for sales of wine at a lower rate for grapes grown in Western Australia than elsewhere. This was precisely the kind of discrimination that section 92 was unquestionably intended to prevent: the law under challenge sought to impose an additional financial barrier to interstate produce. The next case involved people rather than goods. In *R v. Smithers* (1912) 16 CLR 99, the Court decided that a New South Wales law which made it an offence for a person with a criminal conviction to enter the State within three years of being released from prison was invalid. Two of the judges relied on section 92's requirement that 'intercourse' be free. Then followed three World War I cases. The Court did not disapprove of a New South Wales law for compulsory acquisition of wheat, but it did strike down a law preventing the movement of stock from the State when acquisition was not involved. In the third case the Court approved a Queensland law similar to the New South Wales law it had struck down in the second case. This was just the start of the many changes of approach which were to bedevil the Court and the governments which had to cope with its decisions. In 1920, in another Queensland case, the Court reversed itself again. This time the law that was held invalid was intended to fix prices, but it did so in such a way that Queensland sellers were favoured because of the way they could treat transport costs. Although there was no Commonwealth law involved in the case, the Court held that section 92 did not bind the Commonwealth, a decision which it felt was necessary so as not to deprive of all force the Commonwealth's power to make laws with respect to interstate trade (s. 51(i) of the Constitution).

But a decade and a half later the Privy Council decided that the Commonwealth was bound by section 92. The Privy Council struck down a Commonwealth–State scheme to control the production of dried fruits. This followed an earlier decision by the High Court upholding a South Australian law for the compulsory acquisition of dried fruits, a decision later overturned by the Privy Council. The Commonwealth scheme, overturned in 1936, was put in place at the request of most of the industry. At the same time, legislation introduced by the States to protect their railways against interstate road hauliers was held valid.

Throughout the 1920s, 1930s and 1940s competing theories were advanced by Justices on the Court, and by the Privy Council, to try to provide some underlying justification for the way section 92 was being applied. What triumphed in the second half of the 1940s was an 'individual rights' theory. Section 92 protected the freedom of individuals to trade, rather than the overall flow or volume of trade. But regulation of trade, commerce and intercourse among the States was compatible with absolute freedom. Section 92 was violated only when a legislative or executive act operated to restrict such trade, commerce or intercourse directly and immediately, as distinct from creating some indirect or consequential impediment that might be regarded as remote. There was a further rider added by the Privy Council (*Commonwealth v. Bank of NSW* (1949) 79 CLR 497, at 640–1):

> [T]heir Lordships do not intend to lay it down that in no circumstances could the exclusion of competition so as to create a monopoly either in a state or Commonwealth agency or in some other body be justified . . . at some stage of social development it might be maintained that prohibition with a view to state monopoly was the only practical and reasonable manner of regulation and that interstate trade commerce and intercourse thus prohibited and thus monopolised remained absolutely free.

Monopoly power

Despite the Privy Council's rider about monopolies, the High Court struck down laws passed by the Chifley government which were intended to give its airline, Trans Australia Airlines, a monopoly of interstate airline traffic, and its bank, the Commonwealth Bank, a monopoly of interstate banking. These laws were invalid because they prevented the carrying on of interstate trade by other airlines or the private banks. The policy of bank nationalisation was adopted by the Chifley government after the High Court invalidated earlier banking legislation that was designed to force the States and their instrumentalities to bank with the Commonwealth or with State banks, and prevent them doing any business with the private banks. But that decision, in the *State Banking* case, did not involve section 92. The key section was invalid because a majority of the Court thought that it was not legislation authorised under the Commonwealth's powers to make laws with respect to banking. It was, rather, a law with respect to the functions of the States, and not within any Commonwealth power. Bank nationalisation became one of the key issues of the federal elections that followed, which resulted in defeat for the Chifley government.

The Privy Council had not finally determined the true meaning of section 92, however. Its next move was to hold that legislation passed by the States to control interstate road hauliers was invalid. At the same time, the High Court developed reasoning that allowed it eventually to approve the imposition of charges on interstate hauliers for road maintenance. It approved State legislation that controlled the production of margarine for interstate trade, holding that production was not covered by section 92. It also approved Commonwealth action to prevent the importation of aircraft to be used in interstate trade, as it did a law banning trading stamps and a law requiring the grading of eggs to be sold within a State.

Disagreements

Conflict within the High Court increased throughout the 1960s and 1970s and came to a head in the late 1980s. It was highlighted in three cases involving two Commonwealth laws, one concerning telecommunications (*Miller v. TCN Channel Nine Pty Ltd* (1986) 161 CLR 556), the other two, wheat marketing (*Clark King & Co. Pty Ltd v. Australian Wheat Board* (1978) 140 CLR 120 and *Uebergang v. Australian Wheat Board* (1980) 145 CLR 266). The *TCN* case was the last decided before the revolutionary decision in *Cole v. Whitfield* (1988) 165 CLR 360. It was also the last in which Justice Murphy participated (he died on the day judgment was delivered). The case involved a prosecution of TCN for establishing and using a network of transmission stations between Sydney and Brisbane to carry its network programs as an alternative to using the Telecom network. The Wireless Telegraphy Act 1905 made it an offence without proper authorisation to establish, erect, maintain or use a station or appliance for the purpose of transmitting or receiving messages by means of wireless telegraphy. The primary question the Court had to answer was whether section 92 protected TCN from a prosecution. The answer that emerged from seven different judgments was that section 92 prevented a prosecution for 'use', but not prosecutions for establishing, erecting or maintaining the station without authorisation. Only one of the seven members of the Court proposed an order along these lines (Justice Mason) and he said in his judgment that had he felt freed from previous authority of the Court he would have held that section 92 would have no application at all. The other members of the Court demonstrated that such authority as there was provided no sure guide. One member of the Court (Justice Wilson) thought that section 92 prevented a prosecution for erection, maintenance or use. Another two (Chief Justice Gibbs and Justice Dawson) thought that no prosecution could be brought for maintenance or use. One (Justice Deane) thought that a prosecution could be brought for erection or maintenance and declined to rule on use. Two (Justices Murphy and Brennan) thought that section 92 offered no protection at all against a prosecution, but their reasons were incompatible with each other. The result more than justified the remarks of Justice Deane who began his judgment by saying (at 615):

> This is another case about the operation and effect of s. 92 of the Constitution. Both sides argued with apparent conviction on the basis of existing authority to support diametrically opposed conclusions. Perhaps that should not be seen as surprising since the more one becomes immersed in the decisions of the Privy Council and this Court on the subject of s. 92, the plainer the impression becomes that one has entered an area where the ordinary processes of legal reasoning have had but a small part to play and where judicial exegesis has tended to confuse rather than elucidate. Indeed, it is as if many voices of authority have been speaking differently at the same time with the result that, putting to one side some basic propositions, it is all but impossible to comprehend precisely what it is that authority has said.

The *Clark King* case in 1978 involved a challenge against Commonwealth and State legislation that provided for the creation of a nationwide wheat stabilisation scheme, including compulsory acquisition of wheat and a national monopoly on trading for the Australian Wheat Board. The case was heard by a court of just five Justices. Two (Justices Mason and Jacobs) held that the scheme was valid because it provided the only practical and reasonable manner of regulation. This was an example of the exceptional case noted by the Privy Council to justify a government monopoly. Two others (Chief Justice Barwick and Justice Stephen) would have held the legislation invalid, because of its intention to deprive individuals of the right to trade interstate. Validity was guaranteed by the decision of the fifth Justice (Justice Murphy) who maintained his idiosyncratic view that section 92 was concerned only with discriminatory fiscal burdens and had nothing to say whatever about legislation of this kind. The result prompted another early challenge against the Wheat Board's monopoly, which in some ways was resolved even less successfully than the *Clark King* case.

Uebergang v. Australian Wheat Board came before a full bench of seven Justices in the form of a case stated by the Chief Justice. One question for the Court was whether the validity of the New South Wales and Queensland Acts depended 'on the establishment to the satisfaction of the Court of any fact'. If so, what is that fact? A majority of the Court answered yes to the first part of that question, but could not agree on an answer to the second part. Justices Gibbs and Wilson thought that the Wheat Board should be allowed to try to produce facts which might show that the monopoly was the 'only' practical and reasonable course open in the circumstances. Justices Mason and Stephen thought it would be necessary only to produce facts showing that the restrictions imposed in the legislation were 'no greater than were reasonably necessary in all the circumstances'. Chief Justice Barwick and Justice Aickin both thought that what had been established already demonstrated that the legislation was invalid, while Justice Murphy thought section 92 inapplicable. The comments of Justices Gibbs and Wilson showed that they held views similar to those of Barwick and Aickin that section 92 was 'concerned to protect private interests', and that it was unlikely that any evidence could be produced which would satisfy them of the validity of the legislation. But the matter was never put to the test. The costly challenge was abandoned by Mr Uebergang.

The *Uebergang* case was the last section 92 case on which Chief Justice Barwick sat, and it was marked by his caustic reiteration of his views about the meaning of the section, and a refutation of the way in which Justice Mason was developing a 'public interest' interpretation to replace the 'individual rights' approach. He also rubbished the Privy Council's exception which had been relied on by two of the three Justices in *Clark King* to justify the Wheat Board's monopoly (at 284–5):

> I do not believe that it can ever be established that the only way to 'regulate' in the constitutionally acceptable sense interstate trade, commerce and intercourse, including the individual's participation therein, is to deny the individual any participation in such trade, commerce and intercourse. To state such a proposition is, in my opinion, to establish its inherent falsity. It really is a contradiction in terms to say that the only way in which interstate trade, commerce and intercourse could be free is by denying all participation by the citizen in that trade, commerce and intercourse.

He said that the Privy Council exception could not be applied in any areas where it had already considered schemes. 'They have had before them dried fruits in time of glut, dairy products at risk of out of State competition, peanuts in time of market instability, hides and skins in a period of over supply, travel in wartime, air transport with its risk of undue density, and banking in time of challenge to government control.' As for Justice Mason's suggestion that emphasis should be given to the public as distinct from the private character of section 92, Sir Garfield said that until Justice Mason had made his comment 'no member of this Court had at any time suggested that the protection which the individual obtains in his trade, commerce and intercourse between the States is but incidental to some public character of the constitutional guarantee . . .'.

The *TCN* case in 1986 was supposed to provide the Court with a chance to reconsider its position. But as several Justices mentioned in their judgments, they were presented with the standard line of argument, based on the innumerable positions which members of the Court had previously adopted. The only note of near-unanimity was the rejection by other members of the Court of the stand of Justice Murphy. In fact the only judge since the earliest times of the Court who had adopted a position like that of Justice Murphy was Lord Wright, who in a journal article recanted on the views he had written for the Privy Council in the late 1940s. The *TCN* case was not, in any event, the best vehicle for the kind of root-and-branch review which the members of the Court were seeking. It involved a Commonwealth law, and while the States would be free to intervene, this was not an issue likely to excite their interest or promote some common cause to have section 92 properly revised. Indeed, of the States and Territories, only New South Wales bothered to put any argument to the Court.

Review

A year later the Court had the cases it wanted. *Cole v. Whitfield* concerned undersized (according to Tasmanian law) crayfish which had been imported from South Australia, where they were of a legal size. *Bath v. Alston Holdings* (1988) 165 CLR 411 concerned the sale of interstate tobacco in Victoria. Every State and the Commonwealth decided to intervene in the case. More significantly, they prepared what was in effect a joint submission, with the argument divided among the various counsel. The documentation provided to the Court included a summary of every one of the previous 139 cases on section 92 considered by the High Court and the Privy Council and an indication of how each of them would have been decided had the approach now suggested to the Court been applied at the time. The Court deliberated for eleven months before it produced a revolutionary judgment, approved by every one of the Justices, embodying an interpretation of section 92 based not on what the Court had said before, but on the 1988 Court's view of what those who wrote the section had intended. The Court felt free to look at the Convention debates 'for the purpose of identifying the contemporary meaning of language used, the subject to which that language was directed and the nature and objectives of the movement towards federation from which the compact of the Constitution finally emerged' (at 385). Previously, the Court had confined itself to looking at no more than the various drafts produced throughout the Convention. It is doubtful whether many of the Justices who had previously reviewed section 92 would have been greatly assisted by a more rounded historical analysis, but it provided this Court with the way to put to one side all that its predecessors had done before, and produce a more realistic appraisal of the section. They commented (at 392):

> Attention to the history we have outlined may help to reduce the confusion that has surrounded the interpretation of s. 92. That history demonstrates that the principal goals of the movement towards the federation of the Australian colonies included the elimination of intercolonial border duties and discriminatory burdens and preferences in intercolonial trade and the achievement of intercolonial free trade . . . Section 92 precluded the imposition of protectionist burdens: not only interstate border customs duties but also burdens, whether fiscal or non-fiscal, which discriminated against interstate trade and commerce. That was the historical object of s. 92 and the emphasis of the text of s. 92 ensured that it was appropriate to attain it.

The Court concluded its historical survey by saying (at 394):

> The task which has confronted the Court is to construe the unexpressed; to formulate in legal propositions, so far as the text of s. 92 admits, the criteria for distinguishing between the burdens (including restrictions, controls and standards) to which interstate trade and commerce may be subjected by the exercise of legislative or executive power and the burdens from which interstate trade and commerce is immune. The history of s. 92 points to the elimination of protection as the object of s. 92 in its application to trade and commerce. The means by which that object is achieved is the prohibition of measures which burden interstate trade and commerce and which also have the effect of conferring protection on interstate trade and commerce of the same kind. The general hallmark of measures which contravene s. 92 in this way is their effect as discriminatory against interstate trade and commerce in that protectionist sense . . .

The Court went on to examine some of the history of the interpretation of the section, finding support for their new formula ('freedom from discriminatory burdens in a protectionist sense') in the words of the dissenting judgment of one member of the Court in a 1920 case. Other doctrines were referred to by the Court but rejected. The Court considered the relationship of section 92 to the trade and commerce power in section 51(i), and pointed out that such laws 'will commonly not appear to discriminate in a relevant sense if they apply to all transactions of a given kind within the reach of the Parliament'. So far as State laws were concerned, the Court would have to consider the nature of the law. If it applied to all trade and commerce, both interstate and intrastate, it was less likely to be protectionist than if there was discrimination appearing on the face of the law. But the law would offend section 92 if its effect were to discriminate in a protectionist way.

The Court conceded that application of the test would not always be easy, a fact it demonstrated just a few weeks later when it applied the new test in *Bath v. Alston Holdings* (which had been argued at the same time as *Cole v. Whitfield*) and held, in a split 4–3 decision, that part of the Victorian licensing law that dealt with cigarettes brought from interstate was invalid. But the decision caused the Victorian government little pain. Under the new approach adopted by the Court it would be relatively simple for the legislation to be rewritten to ensure that it was not discriminatory in a protectionist sense. The aim of the law was to raise money from all cigarette and tobacco sales in the State, not to favour Victorian producers. Interstate cigarettes had been treated differently for administrative reasons, and new administrative techniques that were not discriminatory could readily be found.

The significance of the Court's decision cannot be overstated. Its impact can be seen from the material the States provided to the Court in support of a new test which was considerably more cumbersome than the one the Court actually adopted. (The States and the Commonwealth took two pages to outline and define their test; the High Court adopted a one-sentence test.) The new rule would have meant that in about 42 cases where legislation had been invalidated by the High Court or the Privy Council there would probably have been a different decision. Predominantly, these cases concerned transport regulation and primary produce marketing schemes. Other cases concerned fauna conservation, control of firearms (in the State sphere), telecommunications (the *TCN* case) and bank nationalisation. But the impact of the previous approach(es) of the Court went far beyond this. For half a century the Commonwealth and the States simply did not proceed with policies and legislation which they were sure would fall foul of the Court. It was only where they thought they might pass the Court's tests that they proceeded. Policy-making and legislative and administrative action were compromised by the High Court's approach to section 92. The quite extraordinary situation developed where a national marketing scheme approved by the Commonwealth and every one of the States could be rejected by the Court to uphold the absolute right to trade interstate of an individual grower who did not want to be covered by the scheme. The way the High Court interpreted section 92 meant that interstate traders had a special privilege not enjoyed by intrastate traders. There was nothing to stop a State from exercising its legislative powers to monopolise the ownership or trade in any matter that did not have an interstate element. But the fact that someone who would otherwise be subject to the State's laws traded interstate put him or her in a privileged and protected position. In the marketing situation the interstate trader was specially privileged and held a great financial advantage. The whole idea of most of the marketing schemes was to consolidate local and overseas markets, so that all growers would be able to share in the market that produced the highest prices. The interstate trader was able to avoid the markets that produced low or negative returns and concentrate on maximising profits. So the High Court's interpretation of section 92 discriminated against the development of a State's internal trade.

The other criticism largely met by the new formulation was the degree to which previous decisions had required the Court to become involved in political decision-making. As the Victorian solicitor-general pointed out during the argument of *Cole v. Whitfield*, the old cases had left the High Court with the task of determining whether the particular regulation of interstate trade that parliament had decided on was 'reasonable'. In making a decision of that sort, he argued, the Court was making a policy or legislative decision, to put it politely, or (putting it more accurately) 'a political decision'.

The Court's radical new approach won the support of governments throughout the country, but it was derided by former Chief Justice Barwick. In an interview for the New South Wales Bar Association newsletter (Summer 1989, p. 19) he remarked that the Court had included 'a magnificent remark' in its judgment 'that the Constitution might provide the text but not the test':

> So then they proceed to say that what they were worried about at Federation was protection for free trade and what they were intending is that interstate trade should be relatively free, it should be just as free as other trade. But they said absolutely free so you don't take any notice of the text. You find the test is whether the law is passed from a protectionist point of view. It's really laughable. I'd have great fun appealing from that with the Privy Council. Dear me, it's terrible tosh, you know. That

is a remarkable sentence when you analyse it: the Constitution might provide the text but not the test. Very sad.

But of course now there is no appeal to the Privy Council. The High Court has rewritten the meaning of the constitutional text, bearing in mind the probable intentions of those who wrote it and the difficulties the Court had had in applying other tests, such as that which Sir Garfield Barwick had applied.

IMPLICATIONS

The issue today is not what might have been, but what remains. The removal of the old approaches to the interpretation of section 92 opens the way to a reappraisal of section 51(i). The Commonwealth's power to make laws with respect to interstate trade and commerce is no longer limited by the High Court's destructive interpretation of section 92's guarantee of the freedom of interstate trade and commerce (and intercourse). Each now may have an independent and meaningful operation. Section 51(i) provides that the Commonwealth parliament may make laws with respect to 'Trade and commerce with other countries, and among the States.' This apparently wide power has been limited by the High Court in two major ways. First, the Court applied the reserved powers doctrine to its interpretation, in effect holding that the control of intrastate trade and commerce was reserved to the States, and hence that the Commonwealth's power over interstate trade and commerce could not be allowed to intrude over the States' powers. Second, the Court had to match the legislative power in section 51(i) with the prohibition in section 92 which guaranteed that trade and commerce among the States shall be absolutely free. To do so the Court tended to limit the concept of interstate trade. As Chief Justice Mason explained to the Corporate Lawyers Association of New South Wales in 1988, the Court had 'construed the concept of interstate trade to cover movement and communications across State borders and contracts calling for interstate delivery down to the first sale by an importer in another State. Yet, the Court has not accepted the view that production generally for interstate trade falls within the power though the Court has conceded that in some circumstances the power might extend to production' (*Australian Law Journal*, p. 756). He suggested that if a broader meaning were given to the phrase it could give section 51(i) a reach as all-encompassing as the commerce clause of the United States Constitution and said that under the prevailing doctrine in the United States *anything* that affects the economy falls within the reach of the power (Sir Anthony Mason's emphasis). He said the Court's formal distinction between interstate and intrastate trade might well have been appropriate in an era of localised economies, but there was a question of whether it was appropriate today. And he suggested that in times to come the Court might take account of commercial realities in construing the power. Those commercial realities might, for example, have resulted in the Court reaching a different decision in the 1977 case when it held that section 51(i) did not authorise the Commonwealth to permit its own airline, operating in interstate trade, to make an intrastate flight without a licence from the State government—even if the additional landing(s) within the State would be conducive to the efficiency, competitiveness and profitability of the interstate activity (*Minister for Justice (WA) v. ANA Commission* (1977) 138 CLR 492).

The High Court's decision to read section 92 as a limitation on discriminatory regulation of trade, commerce and intercourse makes it more likely that the Court will adopt a far more realistic interpretation of the trade and commerce power. Although it may not give the Commonwealth as powerful a legislative weapon as the US Supreme Court has given to the United States Congress, it nevertheless would provide it with most of the economic control measures that governments and political parties have sought in the past. And while present policies advanced by political parties favour deregulation rather than an extension of controls, it seems inevitable that governments will begin to explore the possibilities that the Court has now opened up.

Part III

Institutions

10

Nationhood: slowly, an independent nation

The Australia which was created by the Constitution Act and which came into being on 1 January 1901 was in no sense an independent nation. In modern terms it was more like a self-governing colony, similar to the status enjoyed by Papua New Guinea between the time it elected its first parliament and when it gained full independence from Australia on 16 September 1975. Determining the date of Australia's full independence is less easy, though the final formal signal of independence may be identified. It occurred on 3 March 1986. On that day two Australia Acts came into force, one an Act of the Commonwealth parliament, the other an Act of the British parliament. They were assented to by Queen Elizabeth, as Queen of the United Kingdom in relation to the British Act, and as Queen of Australia in relation to the Australia Act. It may be argued that there is still some tidying up to do to make the Constitution reflect the political and legal independence which Australia has now achieved. For example, there are sections of the Constitution that reserve a role for the monarch which could not properly be exercised now, except on the advice of the Australian government. There are also sections that deal with the Privy Council, including one which permits the High Court to grant certificates for appeals in certain cases. There are the 'covering clauses' of the Constitution—those sections of the British Act of 1900 which precede the strict text of the Constitution. There is the position of the monarch, who is recognised by Australian legislation, but selected by British law and imposed on Australia, like it or not. But these changes, and others recommended by the Constitutional Commission in 1988, would be merely symbolic. The changes effected by the Australia Acts were more than symbolic: they were real and for the States, in particular, essential to allow the remaining colonial ties between Australia and Britain to be totally removed. Among other things, the Australia Acts finally prevent Britain from passing legislation that can have legal effect within Australia, they allow the States to make laws that would previously have been invalid under Australian law because they conflicted with British laws which continued to be effective in Australia, and they abolished appeals from State courts to the Privy Council. They also dealt with political relations between the States and the monarch.

The Commonwealth's colonial status in the early years after federation can be demonstrated by the events that surrounded the visit to Australia by the Great White Fleet in 1908. The sixteen white-painted battleships formed a large part of the United States Navy. In 1907 President Theodore Roosevelt decided that they should be moved from their bases on the Atlantic coast to the Pacific (via Cape Horn: work on the Panama Canal had only just begun) to demonstrate that they could be moved, and as a warning to Japan and others that the United States regarded itself as a Pacific power. Lacking the proper facilities to maintain the fleet on the west coast for very long, Roosevelt decided to return the fleet to their bases through the Suez Canal, though he had no particular itinerary in mind. When word of the proposed trip was published in Australia on 20 December 1907, Prime Minister Alfred Deakin took an immediate interest. Four days later he began the process which led to the fleet visiting Australia in August 1908, its entry into Sydney Harbour being witnessed by almost half a million people, while a similar number later saw it in Melbourne.

Deakin's invitation was issued in a roundabout way. First he called on the American consul in Melbourne, then he wrote to the American Ambassador in London. Finally he wrote to the

Australian Governor-General, asking him to cable the British Secretary of State for the Colonies to issue a formal invitation to President Roosevelt (though he didn't mention his own American contacts). In fact, the British authorities were hesitant and did not send the formal invitation until after Roosevelt had announced that he had decided to accept Deakin's informal approach.

This curious methodology was forced on Deakin by Australia's accepted colonial status. Australia was part of the British empire. Foreign relations were the responsibility of Britain, not Australia. Relations between Australia and Britain were generally conducted through the Governor-General, who was responsible to the British government, not the Australian government.

Deakin's reason for inviting the fleet was at least partly influenced by his desire to establish an Australian navy. On 9 December 1907 he told the House of Representatives of the progress (or lack of it) in negotiations with Britain on the creation of a separate navy. He reported on Britain's reluctance (it preferred the colonies simply to pay money for the upkeep of the Royal Navy) and the statement by the British prime minister at the 1907 Colonial Conference that the control of naval defence and foreign affairs must always go together. Deakin said the statement implied 'that for the present, seeing that we have no voice in foreign affairs, we are not obliged to take any part in Imperial navy defence. It implies, also, with equal clearness, that when we do take a part in naval defence, we shall be entitled to a share in the direction of foreign affairs' (Parliamentary Debates Vol. XLII, p. 7512). Deakin virtually suspended his negotiations with the Admiralty between the time Roosevelt accepted the invitation and when the fleet departed. The visit apparently persuaded the Admiralty that Deakin's scheme did have popular support, as well as parliamentary approval (£250 000 was put in a trust account in 1908).

It was left to Deakin's successor as prime minister, Andrew Fisher, to benefit from Deakin's efforts. In early 1909 Australia ordered three destroyers from Britain, using the money Deakin had set aside. The Admiralty finally agreed to the Australian proposals for the way the new navy should be controlled, this having been the central problem faced by Deakin. Britain had earlier insisted that the prime requisite was that there should be one (British) navy, with unity of command. If the colonies were to have a navy, it should comprise only very small ships, suitable for little more than harbour defence. Its preference was that Australia and the other colonies should simply send money. But if some ships were owned locally, they were to be controlled in time of war by the Royal Navy. Fisher persuaded the Admiralty that Australian ships in Commonwealth or territorial waters would be completely under the control of the Commonwealth government. Elsewhere they would be under the control of the senior Royal Navy officer in the area. In time of war the Australians would operate under sealed orders which would deliver their operational control to the Royal Navy.

Thus, in the first decade of the new Commonwealth, foreign affairs and defence were recognised by Australia as being essentially a British responsibility. But there was also an appreciation that local political interests did not always coincide with what might be determined in London. And it was possible sometimes to do something to advance those local political interests.

Judicial colonialism

Australian judges faced a similar position, because of the position of the Judicial Committee of the Privy Council as an ultimate court of appeal in most matters. This had not been the intention of the men who wrote the Constitution, though there had been several different proposals considered and adopted by the succeeding Conventions. The final version taken to London would have allowed the parliament to limit appeals to the Privy Council as it wished. But there would have been no appeals on matters affecting the Commonwealth or State Constitutions unless 'the public interests' of some other British Dominion was involved.

The British government was not happy with a clause which would have disentitled commercial and financial interests from appealing important cases to the Privy Council in London. And remarkably, the Chief Justices in the Australian colonies also wanted a general right of appeal to the Privy Council preserved, presumably fearing what would happen to them under the supervision of the new High Court. Negotiations between the Australians who had gone to London to see the Constitution safely through the parliament at Westminster and the British Colonial Secretary, Joseph Chamberlain, finally resulted in a compromise of sorts. (The story is detailed in La Nauze 1972, pp. 260–9.) No appeal would be permitted from any High Court decision involving 'the limits *inter se* of the Constitutional powers of the Commonwealth and those of any State or States' or the *inter se* limits between any States, unless the High Court granted a certificate for such an appeal. Otherwise there was no constitutional limit on appeals to the Privy Council from the High Court, but the parliament could make laws limiting the matters in which such leave to appeal might be asked.

It is interesting to note that both the Commonwealth parliament and the High Court tried to circumvent, or at least limit, the effect of this provision which made Australian laws subject to review by what was in effect a British court. (Strictly speaking, the Privy Council merely 'advised' the sovereign about the legal rights involved in a particular case. But the Judicial Committee of the Privy Council was constituted primarily of judicial members of the House of Lords, and though theoretically applying the law of the country from which the 'appeal' was brought, and in particular having to determine the validity of legislation according to a written Constitution, the Law Lords tended to apply the same principles that the House of Lords would have applied had it been sitting on the case.) In the 1903 Judiciary Act the parliament tried to ensure that Constitutional cases were brought to the High Court from any Supreme Court where they had begun, before the lower court made any final decision on them. This was made mandatory in the case of *inter se* cases being heard in State Supreme Courts. The aim of the legislation was clear: to ensure that the High Court had an opportunity of ruling on all constitutional cases, and was able to control the flow (if any) of *inter se* cases litigants wanted taken to the Privy Council. These provisions were tightened in amendments made to the Judiciary Act in 1907 to make it almost impossible for a constitutional case to go direct from a Supreme Court to the Privy

Council. The revisions to the Judiciary Act followed a decision by the Privy Council in *Webb v. Outtrim* (1906) 4 CLR 356, in which the Privy Council made it clear that it disapproved of this attempt to evade its authority. The judgment approved statements by Justice Hodges in the Victorian Supreme Court that it was not reasonable to suppose that the British parliament ever intended to abolish appeals from the States by 'indirect or circuitous methods' (at 361).

That particular case was part of an important battle over whether the Commonwealth and the States could tax each other and each other's public servants. The first relevant decision was made by the High Court in its first major constitutional case, *D'Emden v. Pedder* (1904) 1 CLR 91. It too concerned taxation. At issue was whether Commonwealth employees had to pay State stamp duty on receipts for their Commonwealth salaries. The High Court, following what it said was United States precedent, decided that the States could not tax a Commonwealth activity. It took the same attitude in several other cases in the next few years, and, as noted in chapter 8, applied a similar and related doctrine to protect the States against Commonwealth interference in the *Railways Servants* case.

It was these cases which were contradicted by the Privy Council at the end of 1906 in *Webb v. Outtrim*. But within six months the High Court had reasserted its position. It held in *Baxter v. Commissioner of Taxation (NSW)* (1907) 4 CLR 1087 that because this particular issue involved the *inter se* powers of the Commonwealth and the States it was not bound by the Privy Council's decision. By a 3–2 majority it decided to follow its own earlier decisions rather than that of the Privy Council. It refused a certificate for a further appeal to the Privy Council. Several Justices suggested ways in which the parliament could prevent a similar embarrassing clash from occurring again. The parliament responded a month later, amending the Judiciary Act to ensure that there would be no further cases of a constitutional nature taken directly from a State Supreme Court to the Privy Council. In a series of cases the Court also laid down strict criteria to govern its own grant of a certificate to allow appeals to the Privy Council in *inter se* cases. The special reasons required by the Court were satisfied in just one case, *Colonial Sugar Refining Co. Ltd v. Attorney-General* (1912) 15 CLR 182, and then only on a limited issue.

The effect of these decisions and legislation was to ensure that the High Court was able, after 1906, to deal with all cases involving the interpretation of the Constitution, even where an appeal might still be taken on to the Privy Council in non-*inter se* matters. (See the discussion in Sawer 1967, pp. 23–30.)

In non-constitutional matters the High Court tended to take the view that it was important to maintain Australia as part of the (English) common law system. The Court tended to defer to decisions not only of the House of Lords but also of the English Court of Appeal (the next court down the hierarchical ladder in England). But that deferential attitude ended in the 1960s, in part at least because the House of Lords made a decision which Australian judges regarded as quite wrong. The House of Lords, at that time, considered that it was unable to overturn decisions which it, the House of Lords, had made on an earlier occasion, so any error was necessarily perpetuated.

Assertions of Independence

The controversial decision was in *Director of Public Prosecutions v. Smith* [1961] AC 290. In *Parker v. The Queen* (1962–63) 111 CLR 610, Chief Justice Dixon, in a statement specifically approved by all the other members of the High Court, referred to the fact that in an earlier case the High Court had said, 'The introduction of the maxim or statement that a man is presumed to intend the reasonable consequences of his act is seldom helpful and always dangerous.' He then continued (at 632):

> That was some years before the decision in *Director of Public Prosecutions v. Smith*, which seems only too unfortunately to confirm the observation. I say too unfortunately for I think it forces a critical situation in our [Dominion] relation to the judicial authority as precedents of decisions in England. Hitherto I have thought that we ought to follow decisions of the House of Lords, at the expense of our own opinions and cases decided here, but having carefully studied *Smith's Case* I think that we

> cannot adhere to that view or policy. There are propositions laid down in the judgment which I believe to be misconceived and wrong. They are fundamental and they are propositions which I could never bring myself to accept . . . I think *Smith's Case* should not be used as authority in Australia at all.

This statement was not considered by the Privy Council when it heard and upheld an appeal in this case: (1964) 111 CLR 665.

Three years later the High Court explained the implications for the Supreme Courts of the States of its rejection of English judicial authority. The States should follow decisions of the High Court rather than the House of Lords. Only the High Court or the Privy Council could decide that a decision of the High Court should not be followed. But of course decisions of the House of Lords were to be treated 'with all the respect that is rightly due to decisions of the ultimate appellate tribunal in England' (Justice Owen, at 138–9). Justice Windeyer referred to the fact that 'our ancestors brought the common law of England to this land. Its doctrines and principles are the inheritance of the British race and as such they became the common law of Australia' (at 134). He noted that 'conditions' in Australia and England were not always the same, and this could lead to differences in the law (at 135).

Then the Commonwealth parliament re-entered the fray. With nationalist-minded John Gorton as prime minister, the government pushed ahead with the Privy Council (Limitations of Appeals) Act, a legislative scheme first approved a year earlier by the Holt government in 1967. This directed that special leave to appeal from the High Court to the Privy Council could only be asked if the decision involved a decision of a Supreme Court that had not been exercising federal jurisdiction, and that did not involve the application or interpretation of the Constitution or a law of the Commonwealth. In 1975 the Whitlam government went further and passed the Privy Council (Appeals from the High Court) Act which said that leave to appeal should not be asked in the case of High Court appeals not covered by the Gorton legislation. The effect of these two pieces of legislation was to eliminate all appeals from the High Court to the Privy

Council other than those where the High Court granted a certificate in an *inter se* matter. The only appeals that might then be taken to the Privy Council were appeals taken directly from a State Supreme Court, on matters not involving any aspect of federal jurisdiction. The Commonwealth seemed to have no direct legislative power to control this, though perhaps it might at a later stage (with a different High Court to validate its move) have relied on the external affairs power—the Privy Council being an external court established under English law, and conducting its business in England. (The High Court, in *Polyukhovich v. The Commonwealth* (1991) 172 CLR 501, held that the Commonwealth could legislate under the external affairs power in relation to matters external to Australia.)

The Privy Council had occasionally recognised that the law in Australia might develop differently from that in England. In *Australian Consolidated Press v. Uren* (1967) 117 CLR 221, it refused an appeal in a case in which punitive damages had been awarded in a defamation action, contrary to the law that then applied in England. The Privy Council noted (at 241) that the issue that had faced the High Court in this case was whether the law as it had been settled in Australia should be changed. It was 'not prepared to say that the High Court was wrong in being unconvinced that a changed approach in Australia was desirable'.

However, it was not to be expected that in every case the Privy Council would defer to the High Court. In *Viro v. The Queen* (1978) 141 CLR 88, Justice Gibbs referred to the difficulty this created for State courts, bound by precedent in some cases to follow the decisions of both the High Court and the Privy Council. But he didn't think there would be a problem. Just as the High Court, though not bound by the House of Lords, recognised the 'highly persuasive value' of its decisions, so would the Privy Council take similar account of High Court decisions. He referred to parliament's intention when it made the High Court an ultimate court of appeal, and said, 'It is for this Court to assess the needs of Australian society and to expound and develop the law for Australia in the light of that assessment.' It would be an impediment to that duty for it slavishly to follow the decisions of the Privy Council (at 120–1). Justice Mason said it was 'well recognised that the common law may develop differently in Australia from the common law as it develops in England and other countries from which an appeal lay or now lies to the Privy Council' (at 135). (The notion of a separate Australian common law was not finally recognised by the parliament until 1988 when in an omnibus Law and Justice Legislation Amendment Act there was included a change to the Judiciary Act. The relevant section had previously provided that where courts were exercising federal jurisdiction and there was no relevant constitutional provision, or Commonwealth, State or Territory law, they should apply the common law of England. This was changed to read the 'common law in Australia'. The explanatory memorandum said 'the reference to the Common Law of England is no longer appropriate because in some respects the common law in Australia has diverged from the common law in England'.)

In the *Viro* case, Justice Murphy's historical analysis was far blunter than that of other members of the Court, tracing the way in which the Privy Council had been used to have British colonies follow English law rather than their own. Now it was 'an eminent relic of colonialism, representing a dwindling influence'. He referred to an extraordinary and recent example of how the Privy Council did not understand Australian law, and intervened in areas where, according to the Constitution, it should not have ventured. This was *Oteri v. The Queen* (1976) 11 ALR 142, in which a highly reputable bench had been ill-advised enough to say, 'The legislative power of the Commonwealth of Australia does not extend to criminal law. That lies within the competence of the States.' Justice Murphy pointed out that each year thousands of people were convicted of offences against the Commonwealth Crimes Act. And that in any event this was an opinion on the powers *inter se* of the Commonwealth and the States where the Privy Council had no right to trespass.

The Queensland reaction

Not all Australians were convinced of the desirability of eliminating appeals to the Privy Council, nor of the effectiveness of the measures that the Commonwealth parliament had approved. As part of its political campaign against the federal Labor government of the time, the National–Liberal government in Queensland headed by Sir Joh Bjelke-Petersen had the Queensland parliament pass the Appeals and Special Reference Act 1973. The law attempted to give the Privy Council jurisdiction to hear any question or matter which arose under or concerned any law in force in Queensland, or which related substantially to the peace, order and good government of Queensland. A certificate that a matter warranted being referred to the Privy Council could be issued by the Queensland Supreme Court on the application of the Queensland attorney-general. The first application made by the attorney-general sought Privy Council advice on a series of questions, including whether Queensland could pass a law that included in the Queen's titles 'Queen of Queensland' and whether the Commonwealth's Royal Style and Titles Act of 1973, which gave her in Australia the title 'Elizabeth the Second, by the Grace of God Queen of Australia and Her other Realms and Territories, Head of the Commonwealth', altered the manner in which the Queen could receive and act on advice from her British or Queensland ministers in relation to matters affecting Queensland. The High Court, intervening at the request of the Commonwealth, was unanimous in declaring the relevant sections of the Queensland Act invalid, because they conflicted with Chapter III of the Commonwealth Constitution. Justice Gibbs said it was implicit in Chapter III that it was not permissible for a State by legislation to provide a procedure by which the Privy Council was enabled to consider an *inter se* question without a certificate from the High Court, or any other matter involving federal jurisdiction when the Commonwealth had limited such appeals. He said (at 315) that the relevant principles underlying Chapter III are that:

> . . . questions arising as to the limits of Commonwealth and State powers, having a peculiarly Australian character, and being of fundamental concern to the Australian people, should be decided finally in this Court, unless for special reasons this Court decides to allow the matter to proceed to the Judicial

> Committee, and that the Parliament should be entitled to ensure that other questions arising in the exercise of federal jurisdiction should, for similar reasons, be finally determined in this Court and not in the Judicial Committee.

Justice Murphy went further: he said that the Queensland legislation purported to confer on an organ of the government of another country power to give advice to Queensland, and was inconsistent with the integrity of Australia as an independent sovereign nation.

The Queensland legislation followed an attempt by the Queensland government directly to ask the Queen to refer to the Privy Council issues concerning the sovereignty over the sea-bed adjacent to Queensland. The Queen refused the request on the advice of both the British and Australian governments, though primarily because she considered she should act on the advice of Commonwealth ministers, who pointed out that the dispute would be determined when the High Court considered the validity of the Sea and Submerged Lands Act. (The relevant material is contained in Justice Murphy's judgment in the *Commonwealth v. Queensland* (1975) 134 CLR 298, at 334–5.)

The Statute of Westminster

In parallel with the High Court's desire to be independent of the Privy Council and the House of Lords, there were stirrings on the political front. When World War I erupted, few political leaders gave any consideration at all to the possibility that Australia might not be involved in the war. If Britain was at war, the whole Empire was at war. Decisions of that nature were taken by the King. Australia had no choice but to be involved. Of course the level of involvement was a different matter. Two bitterly fought referendums decided that Australia would not adopt conscription for overseas service. But over 300 000 men volunteered and about 60 000 were killed. That cost prompted Australian and other Dominion leaders to seek a part in the conduct of the war, and undertakings that they must never be dragged into another conflict without having been fully consulted 'before the die was cast' (Millar 1978, pp. 73–7). Australia participated in the Imperial War Cabinet and Conference and Prime Minister W. M. Hughes, against the wishes of his own Cabinet, won for Australia the right to an independent voice at the Paris Peace Conference in 1919. Australia was an independent signatory to the peace treaty, and a full member of the new League of Nations, though Britain generally maintained its overall right to speak in foreign affairs on behalf of the whole Empire, including the 'independent' Dominions. But by 1926 the Balfour declaration which emerged from that year's imperial conference declared the Dominions to be autonomous communities within the Empire, equal in status and in no way subordinate in internal or external affairs. The declaration also changed the status of the Governor-General, who was no longer to act as a representative of the British government, but rather as the Crown's representative. This last issue was tested by the Labor government in 1930, when it insisted also on the right to nominate an Australian as Governor-General. It chose the then Chief Justice of the High Court, Sir Isaac Isaacs.

The Balfour declaration took legal form in the Statute of Westminster, which was approved by the British parliament in 1931. It dealt with some of the legal constraints on the Dominions which, independently of their own Constitutions, had prevented them from being truly sovereign nations. Britain had not surrendered the power to make laws affecting them, and some British laws which predated the Constitutions had remained in effect. The most important of these was the Colonial Laws Validity Act 1865, which declared void any colonial legislation that was inconsistent with English law that extended to the colony. The Statute of Westminster said that this was no longer to apply: that in future the Dominions could make laws having effect extra-territorially; and that no future Act of the British parliament would extend to a Dominion unless that Dominion had expressly requested and consented to the legislation. The fact that such legislation needed to be passed to free the Dominions demonstrated that they had not previously been entirely free of colonial chains. What was remarkable in Australia, however, was that there was little desire in the 1930s to break those chains.

The Commonwealth parliament did not ratify the Statute of Westminster until 1942, the ratification being backdated to the outbreak of World War II, on 3 September 1939. Yet in that war also Australian politicians assumed that the declaration of war by Britain meant that Australia was also involved in the war. Prime Minister Menzies broadcast that Great Britain had declared war on Germany and that, as a result, 'Australia is also at war'. But it was different in 1941 when Japan entered the war. The King, at the request of the Australian government, assigned power to the Governor-General to allow a specifically Australian declaration of war to be made. Since then, declarations of war have gone out of fashion, as has the automatic commitment of Australian forces to support any British war effort.

While the politicians in Canberra were unhurried about bringing the Statute of Westminster into effect, those in the States were positively antagonistic towards it. They did not want to shed their colonial ties. They thought they could rely on London to protect them against the depredations of Canberra. They feared that the Statute of Westminster would allow the Commonwealth to further expand its powers at their expense. They insisted that they should not be freed from the colonial status accorded to them under the Colonial Laws Validity Act. Australia was therefore in the anomalous position of having a national government that was independent and States that were subject to the laws of another (admittedly friendly) country. It was Canberra that was regarded by the States as unfriendly.

The Australia Acts

In 1973 Prime Minister Whitlam initiated discussions with the premiers and with Britain about legislation to apply the Statute of Westminster provisions to the States, and to have appeals to the Privy Council abolished. By the end of the 1970s three States (New South Wales, Victoria and Tasmania) had passed legislation seeking to have their courts exempted from provisions of 19th century legislation which allowed for appeals to the Privy Council. The Commonwealth, however, thought it could not act without unanimity among the States.

A series of cases in the 1970s showed some of the personal difficulties that resulted from the continuation of the colonial ties, the High Court holding in each that provisions of the 1894 Imperial Merchant Shipping Act still limited the liability of shipowners. In one, a seaman who was seriously injured in Sydney Harbour through the negligence of the shipowner was able to obtain only a maximum of £8 per ton weight of the ship, a total in his case of £1489.

After several years of negotiations, the States finally agreed to cut themselves free from Britain. They passed their versions of the Australia Act, requesting and consenting to Commonwealth legislation under section 51(xxxviii) of the Constitution. The Commonwealth passed the relevant law and also requested and consented to British legislation that would end forever the British legislative hold over the States. The States were not to be bound by the Colonial Laws Validity Act any more; the British government would cease to have any function in the appointment or control of their Governors; provisions requiring the disallowance or reservation of State legislation were abolished; the States would have extra-territorial legislative power to the extent that that was possible under the Australian Constitution; appeals to the Privy Council from State courts would end.

Australia, of which the States were an integral part, was finally an independent nation.

The republic

In the eyes of some politicians and, according to the polls, a significant majority of the Australian people, political and legal independence from Britain was not enough. The people also wanted to sever the constitutional links between Australia and the British monarchy. They wanted Australia to become a republic.

This is not a matter which will involve the High Court until after the Australian people agree, at a referendum, to some proposal put forward by the Commonwealth parliament to change the Constitution. But the High Court is regarded by many of those trying to work out proposals for a republican Australia as a stumbling block—and by defenders of the current system as their ultimate weapon. The men who wrote the original Constitution paid little heed to the way it might eventually be interpreted by the High Court which they also wanted to create. Those people proposing to make Australia a republic face the daunting task of trying to anticipate every legal and constitutional difficulty which such a transition would raise.

There are many potential difficulties. Possibly the first is whether a referendum passed by a majority of people, and in a majority of States but not necessarily by a majority in every State, would effectively change the Constitution. A second concerns the effect of a national republic on the government of the States—would they all become republics too? At least two States—Queensland and Western Australia—have constitutional provisions that protect the position of Governor as a representative of the Queen. Do they separately have to pass referendums to transform their State constitutions? Or can they be changed—as they were by the Australia Acts—through legislation of the Commonwealth and the State, plus the national referendum?

The politicians will also have to decide what provision they should make in the Constitution concerning the powers of a president. Should they be written into the Constitution or a statute? This is considered politically too divisive by many of the advocates of a republic. Or should the Constitution state that the powers of the president are the same as those enjoyed by the (former) Governor-General? In either event, the High Court would be likely at some future time to have to decide the extent of some of those powers.

But given the experience of the past 95 years, the politicians might be tempted to try to limit the way in which the High Court may interpret the republican constitution, by specifying the factors that the Court has to consider. Ultimately, the Court's powers will be determined by the precision with which those who write the Constitution set out the relevant powers and duties of those involved in the governance of the Commonwealth.

11

INSTITUTIONAL INTERFERENCE

The separation of powers doctrine is a useful peg on which to hang demands for judicial independence—useful, but not strictly necessary. In Britain, where the independence of the courts and the judges is equally valued, the three arms of state power are curiously entwined. The head of the judiciary, the Lord Chancellor, is a significant member of the executive, with a place in the Cabinet. He is also an active member of the government's legislative team in the House of Lords. The House of Lords is at the one time the second chamber of the British parliament but also the ultimate court of appeal in Britain, the latter function being performed by designated Law Lords. They are not required, however, to confine their public activities to their judicial work: they may participate in the Lords' legislative activities, in the same way as any other member of the upper house. The intermingling of the judicial, executive and legislative arms of government does not appear, however, to affect the independence of the courts. That independence was secured initially by the Act of Settlement of 1701, which gave judges tenure during good behaviour (not, as previously, during the King's pleasure) and provided them with salaries. These two attributes were seen as fundamental features of an independent judiciary when the Australian Constitution was written. It provided in section 72 for federal judges to have life tenure (later reduced to tenure to age 70) and a salary which could not be diminished while a judge held office. The Constitution also made it clear that judicial power was only to be exercised by properly constituted courts (s. 71): 'The judicial power of the Commonwealth shall be vested in a Federal Supreme Court . . . and such other federal courts as the Parliament creates.' The separation of powers was made more complete when the High Court decided in the *Boilermakers* case that the courts could not exercise non-judicial powers which were not ancillary or incidental to a judicial purpose.

It is axiomatic that the courts should be independent of government. As Sir Harry Gibbs, former Chief Justice of the High Court, has written (1990, p. 25):

> It is commonly accepted that the duty of the judiciary in applying the law is to act independently, without fear or favour, and since the law must be applied to the executive government and its officers as well as to the ordinary citizen, the judiciary must be free from pressure or influence from the executive as well as from any other section of the community.

Given that many of the disputes the High Court has to resolve are between the Commonwealth and one or more of the States, the requirement for independence from the parliament and executive government of the Commonwealth is quite fundamental to the acceptance of those of its decisions that concern political power.

But no matter how obvious it is that the courts should be free from political pressures in the exercise of their judicial role, governments tend to have a different understanding of how much freedom the judges need and how that freedom needs to be secured, and governments are often faced with problems (such as financial restraints) which lead them into conflict with the courts.

Governments find it difficult to keep their hands off the courts, but it is true also that there has been an increasing tendency on the part of the courts to interfere with what governments and parliaments do. It has always been generally accepted that the High Court may review legislation to ensure that it is within constitutional bounds, but more recently the courts have been keen to ensure that executive actions (including those of the Crown's representatives) are also reviewable.

Although the High Court has been unwilling to allow its processes to be used to question the internal proceedings of the parliament, in recent years it seems to have been less inclined to regard the parliamentary process as beyond its reach. The classical judicial approach to parliament's sovereign powers was adopted by the Court in the Browne and Fitzpatrick contempt case in 1955. In that case the House of Representatives, relying on its powers under section 49 of the Constitution giving it the same ability to punish contempts as was possessed by the House of Commons in 1901, decided to gaol two men it declared had been guilty of a serious breach of privilege. The men sought, through a writ of *habeas corpus*, to challenge the power of the House to gaol them. The High Court, in a unanimous decision, held that the power did exist (*R v. Richards; ex parte Fitzpatrick & Browne* (1955) 92 CLR 157). The Court said that while Australia had a rigid federal Constitution which required the courts to determine whether any act by the legislature or the executive was beyond power, the words of section 49 were incapable of a restricted meaning. Section 49 provides that 'The powers, privileges, and immunities of the Senate and of the House of Representatives, and of the members and the committees of each House, shall be such as are declared by the Parliament, and until declared shall be those of the Commons House of Parliament of the United Kingdom, and of its members and committees, at the establishment of the Commonwealth.' As for an argument based on the separation of powers, to the effect that the judicial power could only be exercised by the courts, this was not a sufficient reason to give a restrictive reading to section 49 (even though 'theoretically' and perhaps even 'scientifically' these were judicial powers the parliament was exercising). The courts, according to established English practice, could not go behind the declaration by the House that the two men were guilty of a serious breach of privilege. In a 1998 case, *Egan v. Willis* (1998) 73 ALJR 75, the Court was asked to restrict *Fitzpatrick & Browne* solely to the section 49 issue. It was urged to overturn a decision by the New South Wales Legislative Council to punish a minister for failing to produce documents it had demanded. The Court had not published its decision in that case when this book went to press.

The High Court has expressed doubts as to whether it is able to intervene in some other aspects of parliamentary procedure. In *Cormack v. Cope* (1974) 131 CLR 432, the Court was asked to prevent the holding of a joint sitting of the two houses of parliament for the purpose, under section 57 of the Constitution, of considering (and passing) Bills which had been the subject of a double dissolution of both houses several months earlier. Three Justices (out of six) thought the Court should not intervene on any occasion in the process of the joint sitting, though two asserted that it did have the power to intervene at any stage in that process. A year later the Court was to hold, in *Victoria v. The Commonwealth* (1975) 134 CLR 81, by a 4–2 majority, that in relation to one of the Bills passed by that joint sitting, the Petroleum and Minerals Authority Act (the PMA Act), the conditions of section 57 had not been properly satisfied because the Senate had not rejected or refused to pass it. (Three of the Justices in the majority held that evidence of what opposition senators had said, as reported in Hansard, could not be used to show that it was the Senate's intention not to pass it; now that such material may be used, perhaps the High Court would have been required to reach a different conclusion.)

It was the fact that the High Court could undo any impropriety in the holding of the joint sitting by striking down any legislation passed (as it did with the PMA Act) which helped persuade the Court in *Cormack v. Cope* that it should not, in that particular case, intervene in an issue involving the internal workings of the parliament. The fact that most of what parliament does leads ultimately to legislative action (if parliament intends that its wishes should have legal effect) allows the High Court to supervise what parliament does, without interfering with its internal workings.

Political cases

Recently, however, the Court has become increasingly involved in direct political disputes between the government and the opposition. The most recent case concerned the payment of postage allowances to MPs. The government decided eight months before the 1990 election that the stamp allowances paid to members of the House of Representatives should be increased from $9000 (the amount set by the Remuneration Tribunal) to over $30 000, apparently so that Labor MPs could take advantage of a computerised direct mail campaign the party had developed. Senators were not given the increase. The opposition challenged the move in the High Court and won. The Court declared that having established the Remuneration Tribunal to carry out this function, the government could not by executive fiat increase the allowance that had been determined. The Court also laid down some strict guidelines as to the use that could be made of the Appropriation and Supply Acts to provide money for such purposes. The decision applied something of a straitjacket to the implementation of government initiatives. Putting a spending proposal in the Budget would no longer be a sufficient indication that a policy previously endorsed by the parliament was to be changed.

Another High Court decision which involved it directly in the political process concerned the 1988 referendum proposals. The opposition enlisted the Court's aid to stop the government from televising several advertisements, complaining that they breached the provisions of the Referendum (Machinery Provisions) Act as they were intended to support the government's 'yes' case in the referendums and not merely encourage people to vote in them. The Court granted the opposition's injunction against the advertisements (*Reith v. Morling J.* (1988) 83 ALR 667).

The Court's involvement in 'political' matters has sometimes been justified as reflecting the apparent decline of parliament as an institution, and the development of the overweening power of the executive in relation to the House of Representatives. Sir Gerard Brennan, at a time when he was a Justice of the High Court, said in the Blackburn lecture in 1990, 'As the wind of political expediency now chills Parliament's willingness to impose checks on the Executive and the Executive now has a large measure of control over legislation, the Courts alone retain their original function of standing between the government and the governed' ((1991) 65 ALJ 32, at 35) Justice Brennan was at pains to meet the objection that the 'check imposed by the Courts on the actions of the political branches of governments' was seen by some as anti-democratic because 'the judges are not elected by the people'. That view, he said, 'misconceives what is involved in the exercise of judicial power. The Courts do not seek to interfere with lawful policy: that is the proper domain of the political branches. But the Courts are concerned to subject the political branches of government to the rule of law, for that is the constitutional imperative which binds all branches of government.' The Courts could review legislation that was unconstitutional, but not legislation that was unjust or oppressive, though the courts do use the rules of statutory interpretation to moderate such laws when they can. It is a different matter, however, when it comes to the review of executive action. Sir Gerard continued (at 39):

> . . . the doctrine of legislative supremacy requires the courts to determine whether any exercise of executive power—including the power to enact rules and regulations—falls within parliament's grant . . . The courts insist that executive and administrative power be exercised in good faith according to law and for the purpose for which it was conferred, having regard to all relevant considerations and to none which are irrelevant, that natural justice be done in exercise of power, and that an exercise of power must not be so unreasonable that no reasonable repository of the power could have so exercised it.

THE EXECUTIVE UNDER FIRE

Three cases demonstrate the extent to which the High Court will intervene to review executive action. Until quite recently, it was accepted in Australia that action taken by the Governor-General or a Governor of a State under a power conferred on him or her by a law to act 'if he is satisfied', or 'if it appears to him' that certain circumstances existed, was not reviewable by the courts (see the article, 'Judicial Review of Action by the Crown Representative' by P. W. Hogg, in *Australian Law Journal*, vol. 43, p. 215). That principle was rejected by the High Court in the

1980s. In *R v. Toohey; ex parte The Northern Land Council* (1981) 151 CLR 170, the Court, by a 5–1 majority, ruled that decisions of the Administrator of the Northern Territory, acting on the advice of the Executive Council, were reviewable for bona fides even though they properly conformed with the powers apparently conferred on him by legislation. At issue was whether the Northern Land Council could attack a decision of the Northern Territory government placing a large area of land outside Darwin within the City of Darwin for town planning purposes. The decision meant that the land was not capable of being the subject of a land rights claim. The Court held that even if the Administrator was 'the Crown', his decision could be attacked for lack of good faith. The old rule was no longer valid. Actions of the Crown in relation to legislative power delegated to the Crown could be impugned for bad faith, and perhaps even actions under the prerogative could be challenged. The dissenting judge was Justice Lionel Murphy, who asserted that: 'Inquiry by the judicial branch into the misuse of legislative powers . . . is inconsistent with the separation of legislative and judicial powers. The judicial branch is not empowered to inquire into the good faith of the Senate, or the House of Representatives, or the Governor-General in participating in the enactment of legislation.' Nor could it inquire into the good faith of those to whom the parliament had delegated legislative functions (at 228–9). The majority view, as expressed by Justice Stephen (at 215), was that the Court's decision involved 'no intrusion by the courts into the sphere either of the legislature or of the executive. It ensures that, just as the legislatures of constitutionally limited competence must remain within the limits of their power, so too must the executive, the exercise by it of power granted to it by the legislature being confined to the purposes for which it was granted.'

Six months later, in a 6–1 decision, the Court extended the principle a step further. A State Governor, the Court decided, was obliged to comply with the principles of natural justice, and did not, as the Victorian Supreme Court had held, have unfettered discretion. The issue in this case (*FAI Insurances Ltd v. Winneke* (1981–82) 151 CLR 342) concerned a decision not to renew a licence to conduct an insurance business. The problem was that the company had not been given a full opportunity to put its case for renewal, before the relevant minister recommended to the Governor that the licence be not renewed. The principle of ministerial responsibility was no reason for denying the availability of judicial review for excess of power, including improper purpose. Once again Justice Murphy dissented. He argued that there was no power in the courts to inquire into questions of good faith, observance of natural justice or other propriety of an act of a Governor-in-Council which was otherwise within power. He said certain governmental functions were committed to the executive branch of government to be determined not in a judicial or quasi-judicial way but in an executive way, and the standards that were applied were political standards enforceable by the political process (at 373–4).

The next major development in this field came in *Commonwealth v. Verwayen* (1990) 170 CLR 394, which suggested that the Court could impose on governments a somewhat higher standard of ethical behaviour than applies to other litigants. The Court decided that the Commonwealth was bound by statements by government officials to the solicitors of a man seeking to sue the Commonwealth for damages over the 1964 *Voyager* disaster that the Commonwealth would not plead that it owed the man no duty of care and nor would it raise a defence based on the Statute of Limitations. Two Justices held that the Commonwealth was estopped from changing its defence, two held that it had waived its right to rely on the defences that would otherwise have been available, and three Justices dissented. Professor Paul Finn (1991) has suggested that the decision in *Verwayen* is best explained on grounds related to the 'moral exemplar' role of government, and says, 'there clearly are circumstances in which the government, far from being treated in a fashion similar to the ordinary individual, warrants being dealt with less favourably than the individual and because it is the government'. In this context it is worth noting another recent High Court decision that met with the government's disapproval. In *Commonwealth v. Evans Deakin Industries Ltd* (1986) 161 CLR 254, the Court interpreted a provision of the Judiciary Act requiring the Commonwealth, as a litigant, to be treated as nearly as possible the same as any other litigant as exposing it to provisions of State legislation concerning the payment of subcontractors. The Commonwealth spent four years developing a major piece of legislation which was intended to allow the government to be exempted from such State legislation in the future (though allowing it to 'opt in' when it wished), but this legislation was ultimately withdrawn from the parliament.

The executive was brought to account in a different way in the *Teoh* case (*Minister for Immigration & Ethnic Affairs v. Teoh* (1995) 183 CLR 273). That case concerned the deportation of a Malaysian citizen who had lived in Australia for some years and was the father of a number of children who were Australian citizens. The issue in the case was whether officials who considered his status should have taken into account the 'best interests' of the children. In 1991 Australia had ratified an international convention on the rights of the child, which required various domestic authorities 'in all actions concerning children' to take into account the best interests of the child. The High Court decided that, although the convention had not become part of Australian domestic law, there was a legitimate expectation that Australian officials would observe the undertakings it had made. However, the Court said that the government could, by executive or legislative action, indicate that it would not follow particular requirements of such treaties.

The *FAI Insurances* case and the *Northern Land Council* case impact far more on the freedom of the executive branch of government than was envisaged by the parliament when it established in the 1970s what, at the time, was a radical new structure to cope with administrative law problems. The new system had three major aspects: legislation creating the Office of Ombudsman, an officer who would possess merely advisory powers; legislation establishing an Administrative Appeals Tribunal (AAT) to review the application of policy by departmental officials; and legislation giving the new Federal Court the power under the Administrative Decisions (Judicial Review) Act to supervise the legality of administrative action, including in particular the application of natural justice doctrines.

LIMITING THE COURTS

The new system, and the development of additional doctrines by the High Court allowing citizens to restrict and restrain the actions and determinations of governments, has not been welcomed by governments in the same spirit of adventure with which the new administrative law regime was created. The tendency has been for governments to step back from full and free disclosure, and to try to limit the interference of the courts and quasi-judicial bodies (the AAT) with the decision-making processes of government. For example, in 1990 the Commonwealth introduced major legislative changes to the Migration Act. The effect of the changes was to remove or limit ministerial and departmental discretions, particularly in relation to the deportation of people who had overstayed visa requirements. There was no longer the need for a minister or the Secretary of the Department to weigh up whether the person should or should not be deported—deportation was to be automatic. The fact that deportation was an automatic process meant that the courts and tribunals could not be used successfully to overturn ministerial decisions as they had on many previous occasions. There was some power left to the government to dispense with this harsh result in particular cases, but the power was written in such a way that it would rarely be possible for the courts to be used to upset a ministerial determination. The effect of the new scheme was to largely remove the ability of disaffected would-be migrants to use the courts to overturn governmental decisions or policies—an object achieved by imposing 'a significant degree of rigidity upon the administration of the migration laws' (*Pak Siu Ling & ors v. Minister for Immigration*, French J, Federal Court of Australia, 15 February 1991, p. 26 of pamphlet of judgment). Appeals over such discretions as remained in the legislation, particularly in relation to the granting of various kinds of visas, were to be handled by a new tribunal dealing only with migration matters, one that would become more familiar with (and presumably sympathetic to) the actual policies of the Department than the AAT might have been expected to be, particularly as the new tribunal was to be required to abide by ministerial guidelines, guidelines which could be altered by the minister to ensure that his or her policies were implemented without quasi-judicial interference.

The separation of powers doctrine has led the Commonwealth government into an increasing reliance on what are referred to as 'quasi-judicial' bodies to review administrative action and to undertake strictly non-judicial functions which either need to be performed in a judicial way or which it is advantageous for governments to have the public believe are being carried out with judge-like independence (contrasted with the political decision-making function referred to by Justice Murphy in the *FAI Insurances* case). The Administrative Appeals Tribunal, for example, is headed by a Federal Court judge, though it does not function as a court. The Remuneration Tribunal is also headed by a judge, as are the Electoral Commission and the Law Reform Commission. What is notable about most of these bodies is that they do not have the power to make binding decisions. If their decisions suit the government of the day, they can be given effect to and they carry with them the prestige of being made by an autonomous body. If they don't, the 'decisions' or recommendations can be overruled or not implemented. The fact that these bodies lack full independence in the sense that federal courts may be said to be independent became an issue only in the late 1980s, following the Hawke government's decision to reconstitute the former Conciliation and Arbitration Commission as the Industrial Relations Commission (IRC).

The major result of the transformation of this Commission was the shedding of one of the presidential members, Mr Justice Staples. As mentioned in chapter 8, every member of the Commission but he was appointed to the equivalent position on the IRC. Justice Staples was (not by name) the subject of a special provision in the transitional legislation, which provided that any member who was not reappointed would be 'deemed' to have reached retiring age and be paid his retirement pension. Justice Staples was some months short of his 60th birthday (the earliest date on which otherwise he would have been able to retire and collect a pension) when the law came into effect. The government gave no reason for singling out one member of the

Commission for this treatment, though later the prime minister complained that Mr Staples had not been a productive member of the Commission. As it turned out, that was because he had been sin-binned by two successive presidents of the Commission, the first restricting him to full-bench work, the second giving him no work at all and refusing even to discuss his position. A parliamentary committee which later investigated the dispute was unable to persuade either of those presidents to explain their actions. Mr Staples claimed, and his claim was not contradicted, that he was the victim of decisions by Liberal and Labor governments who disapproved of the decisions he had arrived at on the bench and of his approach to the work of the Commission. But he was never given the opportunity to confront his critics. He was 'retired' against his will without any public complaints having been made about his work, and without being given the opportunity to put his own point of view. More significantly, he was removed from his office despite a provision in the Conciliation and Arbitration Act which mirrored the constitutional protection given to Federal Court judges: namely, that he could not be removed from office except upon an address by both houses of parliament, and on grounds of proved misbehaviour or incapacity. There would have been no basis for such resolutions—but as the government demonstrated, there was no need for dramatic and drastic (and potentially unsuccessful) parliamentary action. Instead the government could do what other governments before had done: abolish the Court or Commission from which it was otherwise impossible to remove him, and give other judicial or equivalent employment to those members of the Court or Commission who were not in the government's black-books. The precedent was established at the Commonwealth level in Australia in 1977 when the parliament gave to the Federal Court the jurisdiction previously enjoyed by the Australian Industrial Court. Two of the Industrial Court judges were not appointed to the Federal Court. They were left holding commissions in a court that had no functions, enjoying life tenure. Their compulsory retirement from active work was on full pay.

Unlike those earlier victims of subterfuge sacking, Staples decided to complain publicly about the way he had been treated and to threaten possible legal action. His main achievement was the creation of a joint parliamentary committee to examine the 'Tenure of appointees to Commonwealth tribunals'. It recommended, among other things, that the abolition of a tribunal should not be used to remove the holder of a quasi-judicial office unless the removal procedures applying to that office were followed. The recommendation did not find favour with the government. So this particular means of removing recalcitrant tribunal members, or for that matter judges, remains, and the independence of the judiciary is to that extent reduced. There is no federal court (including the High Court) or tribunal which cannot be effectively abolished by the Commonwealth parliament.

There is only one legitimate way in which judges can be removed from office. Federal judges cannot be removed except by the Governor-General in Council, on an address from both houses of the parliament in the same session, praying for such removal on the ground of proved misbehaviour or incapacity (Constitution, s. 72). Preliminary moves to invoke this section were undertaken in the mid-1980s following a media and political campaign directed at Justice Lionel Murphy. Allegations were based initially on tapes, transcripts and summaries prepared by New South Wales police following telephone intercepts of conversations involving a long-time friend of Murphy. These were succeeded by allegations of other conversations Murphy was said to have had with a judge and with the chief magistrate in New South Wales. Murphy was accused of attempting to pervert the course of justice. He was tried and found not guilty in relation to the judge but guilty in relation to the magistrate. An appeal was successful (members of the jury having explained to the media how they had been confused by the trial judge's summing up) and on the retrial Murphy was acquitted.

The trials were neither the beginning nor the end of the matter, however. They were preceded by two Senate committee inquiries, and followed by the establishment of a parliamentary commission of inquiry. Murphy refused to give direct evidence (other than in the form of a statement) to the Senate committees, arguing (in part) that this would impinge on the separation of powers. All the committees were concerned to understand the way in which the parliament should decide what would constitute misbehaviour, the commissioners taking a fairly broad view. But there was no cause for them to apply their decision. The Commission was terminated when it was discovered that Murphy was dying of cancer. (The 'Murphy affair' is analysed by Professor Tony Blackshield in a chapter in Scutt 1987.)

Paying judges

Security of tenure is one of the two major bases of judicial independence. Pay is the second. And that has not proved to be inviolate either.

When the High Court was established, the parliament was concerned about what the Court would cost. The government was forced to compromise its preferred position of having a five-member Court so that it could get parliament's approval for the establishment of any Court at all. But the three Justices were given salaries which befitted their position as members of the highest court in the land. Their salaries of £3500 for the Chief Justice and £3000 each for the other two Justices were comparable with judicial salaries elsewhere in Australia. They totally overshadowed the salaries paid to members of those first parliaments—£400—and no-one would have claimed that MPs were underpaid by the standards of the day, as they received about eight times the average annual salary earned by Australian men. Translating those figures to the money values of 1990, MPs were being paid in 1903 about $200 000 a year (three times what they are actually receiving now), while the High Court Justices would be getting well over the million dollar mark. Instead, the six Justices each receive (in mid-1998) under $220 000, and the Chief Justice gets $240 140. Few people have suggested that the current salaries of High Court judges are appropriate, nor those of other federal judges and officials whose salaries are set in relation to the High Court. Given its own way, the Remuneration Tribunal would probably have set salaries for the High Court some 50 per cent higher than the salaries actually being paid in 1991. However, the Tribunal has not acted as an independent Tribunal might have been expected to act. Every time the government made it clear that it would not accept what the Tribunal truly thought were the appropriate judicial salaries, the Tribunal has given way and made lower recommendations, and even those lower proposed salaries have then been adjusted downwards by the government. The judges didn't protest publicly, but their dissatisfaction was evident. Chief Justice Mason, in a letter to the Remuneration Tribunal complaining about proposals for increased salaries for senior legal officers in the executive branch of the government (the Solicitor-General, the Director of Public Prosecutions and the head of the National Crime Authority) and writing with the concurrence of other members of the High Court, said:

> The present procedures governing the determination of remuneration and conditions of judicial service have proved to be manifestly unsatisfactory. The remuneration and conditions of service have been eroded to the point that there is a distinct possibility, if not a likelihood, that the quality of the Federal Judiciary will be impaired. The difficulties encountered in federal and State jurisdictions in attracting suitable appointees is indicative of what has happened. And, as you know, some members of the Judiciary have resigned their offices. This situation threatens the maintenance of a strong and independent Judiciary.

The problem of quality is a real one, particularly for the States and the Federal Court. State and Commonwealth attorneys have found it increasingly difficult to get leading members of the Bar to accept appointment as judges. One State attorney in the 1980s was informed that the first eighteen people who had been offered a position as a Supreme Court judge had declined the offer. The position is not as serious with the High Court, where the prestige (and power) associated with being at the top of the legal profession counts for a great deal. But even there appointments have been refused, though not always for monetary reasons. The problem of judicial resignations is perhaps even more directly related to financial concerns. Some judges appointed in their 40s and early 50s have found their new salaries inadequate to support the educational needs of their families and the lifestyles they assumed while at the comparatively well-paid Bar.

However real the problem is, it does not manifest itself as a political problem for governments. The Court system continues, whether the best people are appointed as judges or not. The quality of the judiciary is not perceived to be a governmental problem. The government is not answerable for the mistakes that a less-than-best quality judiciary might deliver. Besides, who would know?

The current judicial salary issue needs to be seen in some kind of perspective. There have been previous clashes between the High Court and the government of the day about judicial salaries and allowances. Perhaps the worst occurred early in the life of the Court when the Commonwealth attorney-general, Sir Josiah Symon, decided to question the Court's early decision that it should be an itinerant body, sitting in the major capital cities instead of spending all its time in Melbourne which was designated as its principal seat. He told the Court he wanted it to sit primarily in Melbourne, but he was prepared to allow it to sit in Sydney also. The High Court refused to consider this proposal and a vitriolic correspondence followed. The cost-cutting which Symon insisted on included a refusal to pay for shelving for Griffith's law library in Sydney, a library the Chief Justice had moved from Brisbane where he was the Queensland Chief Justice before his appointment to the High Court. The dispute ranged over where the Court could sit, what staff the Justices could take with them when they travelled, and even how many telephones the Court could have. The attorney-general, in a letter of 26 April 1905, complained that there were seven telephones for the Court in Sydney, five at the Court and two in the homes of two of the Justices, and that they were costing the Commonwealth £70 10s a year. He proposed that there should be just one telephone for the Court in Sydney, to be placed 'wherever in the building the Justices may think it most convenient'. The Justices responded by postponing for a week their May sittings in Melbourne, and made a public statement explaining their problems with the attorney-general. Symon expressed his profound regret at the way the Justices had used the Court 'as the arena for a public and non-judicial animadversion on the Executive' (letter dated 9 June 1905). The dispute ended only when there was a change of government and Isaac Isaacs became attorney-general. The new government then gave way on every point raised by Symon.

During the Great Depression of the 1930s, the government sought to persuade the Court that salaries paid to the Justices should be reduced, in line with reductions generally applying through the public service. The Court refused, though three Justices agreed to forgo travelling allowances and three others made payments back to the Treasury from their salaries. The Court's visits to outlying capitals were curtailed for several years, resulting in a considerable saving for the Commonwealth.

Commissions of inquiry

Another area of dispute between the government and the Court during its earlier history was over the appointment of judges as Royal Commissioners. Between 1919 and 1928 governments made repeated requests to the Chief Justice to make judges available for these executive inquiries. As Sir Adrian Knox wrote in a confidential letter to the prime minister on 7 August 1923:

> . . . a judge who acts as a Royal Commissioner places himself in a false position and is likely to damage the status of the Court of which he is a member. His whole duty as a Judge is to deal according to law and on fixed judicial principles with matters brought before him in a judicial capacity, and his decisions, while subject to correction on appeal, are binding and must be obeyed. When he acts as a Royal Commissioner he may be, and generally is, required to some extent to depart from ordinary judicial methods and his decision is no more than a recommendation which may be ignored by the Executive and has of itself no binding force. He assumes the position of giving advice which need not be accepted, and so detracts from the position of authority occupied by him as a Judge. In a word he ceases to be a Judge and becomes merely an adviser . . .

Coincidentally, the Victorian Supreme Court judges a week later rejected a request by the Victorian premier that one of their number should conduct a Royal Commission into bribery allegations concerning the letting of a contract.

The High Court subsequently maintained its policy of refusing to allow its Justices to be appointed as Royal Commissioners, though during World War II Chief Justice Latham served for thirteen months as Minister Plenipotentiary to Japan and later Justice Dixon accepted an appointment, for two and a half years, as Australian Minister in Washington. That is, both Justices acted as representatives of the executive government and advisers to it. Before he went to Washington, Sir Owen Dixon held other appointments as chairman of various councils and boards which had executive functions. A decade after the end of the war Chief Justice Dixon explained that early in the war he had felt 'very depressed . . . and had not the opinion which we may now have in retrospect, about its outcome. In those conditions, feeling very restless indeed and finding it difficult to accommodate myself to sitting on the Bench throughout the war, I agreed to do other work. Looking back from this point of view, I am not sure that it was right. I do not wish it to be thought that, looking in retrospect, I altogether approve of what I myself did.' (*Australian Law Journal* (1955), 29, 252, p. 292.)

Although most judicial opinion seems to support the view that judges should not perform public functions other than those of their judicial office, some courts and some other judges adopt a different view. The Federal Court and the New South Wales Supreme Court have both allowed judges to participate in Royal Commissions in recent years, and Sir Gerard Brennan, when a member of the Federal Court, supported the appointment of judges to tribunals such as the Administrative Appeals Tribunal and the Trade Practices Tribunal. What needed to be avoided, he suggested, was having judges in a position where they were making 'political' decisions—'policy decisions which affect the community at large' (see Justice Brennan's article 'Limits on the use of Judges' 1978, particularly p. 6). He also stated his disapproval of the Victorian Supreme Court (and High Court) carte blanche refusal to sit on Royal Commissions. He expressed concern that if judicial skills were needed and not made available by the judges, 'the institution of the judiciary may lose its relevance or, at the least, fall short of discharging fully the functions which the community would commit to it' (p. 14). (The issue is debated at length in

Judges as Royal Commissioners and Chairmen of Non-judicial Tribunals, published by the Australian Institute of Judicial Administration Inc. in 1986.)

However, in recent years problems about staffing Royal Commissions have not been an issue of any significance for High Court–Commonwealth government relations, given the readiness of the Federal Court to cooperate with the government, and the expedient the government has adopted of creating personal judgeships. (For example, legislation was passed to give Mr Justice Stewart judicial status when the New South Wales Supreme Court, of which he was then a member, objected to his appointment as Chairman of the National Crime Authority. He retained his personal title when he moved on to become chairman of the Resource Assessment Commission.)

The High Court has begun reducing the non-judicial use that the government can make of other federal judges. In *Wilson v. Minister for Aboriginal and Torres Strait Islander Affairs* (1997) 189 CLR 1, the Court, by a 6–1 majority, held that the appointment of a Federal Court judge to make a report to a minister recommending whether an area of land should receive protection under the Aboriginal and Torres Strait Islander Heritage Protection Act was invalid. The majority said no functions could be conferred on a judge which breached the separation of powers, and that the role intended to be assigned to the judge in this case was a political one.

A year earlier the Court had discussed the same issue when it reviewed the use of judges to issue warrants to allow telephone calls to be tapped by security or police services. This is classed as an administrative not a judicial function, but the High Court has permitted judges to undertake this function so long as individual judges could decide whether or not they wished to do so. In *Grollo v. Palmer* (1995) 184 CLR 348, the Court said that there were some functions that were incompatible with judicial independence. Incompatibility could arise because the involvement in non-judicial functions makes it impracticable to perform the judicial function; or because performance of non-judicial functions compromises or impairs the judicial function; or because performance of the non-judicial function diminishes public confidence in the integrity of the judiciary as an institution or in the capacity of the individual judge. In *Grollo*, only one judge held that federal judges should not be involved in issuing warrants. However, as a result of the Court's analysis of the issue, almost all federal judges decided that they would not in future allow themselves to be involved in issuing warrants. The parliament later passed a law to allow members of the Administrative Appeals Tribunal to perform this function instead of judges.

THE TAX BITE

The question of money, and in particular pay and tax, has been a perennial problem in relations between the government and the Court. The pay problem has been referred to earlier, and was cause enough for alarm by judges. The tax problem emerged unannounced and was an extraordinary blow at the personal circumstances of federal judges. In the 1990 Budget the federal treasurer announced a measure designed to ensure that company directors and others who had avoided making Pay As You Earn (PAYE) payments as they received their salaries and allowances would, from the 1990–91 financial year onwards, be required to make those payments. Federal judges had, until that time, received their pay in monthly instalments, and paid their taxes in the succeeding year. In 1990–91 they were faced with having to pay their tax bills on their 1989–90 incomes plus their taxes on their 1990–91 incomes. For a Federal Court judge earning about $120 000 a year, the tax payable in 1990–91 amounted to about $112 000. The judges saw this as further evidence of the government's desire to diminish their standing. Some Family Court judges considered taking action in the High Court to have the particular section in the tax legislation declared invalid, primarily on the grounds of the legislative and constitutional provision that a judge's income should not be diminished during his tenure of office. In fact, there had been rumblings for some time about the government's failure to adjust judicial salaries to take sufficient account of inflation. These were referred to in a speech by Justice Sir Gerard Brennan who, denying that he was expressing an opinion about the level of judges' salaries, or that the level of those salaries was the problem, said (1990, pp. 25–6):

> The problem relates to the isolation of judges from influence by government, whether the influence by generosity or parsimony. The problem, which could have arisen at any time under an unwritten constitution, now exists under the Constitution of the Commonwealth because inflation and the nominalist theory of money have placed judicial remuneration back in the hands of the Executive. The problem is not merely that Executive control is contrary to constitutional history and intent. The power to fix from time to time the conditions of judicial service is an inappropriate power to entrust to an Executive Government with the capacity to translate its decision into law. It gives rise to a misgiving of some relationship between the Executive Government's periodic decisions on conditions of service and judicial conformity to governmental aspirations of judicial conduct or even judicial decision-making. What is essential, in both Commonwealth and State, is machinery for fixing judicial conditions of service that is as independent of political influence as the courts themselves.

Instead, the government has subverted the work of the judicially-led Remuneration Tribunal, the body established to provide an independent view of politicians and the allowances that should be paid to politicians, public servants and judges at the federal level. In the interests of relations with the trade union movement, the government has made it plain that the salaries and allowances of judges will be determined at the whim of the executive. Although no-one would suggest that this will directly undermine judicial independence (it is more likely that the government, as a litigant, will suffer some inconveniences it might not otherwise have experienced), in the long run it will be damaging to the courts because it will affect the quality of lawyers attracted to judicial office. The resignations that occurred in the 1980s from the Federal Court, for financial reasons, were unprecedented in the Australian and English judiciary, according to the Remuneration Tribunal. Judicial conditions have worsened since those resignations took place, while those who resigned have flourished.

On the government side of the argument, there has been increasing concern at the cost of justice. There has not been any complaint about its quality. There have also been misunderstandings, on both sides, about the impact of parliamentary demands for information about the work of the courts. In the mid-1980s the Court, relying on its protected position in Chapter III of the Constitution, considered itself to be in an entirely different position from other governmental organisations which, like it, were required by legislative direction to provide the parliament with an annual report on their activities. The Court was prepared to account for its finances, but not its judicial activities. It suggested to the parliament that this would be an intrusion into judicial independence. The Senate Committee charged with examining the High Court's annual report disagreed. It thought a line could be drawn between judicial independence and 'the accountability of institutions, be they administrative, legislative or judicial, which are funded by public monies' (Report by the Senate Standing Committee on Constitutional and Legal Affairs 1984–85, p. 5). To prove its point it wrote to a series of legal agencies and professional bodies, asking them what they thought about the High Court and particularly about costs and delays. None of the legal bodies, the Committee noted in its next report, thought that the compilation of the information requested from the Court would interfere in any way with the independence of the judiciary, though the Law Council of Australia initially resisted publicly discussing the administration of the Court. The Committee conducted several public hearings, at which many complaints and suggestions were made. The hearings demonstrated a fair degree of ignorance, even within the legal profession, about the workings of the Court. That, as much as anything else, apparently persuaded the Court to be more forthcoming in its subsequent annual reports, an outcome that pleased the Committee.

More controls

Perhaps the most important way in which the parliament can interfere with the work of the High Court is by directing the way in which it functions. There are two major aspects of this problem, only one of which seems to have excited any judicial concern. Justice Murphy, in *Commissioner of Taxation v. St Helens Farm (ACT) Pty Ltd & ors* (1981) 146 CLR 336, referred to the fact that an earlier tax case had been decided by a 'statutory majority', a majority established under the provisions of the Judiciary Act. Justice Murphy said that such directions were of doubtful validity (at 387):

> If parliament can direct that on an even division a certain judgment follows, for example that in certain cases the opinion of the Chief Justice or, if he is absent, the opinion of the senior Justice present shall prevail, presumably it can direct that in those or other cases the opinion of the junior or some other Justice shall prevail, and of course it can change the directions from time to time. If Parliament can direct that a Full Court consisting of less than all the Justices shall not give a decision on a question affecting the constitutional powers of the Commonwealth unless at least three Justices concur in the decision (see s. 23(1)), presumably it can direct that the decision shall not be given unless it is unanimous. If Parliament can give such directions, why can it not direct that no decision shall be given which invalidates an Act (or on a question affecting the validity of an Act) or challenges the validity of any governmental action, or which is adverse to the Government, unless the decision is unanimous.

He said that section 79 of the Constitution did not authorise directions by the parliament on how the individual opinions or votes of the Justices should be transformed into judgments—this was a matter for the Court.

Justice Murphy believed that the way in which the Court functioned was a matter for the Court itself to determine. He believed that each Justice had a right to sit on any case he or she chose—a view shared by many other Justices, and at times exercised by them, as it was by Justice Murphy himself. Parliament has, as Justice Murphy pointed out, laid down some rules. It has defined a Full Court to mean a Court comprising at least two Justices. It has specified that in constitutional cases a majority must contain at least three Justices. The composition of the Court for any case, however, is normally determined by the Chief

Justice in accordance with the usual practice—at the time—of the Court. Constitutional cases may be determined by a Court of five (the minimum size, given the parliament's requirement about the number who must be in the majority) or six (one judge may be ill or absent, or there may be a vacancy on the Court) or seven. Applications for special leave to appeal in civil cases were, until 1998, heard by three Justices, and criminal special leave cases by three or five. However, pressure of business—the Court now hears more than 20 applications on each special leave sitting day—has led parliament to reduce the number of Justices hearing special leave applications to two, in most cases. In civil appeals it is possible to have as few as three on the bench—tax cases in the Court headed by Sir Garfield Barwick were heard by three or five Justices. The fashion in the 1990s is for appeals to be heard by five or seven. The larger the Court, the less likely it is that the outcome will be determined by the way in which the bench was selected (or even self-selected). Given that many cases are split 3–2, the 'lottery effect' may determine the outcome of a case.

A second issue concerns the way in which the Court interprets legislation. The Commonwealth parliament, since 1981, has determined the main rules about the way legislation should be read in the Acts Interpretation Act. Sections 15AA and 15AB tell the courts that in interpreting Commonwealth legislation they have regard to the purpose or object of the legislation, and that they may use various parliamentary materials to confirm or determine the meaning of a provision. Previously the courts themselves declared the rules of statutory interpretation. While there has been no questioning of the parliament's right to say how its legislation should be interpreted, the Court has rejected any suggestion that the parliament can tell it how it should go about interpreting the Constitution. In particular, in the *Communist Party* case, the Court rejected an attempt by the parliament to determine factual issues which might have brought the proposed law within constitutional bounds.

Nor should it be thought that the entry of parliaments into providing rules about statutory interpretation has freed them from difficulties with the courts in this area. In *Bropho v. Western*

Australia (1990) 171 CLR 1, the High Court changed the common law rules about the intention of statutes in relation to the issue of whether a particular law bound the Crown. The variation in the rule of interpretation which the Court decided on makes it far easier for courts to say that the Crown is bound by its own laws. The decision meant that in future the parliament would have to explicitly exempt the government from provisions of its own legislation if that was what it wanted to do; it could not achieve that objective without saying that that was its intention.

In this as in other areas, there is a continuing tension between the rights and powers of the parliament, the executive and the courts. So long as the courts seek to retain their independence, that is inevitable.

The High Court and the Attorney-General

There has been a tradition that the attorney-general should speak up for the courts if they come under attack. That tradition was abandoned in the 1990s when attacks on the High Court were originated primarily by politicians. The attorney-general, despite the fact that he or she is supposed to approach at least some of his or her tasks in a non-political manner, is a politician, and modern attorneys-general don't wish to publicly confront their ministerial colleagues in defence of the courts. In 1992 Daryl Williams QC, then shadow attorney-general, put the courts on notice when he said, 'The judiciary should accept the position that it no longer expects the Attorney-General to defend its reputation.' As attorney-general in the Howard government, Williams adhered to that position. The judges did not accept that this was correct. Sir Gerard Brennan, in a 'state of the judicature' speech to the Australian Legal Convention in 1997, noted that attorneys were 'politically hamstrung' in responding to attacks on the courts by their colleagues. However, he argued that if an attack on the courts came from a political source, the response must be from a political identity.

> If it be politically unrealistic to expect an Attorney publicly to defend the integrity of the judicial process, it must be because governments now perceive the courts to be players in the political game. That is a false perception but—frightening though the thought may be—governments have the power to make that perception a self-fulfilling prophecy. Political attacks on courts will inevitably lead some judges into political responses. Treating courts as political players will lead politicians to make political appointments, to offer personal or institutional rewards for judicial conduct that is politically desirable and to impose penalties for decisions that are politically unacceptable.

It is already beginning to happen, and it won't be reversed merely by the attorney-general taking up cudgels on behalf of the court. Too many politicians resent the way the High Court has reduced their effective power and created political problems for government (as with its native title decision).

12

What the People Say

Hundreds of decisions of the High Court have helped shape the Constitution as a working document. Scores of referendums seeking changes to the Constitution have been submitted to the people by politicians. But on only a relatively few occasions have the people of Australia actually given their agreement to a change in the wording of the Constitution.

Almost invariably the politicians have sought to change the Constitution so as to increase the powers of the Commonwealth. Frequently they have been moved to act by a High Court decision denying the parliament a particular power which the politicians thought they had, or thought they should have. Not one of the many referendums put to the people by the parliament has sought to diminish the Commonwealth's powers. Only once, apparently, has it been even suggested to the parliament that a limitation might be placed on a power that the Court had held to exist. That was a scheme suggested by the shadow attorney-general, Senator Peter Durack, to limit the external affairs power following the High Court's decision in the *Koowarta* case. Like scores of other proposed changes (generally suggested by oppositions) it failed to gain parliamentary approval and thus never reached the referendum stage.

The people, through referendums, may change the wording of the Constitution, and the High Court, through its decisions, can change the way the Constitution works. The power of the politicians is more limited. At the federal level, politicians decide which proposals for constitutional change should be put to the people for their approval—and which should not. State politicians have no influence at all over referendum topics, though widespread opposition by them to any proposal will normally result in the failure of the referendum. This is a very different scheme from what was proposed at the first Constitutional Convention in Sydney in 1891. That Convention wanted to exclude the people from the process altogether and share the ability to change the Constitution among federal and State politicians. It decided that the Constitution should be changed only after a proposal had received an absolute majority in both the House of Representatives and the Senate, and was then approved by Conventions in a majority of States, so long as the States that approved the proposal contained a majority of the people of Australia. This was representative democracy, not participatory democracy. The people would not have a direct vote on changes to the Constitution. Instead they would elect representatives (politicians, by definition) in a manner to be determined by the Commonwealth parliament at a later time. The scheme was intended, deliberately, to give the States a double chance to negative any proposal, first through their representatives in the Senate, then through the requirement that Conventions in a majority of States should approve any changes. The final element, that a majority of the whole population should be in those States which approved of any changes, was intended to protect the interests of the two largest States, New South Wales and Victoria, against any ganging up by the other, smaller States.

The scheme was also meant to prevent any quick and easy changes to the Constitution. Mr Donaldson admitted bluntly, 'For my own part, I wish to make the amendment of the constitution as difficult as possible' (Convention Debates, vol. 1, p. 887), and Alfred Deakin thought the scheme, if adopted, would fulfil Donaldson's desires and make 'reform almost impossible' (p. 888).

The mood changed between 1891 and 1897 when the matter was next considered. Democratic principles, such as one man, one vote, were established in the meantime in all of the colonies, and South Australia had gone so far as to give the vote to women, a matter which caused some difficulties for delegates who thought that this would mean that South Australia would have twice as many votes as it would otherwise be entitled to. The Sydney Convention in 1891 had even rejected the notion of the proposed Constitution being put to a vote of the people before it was sent to London for the approval of the parliament at Westminster. By 1897 there was no questioning of the fact that the Constitution would have to be approved by the people in a series of referendums in the different colonies. Indeed, that fact was used by many delegates to argue for the liberalisation of the contents of the document—unless it was made more democratic it would not gain the approval of the people.

By 1898 there had been a significant change in the amending provision of the proposed constitution: not only had a direct vote of the people replaced the notion of conventions, but the requirement for an absolute majority of both houses of parliament had been set aside, so that either house could initiate a referendum. That, as it turned out, was a change which made no difference, because although the parliament might determine the questions that should be submitted to the people it could only be the government of the day, through its advice to the Governor-General, which would determine which questions were in fact submitted to a referendum. More practically, where there was a difference between the houses, the prospect of a referendum achieving the required popular majorities was utterly unlikely.

The expectations of those who wrote the conservative amending section in the Constitution were largely met. Of 110 Bills presented to the parliament in the first 95 years of federation, 38 became proposals that were submitted as referendums but only eight were approved by the electors. Another five were approved by a majority of voters but did not pass because they did not obtain a majority of votes in a majority of States. One of those which failed, the most 'popular', was the Fraser government's proposal in 1977 for simultaneous elections. It obtained a national vote of over 62 per cent, but won majorities in only three States.

The referendums that did win the approval of the voters were not controversial and not one of them was intended to overturn a High Court decision. The largest group of successful referendums comprised proposals that were seen as making merely mechanical changes (changing the date on which Senate elections would be held, giving voters in the Territories a say in referendums, defining the way Senate vacancies should be filled, and allowing Aborigines to be counted in the census). Several others approved arrangements that had been agreed between the Commonwealth and the States (over State debts and loans), while others were to guarantee benefits which almost all voters wanted or thought should be provided (social security benefits). There was also an amendment approved to limit the age to which federal judges could serve, which could be thought of as procedural and/or as eliminating a discriminatory provision in the Constitution, and another which was seen to remove discrimination against Aborigines (but in fact gave the Commonwealth additional legislative powers).

What have not been approved by the electorate are increases in the real powers of the Commonwealth to make laws over monopolies, corporations, industrial matters, prices (all these proposals submitted on more than one occasion), aviation, railway disputes or trusts. These unsuccessful referendums were frequently prompted by particular High Court decisions. The Court's decisions in the *Union Label* case (*Attorney-General (NSW) v. Brewery Employees Union of NSW* (1908) 6 CLR 469) and *Huddart, Parker* in 1908 and 1909 were seen by Labor as attacking fundamental aspects of its legislative program. Private members introduced referendum Bills into the Senate in 1909 to deal with the nationalisation of monopolies and with industrial conditions. They failed to gain majority support. When Labor took office in 1910, it moved quickly to hold referendums to overcome the deficiencies which the High Court had held to exist in Commonwealth power. They sought two changes. One, which was labelled 'legislative powers', would have given the Commonwealth full power over trade and commerce, corporations, labour and employment conditions and monopolies. The second would have allowed the nationalisation of monopolies. Both were soundly defeated when put to the people in 1911. In 1912 a package of six proposals was introduced into parliament, containing the same kind of proposals as those rejected in 1911. The referendums were held in conjunction with the 1913 election. They were only narrowly defeated, winning majorities in three States and overall just under 50 per cent of the national vote. One additional matter in this package was railway disputes, which belatedly took up the problem exposed in the *Railway Servants* case. The parliament considered similar Bills again in 1913, 1914 and 1916, but they were not submitted as referendums. Proposals similar to those produced by Labor in 1911 were put by the Nationalist government in 1919, but suffered a similar fate. In 1926 the Nationalist–Country Party government sought control over essential services as well as a legislative powers package, but again failed. In 1936 there was something new, a proposal to give the Commonwealth power over 'air navigation and aircraft' and a power to exclude primary produce marketing schemes from the restrictions of section 92. Both were the parliament's response to judicial limitations on power, the former by the High Court in *R v. Burgess; ex parte Henry* (1936) 55 CLR 608, the second by the Privy Council in *James v. Cowan* (1932) 47 CLR 386. Both failed at the referendum stage.

Without detailing the remaining history of the changes sought by referendums, it is necessary to mention just one other change that was specifically related to a High Court decision. That was the referendum held by the Menzies government in 1951, seeking approval for the Communist Party Dissolution Act of 1950, which had been invalidated by the High Court. Chief Justice Latham, who was the sole dissentient in that case, provided 'informal' advice to the prime minister about the constitutional amendments necessary to overcome the Court's decision (see Lloyd, 1987).

Since the 1960s the nature of the issues raised in referendum proposals has changed, with only one (once repeated) taking up and trying to reverse a High Court decision. That one concerned 'democratic elections'. An unsuccessful attempt was made in 1975 in the *McKinlay* case to persuade the High Court that a provision in section 24 of the Constitution that members of the House of Representatives should be 'directly chosen by the people' ought to mean (as a similar section in the United States Constitution had been interpreted) that electorates should have an equal number of voters. Electoral and parliamentary issues tended to dominate other referendums through this period, but were unrelated to anything said by the High Court.

Investigating the Constitution

Politicians, recognising that the public might discern a certain degree of self-interest in their pleas for increased powers, have occasionally sought to establish impartial, or at least bipartisan, inquiries into the workings of the Constitution. There have been four significant exercises of this kind. The first was a Royal Commission established by the Bruce government in 1927 to inquire into the Constitution. This form of inquiry was adopted because the Labor Party refused to participate in a bipartisan parliamentary inquiry. The Labor Party changed its mind 40 years later when another parliamentary inquiry was proposed by the Menzies government. Although that committee produced many unanimous all-party recommendations for changes to the Constitution, they were never taken up by the government which had established the inquiry. Those recommendations indicate the range of issues which the politicians of the late 1950s considered to be important. They consisted, first, of a series of proposals concerning the Commonwealth's legislative machinery, including one proposal for the abolition of the nexus between the sizes of the two houses which was eventually (in 1967) put to the people in a referendum but was soundly defeated. Other recommendations dealt with disagreements between the two houses, the terms and rotation of senators and casual vacancies in the Senate.

More importantly, there was a series of recommendations dealing with legislative powers. One proposed that the Commonwealth should have the power to make laws generally about navigation and shipping; another that it should have power over aviation; a third that it should have the power to make laws concerning scientific and industrial research; a fourth that it should be able to make laws concerning nuclear energy and ionising radiation; a fifth that it should have express powers over broadcasting and television and other like media; a sixth, with one dissent recorded, that the Commonwealth should have the power to make laws with respect to the terms and conditions of industrial employment; a seventh would have allowed the Commonwealth to enact a uniform companies code but would have prevented it regulating the business activities of corporations (there was a dissenter here too); the eighth would have provided a specific power over restrictive trade practices and also would have encouraged the re-creation of the Inter-State Commission; and the ninth would have permitted the creation of primary marketing organisations under specified conditions. Under the heading 'economic powers' the committee recommended additional powers to allow Commonwealth control over capital issues, consumer credit and interest rates in connection with loans secured by mortgages of land. The final major issue concerned section 92, where the proposal was that the States should be able to make reasonable charges on road hauliers. There were also recommendations about the creation of new States and about adopting a different way of changing the Constitution.

What is noteworthy about these proposals is that most of them would no longer be considered necessary because the High Court no longer stands in the way of the Commonwealth legislating in these areas. But it is also true that these days it would be all but impossible to get the three major parties to agree on a package of reforms which was biased in favour of increased Commonwealth powers. These days the Liberal and National parties would begin with a series of propositions which would reduce the Commonwealth's powers particularly in relation to external affairs.

In the early 1970s there was still a desire among politicians to revise constitutional arrangements. The Whitlam Labor government adopted a suggestion by the Victorian Liberal government for a series of constitutional Conventions which would include representatives of federal and State (and later local) governments, from all the major political parties at each level. Although this might have been the way to go to assure any referendum proposal that emerged received all-round support, in fact there were very few areas of agreement.

The most recent attempt to produce a comprehensive examination of the Constitution was undertaken by the Constitutional Commission appointed by the Hawke government in 1986. It made use of ex-politicians from Commonwealth, State and local government and from most major parties, but also included judges, lawyers, journalists, economists, business people, trade union leaders, political scientists and other 'experts', as well as representatives of various community and 'ethnic' groups, to try to broaden the range of opinions that could be tapped. The report it produced largely favoured an increase in Commonwealth powers, though in many respects its recommendations would have strengthened the existing roles of the States. It would also have tidied up the existing provisions of the Constitution, making them reflect the way the parliamentary and governmental systems actually work. But the government sacrificed whatever good the Commission might have achieved when it required it to produce an interim report covering some of the areas it thought might win referendums during the celebration of the bicentenary of European colonisation of the continent. In fact the government was not entirely content with the interim report and substituted its own proposals on which it had needed no advice from anyone. The referendums failed dismally.

The Constitutional Commission did produce reports of considerable value and sponsored research which shows why so many referendums are doomed. The most telling study was a public opinion poll conducted for the Commission which showed that almost half the population were unaware of the fact that Australia had a Constitution—54 per cent said it did have a Constitution, 23 per cent said it did not, while 23 per cent admitted they did not know. Women and the young were the most ignorant, with only 31 per cent of people between 18 and 24 and 44 per cent of women of all ages saying that they knew Australia had a Constitution. Only a quarter of those asked thought the Constitution had a major effect on life in Australia. It was almost a non sequitur but people were also asked whether they favoured changes to the Constitution. Overall 38 per cent were in favour of non-specific changes, only 12 per cent said they were against, and half of those polled said they did not know. Among the favoured reforms were industrial relations, controls of company takeovers, the length of parliamentary terms, protection of the individual, the external affairs power, the Senate's power over supply, and the powers of the Governor-General. Support for the possible changes ranged from almost 60 per cent to just over one-third, but it is difficult to take much notice of any of these details given the original confessed (or more accurately perhaps, discovered) popular ignorance, particularly as the 1988 referendum on parliamentary terms and protection of the individual attracted the support of only about one-third of voters. The figures pointed to a desperate need to provide the people of Australia with basic education about the way their country is governed.

The results of the Constitutional Commission's survey were confirmed in research in 1993–94 undertaken by the Civics Expert Group, chaired by Professor Stuart Macintyre. That committee found that there was a 'high degree of community ignorance about Australia's system of government and its origins' and said that there was a 'demonstrable need for a non-partisan program of public education and information on the Australian system of government, the Constitution, Australian citizenship and other civics issues'. It proposed that the Commonwealth should institute a national civics education process involving schools, Technical and Further Education colleges and higher education institutions—a proposal essentially accepted by the Keating government and subsequently by the Howard government.

In the absence of such an education program, it is not surprising that people have supported referendums only (1) when they could be persuaded that they would get a financial benefit from the change (e.g. the social security referendum in 1944) or (2) when the proposal was not opposed by any formidable political block and the proposal seemed either to be structural (Senate election dates, State debts) or 'right and proper' (Aborigines, replacement of senators, a retiring age for judges).

Since the early 1980s Commonwealth governments have felt less need to press for constitutional changes that would give them more power, largely because of the way the High Court had been supporting the expansion of the Commonwealth's powers in that period. The Court's decisions in the *Uniform Tax* cases and over the section 96 grants power gave the Commonwealth the power to invade almost any policy area which was within the sphere of State's powers, particularly where large sums of money were needed, as was the case with education, housing, roads and health. Sir Robert Menzies was able to have the Commonwealth take over a higher education policy by offering money. He had no need to seek a constitutional amendment. The Court's decision in the *Concrete Pipes* case reduced the need for a new monopolies power or for changes to the corporations power. A series of decisions in the arbitration field and in relation to the corporations power overcame many of the complaints about the narrowness of the arbitration power. A new attitude to the external affairs power provided the Commonwealth with a way of determining major environmental issues, while there remain other significant sections of the Constitution where the extent of the Commonwealth's power has yet to be fully explored. This means that the 'wish list' of those wanting more centralised power has largely been satisfied, not by changes to the Constitution, but by changes in the approach of the High Court, changes which the politicians had been unable to procure through the referendum process.

By the end of the 1980s the pressures for constitutional reform were quite different from that agenda. Difficulties of political management at both the Commonwealth and State level persuaded Prime Minister Hawke and the New South Wales premier, Nick Greiner, in 1990 that they should try to initiate a process that would lead to different power-sharing arrangements between the Commonwealth and the States. The process was undermined by Paul Keating when he was battling to take Hawke's place as prime minister. It eventually resulted in the creation of COAG, the Conference of Australian Governments. That was not enough, however, for the States, which through the 1990s continued to press for financial and constitutional changes that would limit the powers of the Commonwealth to interfere with State activities. The general debate over constitutional reform was, however, subsumed by Keating's promotion of the republic. Academics, lawyers, journalists and others had used centenary anniversary re-enactments of the various Conventions of the 1890s to promote widespread discussions about the need for constitutional reform in areas such as human rights, but by 1995 the republican issue dominated all others. John Howard won the election in 1996 and became prime minister with a promise to hold a people's constitutional convention devoted to the republican issue—though it was well-known he was a confirmed monarchist. That convention, early in 1998, opted for a republic, though in a form which denied the right of Australians generally to elect the president. A referendum about whether to implement these changes was promised for 1999. The convention also proposed that a further convention should be held early in the next century to discuss other constitutional issues. Unless a future federal government agrees to implement that proposal, the prospects for any significant revisions of the Constitution (other than the major alterations associated with the change to a republic) will remain firmly in the hands of the High Court.

The first High Court had its own, idiosyncratic view of what the Constitution was meant to mean. Until that view was rejected by the Court itself in the *Engineers* case, it was reinforced by the refusal of the people to take the many opportunities offered to them by politicians to overturn or displace the decisions of the High Court. Whether it was the voters who were conservative or whether it was the mechanism for changing the Constitution which was conservative, or both, is not absolutely clear. But events have demonstrated the validity of warnings which were given to the constitutional Convention in 1898 by Mr Glynn, when he was dealing not with the powers of the High Court but with the means chosen for constitutional amendment by the people.

'We are creating,' he said, 'a Judiciary which will become legislators.' He argued, 'We ought not to create the evil of making the Judges not merely interpreters, but the extenders of the Constitution, and we ought to give the Constitution such a degree of elasticity as will render it capable of being moulded to changed conditions as time goes on, and prevent the dangerous alternative of judicial expansion.'

13

JUDGING JUDGES

Who is to judge the judges? Although many do so informally (e.g. their fellow judges, the legal profession generally, the media on occasions, and certainly the litigants who utilise their services, successfully and unsuccessfully), the only people who really count are the politicians. And they have to make their decisions before the judges actually become judges. What they weigh up in relation to prospective High Court judges is not just whether a particular nominee is appropriately qualified for appointment to the highest court in the land, but also what effect the appointment will have on the way the Court interprets the Constitution. Or should that second issue be altogether disregarded?

The Americans don't believe so. The US Supreme Court has a far more limited jurisdiction than that enjoyed by the High Court: its work is primarily concerned with interpreting the Constitution, and particularly its Bill of Rights. One consequence of this is that the United States President and the Senate (which has the responsibility of confirming or refusing any nomination made by the President) are particularly conscious of the political impact of the Supreme Court's decisions. And being conscious of that impact, they take account of it. A President will normally seek to appoint to the Supreme Court men and women who support the President's particular political views, be they conservative or liberal. The Senate may seek to deny confirmation to a nominee whose views are hostile to those of the majority party in the Senate, though it will generally not do so on what can be perceived as strictly partisan political grounds. Nevertheless, the nomination and confirmation process will be seen normally as a political act. And on all sides it is thought proper that the prospective appointee should be asked about his or her judicial attitudes. As United States Chief Justice William H. Rehnquist told the Australian Legal Convention in 1988:

> It is generally accepted in our country that the appointing authority . . . is entirely free to take into consideration the judicial philosophy of a prospective nominee. It is also accepted, though not quite so generally, that the Senate, too, may consider the nominee's judicial philosophy in the exercise of its constitutional function of advising and consenting to the nomination . . .
>
> When a vacancy occurs on a constitutional court, it is only natural that the appointing authority outside the court may have a preference for one view of the constitution as opposed to another. It would be quite surprising if the appointing authority did not attempt to fill the vacancy with a judge whose views it thought were consistent with those it wished to have prevail on the Court.

Chief Justice Rehnquist expressed some disapproval of the way in which the Senate had gone about its task when Judge Robert Bork was nominated by President Reagan (but denied appointment by the Senate). However, he said, 'surely the question of who shall sit on the constitutional court of last resort of any nation is a vitally important question, one in which the public-at-large as well as the Bar is entitled to have a say'.

His reference to the Bar was a reference to the one Australian case in which it is known that a prospective appointee to the High Court was asked in advance of his appointment about his approach to constitutional issues. This was in 1913, and the then attorney-general, W. M. Hughes, was considering who should fill a vacancy on the Court. It was the first time a Labor government had had the opportunity to make appointments to the bench of what everyone knew at that stage was a

States-rights-minded High Court, and which had struck down important legislation that Labor had ardently supported over the previous ten years. Hughes thought to appoint Albert Piddington, a Sydney barrister. But because Piddington was out of the country, Hughes wrote to Piddington's brother-in-law asking him to obtain an assurance that Piddington looked favourably 'upon the national side of things'. Piddington cabled back from Port Said, 'In sympathy with supremacy of Commonwealth powers.'

Chief Justice Rehnquist commented, 'This surely, in a nutshell, is a summary of judicial philosophy.' It was certainly enough for Hughes and the government to proceed with his appointment. But Piddington never sat on the Court; his resignation was volunteered after the Sydney and Melbourne Bars mounted a hostile campaign against him.

Chief Justice Rehnquist suggested that the question Hughes put to Piddington was 'the sort of question that any appointing authority should feel free to put to a potential appointee'. But the Piddington incident virtually guarantees that such a procedure will not be invoked in Australia. This is not because Australian governments are unaware of the desirability of having a Court sympathetic to their own philosophies. Most of them, to put it more bluntly, would like to be able to stack the Court if they could get away with it. But the political and legal culture usually tells against such a development, despite the fact that all the earliest appointments to the High Court were of politicians or ex-politicians, and that throughout the Court's history about half the Chief Justices and Justices have been active in politics at some time in their careers. Those with a political background have come predominantly from the conservative side of politics, but this is hardly surprising given that the leading members of the Sydney and Melbourne Bars, the most likely candidates for appointment to the High Court, are more likely than not to be affluent and associated with conservative interests. The other important factor is that for most of this century conservative governments have been in office at the Commonwealth level. It is also true that when Labor was in office during the early years of the federation there were virtually no prominent lawyers associated with the Labor cause—hence Hughes' need to find out something about the leanings of those who might be appointed. Hughes simply did not have sufficient contact with the leading members of the Bar (or the State judiciary) to know anything about the judicial philosophies of those who might properly be appointed to the Court.

This was not a problem for a conservative attorney-general and prime minister like Menzies, who had practised in the High Court in the constitutional area and would have been well acquainted with the personal views of all the leading counsel. Since 1975 both Liberal and Labor governments have often chosen to appoint judges from the Federal Court or State solicitors-general to the High Court, not least because their views on such key issues as centralism and States rights were well known, or at least could be reasonably predicted.

Once appointed, a judge is under no compulsion to live up to the appointing government's expectations. A judge's views may be influenced by other members of the Court and may vary over time.

It is common for politicians, lawyers and journalists to label particular courts (e.g. as being dominated by notions of reserved powers, or being centralist) and even to predict the outcome of the court's consideration of various issues (e.g. that the Gibbs High Court would split 4–3 in favour of the Commonwealth on federal issues). However, it is important to recognise that 'the Court' is not a static and unchanging entity. This is partly because its membership changes over the years, and partly because some judges do not have an inflexible approach to the legal questions the Court has to determine.

Correcting errors

Any judgment of the work of the High Court must take into account the fact that the High Court itself recognises that it can and does make mistakes, that some of its decisions have been wrongly made and have to be corrected. Not that it is prepared to acknowledge such error lightly. Over the years the Court has evolved guidelines for itself, most recently elucidated in *John v. Commissioner of Taxation* (1989) 166 CLR 417. There were, the

Court said, four matters that would justify departure from earlier decisions, and not all applied in all cases. The first was when earlier decisions did not rest on a principle carefully worked out in a significant succession of cases. The second was the existence of a difference between Justices constituting the majority in one of the earlier decisions. The third was that the earlier decisions had achieved no useful result, but rather had led to considerable inconvenience. The fourth was when the earlier decisions had not been independently acted on in a manner which militated against reconsideration. But in cases of statutory construction, if the Court was convinced that a previous interpretation was plainly erroneous it should declare the true intent of the statute.

However, it has also acted to prevent every case it hears from becoming the vehicle for overturning some previous decision it has made: it now requires counsel who want to challenge a prior decision of the Court to obtain the Court's permission to undertake that task, and permission is not always given (*Evda Nominees Pty Ltd v. Victoria* (1984) 154 CLR 311).

Early in its history the Court held that a decision had to be 'manifestly wrong' for it to be overturned by the Court. But Chief Justice Griffith said, 'it is impossible to maintain as an abstract proposition that the Court is either legally or technically bound by previous decisions. Indeed, it may in a proper case be its duty to disregard them' (*Ex parte; The Brisbane Tramways Co. Ltd* (1914) 18 CLR 54, at 58). It appears from many of the Court's decisions that the Court will more willingly reconsider the correctness of its judgments in constitutional cases than in cases involving, for example, statutory construction. In the latter cases it is usually open to the parliament to change the law if it thinks the Court has misinterpreted legislation. But the Constitution is not so easily corrected.

Stare decisis

It has also been suggested that mere changes in the composition of the Court should not be a reason for reconsidering an earlier decision. The fact that a Court which was differently constituted might have reached a different decision if it had heard the case is not of itself a good reason for reopening the question of its correctness.

But as with most questions considered by the Court, there can be differences even on this fundamental issue. These were demonstrated in the *Second Territorial Senators* case (*Queensland v. The Commonwealth* (1977) 139 CLR 585). In 1975 the High Court heard a challenge to Commonwealth legislation which gave the Northern Territory and the Australian Capital Territory two senators each, the States at that time each having ten senators. In *Western Australia v. The Commonwealth* (1975) 134 CLR 201, the Court held by a 4–3 majority that the law was valid, under section 122, the Territories power. The one major difference between the two *Territorial Senators* cases was that the bench had changed. Justice McTiernan, a member of the majority in the 1975 case, had retired and been replaced by Justice Aickin who, it was confidently expected, would vote to invalidate the law. As none of the other members of the Court had changed their views about validity, the anticipated result was a 4–3 vote against validity. However, two of those who thought the law invalid, Justices Gibbs and Stephen, decided that they were nevertheless bound to follow the 1975 decision of the Court of which they had then disapproved and continued to disapprove. Justice Gibbs explained his position by saying, 'No Justice is entitled to ignore the decisions and reasoning of his predecessors and to arrive at his own judgment as though the pages of the law reports were blank, or as though the authority of a decision did not survive the rising of the Court.' And he bluntly stated the reason the Court was being asked on this occasion to reconsider its decision: '[T]he only possible answer is that one member of the Court has retired and another has succeeded him.'

Chief Justice Barwick justified his refusal to conform to the principle of *stare decisis* by saying (at 593):

> . . . it is fundamental to the work of this Court and to its function of determining, so far as it rests on judicial decision, the law of Australia appropriate to the times, that it should not be bound in point of precedent but only in point of conviction by its prior decisions. In the case of the Constitution, it is the

> duty, in my opinion, of each Justice, paying due regard to the opinions of other Justices past and present, to decide what in truth the Constitution provides . . . The Constitution may be rigid but that does not imply or require rigidity on the part of the Court in adherence to prior decisions. No doubt to depart from them is a grave matter and a heavy responsibility. But convinced of their error, the duty to express what is the proper construction is paramount.

And dealing with the argument that the only difference between this particular challenge and the one two years earlier was that there had been a change on the bench, the Chief Justice said, 'the fact that there has been a change in the personal composition of the Court since an earlier decision was given can be no reason, in my opinion, why any Justice should refrain from expressing what he is convinced is the right conclusion in the matter before the Court'.

That argument aside, it is plain that there is no dispute at all about the Court's ability to reverse its own decisions. And that flexibility applies not just to particular decisions but also to the way in which the Court approaches its task of interpreting legislation and the Constitution, and also the way it approaches its determination of the common law.

CONVENTION DEBATES

Although the High Court has always been ready to change its mind, it has not always been willing to allow its mind to be influenced by all the material that might have been available to help it determine difficult issues. Specifically, in interpreting the Constitution it rejected, until recently, any suggestion that it should examine the words of those who wrote the Constitution to help decide what it was they meant. The first volume of the Commonwealth Law Reports includes the report of argument in a case where counsel sought to rely on the Convention debates to show the meaning of a particular provision. He was rebuffed by each of the three members of the Court, who in so doing established the practice that reference could not be made to the Convention debates (*Municipal Council of Sydney v. The Common-*

wealth (1904) 1 CLR 208, at 213). That 'settled doctrine of the Court' was defended in 1981 by Sir Garfield Barwick, who explained (*Attorney-General (Victoria); ex parte Rel Black v. The Commonwealth* (1981) 146 CLR 559, at 577–8):

> An academic exercise to explain historically why the Constitution was cast in a particular form is one thing. To identify the meaning of the words in which the Constitution is expressed by examination of its discursive development is quite another. The former, in my opinion, has no place in the task of construing the text of the Constitution except perhaps in the case of an ambiguity in that text which cannot otherwise be resolved. But absent the possibility which such ambiguity may present, the task of adducing the meaning of the words constitutionally employed derives, in my opinion, no assistance from a consideration of the process by which that text came into being . . . That is not to say, however, that that meaning must be assigned without regard to the sense in which the words of the text were understood in the day of their expression.

Seven years later, in *Cole v. Whitfield*, the Court unanimously invoked the history of the Convention debates to demonstrate why successive High Courts had, for more than half a century, misinterpreted section 92 of the Constitution. The Court said (at 385):

> Reference to the history of Section 92 may be made, not for the purpose of substituting for the meaning of the words used, the scope and effect—if such could be established—which the founding fathers subjectively intended the section to have, but for the purpose of identifying the contemporary meaning of language used, the subject to which that language was directed and the nature and objectives of the movement towards federation from which the compact of the Constitution finally emerged.

Over the next two years the Court had resort to the Convention debates on at least three more occasions. In the *Corporations* case the majority of the Court used the debates to help determine that the Commonwealth could not legislate to control the formation of companies, only to regulate those companies which were already 'formed'. But at no stage did the Court even acknowledge that it was breaking new ground in referring to the Convention debates, let alone attempt to explain why it was reversing that longstanding rule.

In both *Cole v. Whitfield* and the *Corporations* case, the Court has history to bolster an argument which might otherwise have appeared quite thin, and where precedent either pointed to a different answer (in *Cole v. Whitfield*) or was of dubious value. History was used not as a logical step in a line of legal reasoning, but as a non-legal explanation of why a particular result should be reached: in essence, a political argument. Used in the way the Court suggested in *Cole v. Whitfield*, there is little likelihood that the Convention debates will open the way to an interpretation of the Constitution more favourable to the States—for the Court, in the quotation above, rejects the possibility of using the 'subjective' intentions of the founding fathers to qualify the words they used. Thus, for example, the original intention of the founding fathers that the external affairs power would not give the Commonwealth a treaty-making power is unlikely to be used to limit the words 'external affairs' as actually used in the constitutional grant of power.

It might be argued that the kind of material the present Court is prepared to consider from the historical record is precisely the background information of which the original Justices of the Court were extremely conscious, and that they needed no reminders from counsel of the 'contemporary meaning of language used' or the 'nature and objectives of the movement towards federation', they having been significant members of, and contributors to, that movement. Indeed it was that kind of background which led them to develop a view of the Constitution which included the notion of some powers being reserved to the States and of the doctrine of the implied immunity of instrumentalities. From the time of the *Engineers* case onwards (*Amalgamated Society of Engineers v. Adelaide Steamship Co. Ltd* (1920) 28 CLR 129), the High Court had no need of the historical debates for a different reason: the fashion was then to apply 'strict legalism'. The meaning of the Constitution was to be found in the words of the Constitution alone (or almost alone).

FROM IMPLICATIONS TO *ENGINEERS*

The first Chief Justice, Sir Samuel Griffith, came to that position from the chief justiceship of the Queensland Supreme Court, but before taking that judicial office he had held office as premier and as attorney-general. He had played a very active role in the 1891 Constitutional Convention, where he drafted much of the document which subsequently became the Constitution. He was frequently consulted informally by the leading politicians of the day after his judicial office precluded him from active participation in the remaining Conventions. The other two members of the first High Court came directly from the federal parliament, Sir Edmund Barton from being prime minister and Justice O'Connor from being government leader in the Senate. Justices Isaacs and Higgins, who were added to the Court two years later, had also taken an active part in the Conventions and in subsequent federal governments.

Those five political judges were to determine the original judicial policy direction of the High Court, and the way the Constitution should be interpreted, for seventeen years. Griffith, Barton and O'Connor constituted the political and judicial majority. They were somewhat more conservative than the nationalistic liberals, Isaacs and Higgins.

When it came to interpreting the Constitution, the tests the Court applied probably did represent the mood of compromise which above all else permeated the Conventions. But they were political tests. The Justices applied tests which they thought should override the words of the Constitution.

POLITICAL TESTS

Political tests were intended to give the Constitution the 'balance' the Justices thought was necessary. The first was the 'doctrine of implied prohibitions', the second was the doctrine of 'the implied immunity of instrumentalities'. Both were explained early in the Court's exploration of the meaning of the Constitution. The doctrine of implied prohibitions was based on the notion that, when the colonies handed over particular powers to the Commonwealth, their intention was to fully exercise all the remaining powers that were not enumerated in the Constitution. Section 107 of the Constitution, which preserves the powers of the States, says that the powers of the colonies, unless 'exclusively vested in the Parliament of the Commonwealth or withdrawn from the Parliament of the State', shall continue. To honour the spirit of that reservation of powers to the States, it was necessary to interpret the powers which had been given to the Commonwealth in a narrow way. So the Commonwealth's exclusive power to levy duties of excise was held not to affect a State licensing system which regulated internal trade within the State even though the particular licence in question, to brew beer, was accepted in Australia to be an excise duty (*Peterswald v. Bartley* (1904) 1 CLR 497). And the Commonwealth's power to regulate interstate trade and commerce (in s. 51(i)) had to be interpreted narrowly to prevent any interference with the rights of the States to regulate intrastate trade (the *Union Label* case in 1908 and the *Huddart, Parker* case in 1909).

The implied immunity of instrumentalities was based on a somewhat different notion. This was that there was a kind of equality between the Commonwealth and the States, and unless there was a specific constitutional authority to the point, neither could interfere with the ordinary exercise of the powers of the other—a doctrine of mutual non-interference, as it was later called in the *Engineers* case. As the Court put it in its first major constitutional case, *D'Emden v. Pedder* (1904) 1 CLR 91 (at 111), 'when a State attempts to give its legislative or executive authority an operation which, if valid, would fetter, control, or interfere with, the free exercise of the legislative or executive power of the Commonwealth, the attempt, unless expressly authorised by the Constitution, is to that extent invalid and inoperative'. Similarly, the Commonwealth could not interfere with the powers of the States. So the Commonwealth and its public servants were not liable to pay State income taxes or stamp duties, but nor could the Commonwealth make employees of a State subject to the jurisdiction of the Commonwealth arbitration system (the *Railway Servants* case).

There was resistance to both these doctrines when Justices Isaacs and Higgins joined the bench, but it was not until 1920 that the doctrines were decisively overturned in the *Engineers* case. There the joint judgment of Chief Justice Knox and Justices Isaacs, Rich and Starke laid down new rules for the interpretation of the Commonwealth's powers, devoid of any implied limits. They also revised or explained the decisions in the earlier cases, to take account of the now 'correct' view of the Constitution which they adopted. The doctrine of implied immunities, the Justices pointed out, had been rejected by the Privy Council in *Webb v. Outtrim* (1906) 4 CLR 356 and by the minority of the High Court. The application of the doctrine was based on the political doctrine of necessity. This had no place in the work of the Court. Limitations on powers were laid down in the Constitution, and 'no court has any right to narrow those limits by reason of any fear that the powers as actually circumscribed by the language naturally understood may be abused' (at 151). The extravagant use of the granted powers in the actual working of the Constitution was a matter for the voters, not the courts (at 151–2). The argument that section 107 of the Constitution implied that Commonwealth power should be interpreted narrowly was rejected outright. '[I]t is a fundamental and fatal error to read sec. 107 as reserving any power from the Commonwealth that falls fairly within the explicit terms of an express grant in sec. 51, as that grant is reasonably construed, unless that reservation is as explicitly stated.' In this case there was nothing in section 107 which either cut down the meaning of the expression 'industrial disputes' in section 51(xxxv), or exempted a State when it was a party to an industrial dispute from the operation of Commonwealth legislation under section 51(xxxv). They said that the doctrine of implied prohibition 'finds no place where the ordinary principles of construction are applied so as to discover in the actual terms of the instrument their expressed or necessarily implied meaning' (at 155). Where 'the affirmative terms of a stated power would justify an enactment it rests upon those who rely on some limitation or restriction upon the power, to indicate it in the Constitution' (at 154).

The 'balance' of the Constitution had been decisively changed. The Court would give full weight to any grant of power by the Constitution to the Commonwealth, and there would be no inhibition on the use of the power, either to allow the States full legislative power in 'their' areas of responsibility or to prohibit the application of laws made under the Commonwealth's powers directly to any of the States or their instrumentalities. From this time, the residue of powers remaining for the States would be continually reduced as the Commonwealth exercised its powers. Where there was a legislative conflict between the two, the Constitution proclaimed in section 109 that the Commonwealth should prevail. The Court developed rules which found 'inconsistency' (the word used in s. 109) between Commonwealth and States' laws on an increasingly broader front, so further reducing that 'balance' over which the States prevailed.

AFTER *ENGINEERS*

The *Engineers* doctrine has dominated the High Court's approach to the Constitution since 1920, though there have been occasional blips. The Commonwealth legislative powers in section 51 were given, in its introductory clause, 'subject to this Constitution'. One of the central elements of the Constitution (according to the High Court, in any event) was section 92. All the Commonwealth's powers were held to be limited by this section, and in particular there had to be read into the Constitution limits on the Commonwealth's powers to make laws with respect to interstate trade and commerce, under section 51(i). There was also in the 1940s and 1950s a tendency to read into the Constitution a revised notion of State immunity, as occurred in the *State Banking* case (*Melbourne Corporation v. The Commonwealth* (1947) 74 CLR 31). In that case, Chief Justice Latham took up the question of whether laws that discriminated against a State or unduly interfered with its function could be valid. He thought not, because what was referred to as 'discrimination' showed (at 61):

> . . . that the legislation is really legislation by the Commonwealth with respect to a State or state functions as such and not with respect to the subject in respect of which it is sought to bind the State . . . The Commonwealth Parliament has no power to make laws with respect to State governmental func-

> tions as such, and the State Parliaments have no power to make laws with respect to Commonwealth governmental functions as such . . . Similarly, federal legislation which, though referring to a subject of federal power, is really legislation about what is clearly a State governmental function may be said to 'interfere unduly' with that function and therefore to be invalid.

But the Chief Justice was the only member of the majority to adopt this reasoning, which went counter to the prevailing doctrine of the Court as to how a law should be characterised. The other four members of the majority rested their decision on the basis that the relevant section was a law with respect to banking, but it was invalid because the Commonwealth parliament could not use its legislative powers to discriminate against the States or single them out for special restrictions.

This put something of a gloss on the reasoning in the *Engineers* case. It took up an approach which had been developed by Justice Dixon, initially in a case decided just ten years after *Engineers*. He said that every grant of legislative power to the Commonwealth allowed the making of laws affecting the States and their agencies, first if the State was not acting in the exercise of the Crown's prerogatives and second if the parliament confined itself to 'laws which do not discriminate against the State or its agencies' (*Australian Railways Union v. Victorian Railways Commissioners* (1930) 44 CLR 319, at 390). The second qualification formed the basis of the Court's decision in the *State Banking* case, with Justice Dixon saying that there was to be implied from the federal nature of the Constitution a prohibition against a Commonwealth law 'which discriminates against the States, or a law which places a particular disability or burden upon an operation or activity of a State, and more especially upon the execution of its constitutional powers' (at 79–82).

By the 1980s this principle had been discussed in a number of cases, but on only one occasion (the *State Banking* case) had it actually been applied so as to invalidate a Commonwealth law. However, in the *SEQEB* case (*Queensland Electricity Commission v. The Commonwealth* (1985) 159 CLR 192), the Court once again struck down a Commonwealth law because it discriminated against a State. The law in question was passed by the Commonwealth parliament as a political response to a battle between the Queensland government and the South-East Queensland Electricity Board (SEQEB) on the one hand and Queensland trade unions on the other. Almost 1000 linesmen were sacked, and massive strikes and ugly confrontations between workers and strikers forced a lengthy close-down of business in mainly the Brisbane area. The Commonwealth legislation was intended to remove the dispute from State government control by requiring the making of a Commonwealth industrial award. The legislation in effect required the making of an award, thereby removing from the Commonwealth Arbitration Commission its power, under the Conciliation and Arbitration Act, to decline to make an award or to refer the matter to a State Commission. The law was plainly discriminatory, and the government had virtually acknowledged the fact when it introduced the legislation. It was deliberately intended to interfere in the battle between Sir Joh Bjelke-Petersen and the Queensland trade unions.

All six members of the Court who heard the case found that all or some of the Act was invalid. Each wrote a separate judgment using slightly different words to describe what now was to be regarded as the implied limitation on the Commonwealth's use of its heads of power in relation to the States. As formulated by Justice (later Chief Justice) Mason, the principle had two elements (at 217): '(1) the prohibition against discrimination which involves the placing on the States of special burdens or disabilities; and (2) the prohibition against laws of general application which operate to destroy or curtail the continued existence of the States or their capacity to function as governments.' The principle was accepted and applied in the *Industrial Relations Act* case in 1995, where the Court held that only the top echelons of a state public service are exempt from Commonwealth industrial relations regulation.

While this is not pure *Engineers*, it is a far cry from the doctrines of implied prohibitions and the immunity of instrumentalities of the pre-1920 Court. The new doctrine protects the States but not their powers. Commonwealth legislation which is supported by one of the heads of power in section 51 of the

Constitution will not be invalidated simply because it reduces or removes a power previously enjoyed by the State, so long as the State's very existence is not threatened. There is no place here for any balancing of Commonwealth and State interests: the Court is prepared to imply a prohibition on Commonwealth power only where it reaches into the most vital areas of State government functioning.

Strict legalism

The Court's now-settled policy of interpreting the powers given to the Commonwealth uninhibited by the prospect of the Commonwealth intruding into what had previously been State matters sets one of the parameters for the way it approaches the Constitution. But there are other various methods of interpretation open to judges. Which methods they apply will in many cases affect the outcome of a case. For many years the predominant approach was that expounded by Sir Owen Dixon when he was elevated from a Justice of the Court to Chief Justice ((1971) 125 CLR 93):

> Federalism means a demarcation of powers and this casts upon the court a responsibility of deciding whether legislation is within the boundaries of allotted powers. Unfortunately that responsibility is very widely misunderstood, misunderstood largely by the popular use and misuse of terms which are not applicable, and it is not sufficiently recognised that the court's sole function is to interpret a constitutional description of power or restraint upon power and say whether a given measure falls on one side of a line consequently drawn or on the other, and that it has nothing whatever to do with the merits or demerits of the measure. Such a function has led us all I think to believe that close adherence to legal reasoning is the only way to maintain the confidence of all parties in federal conflicts. It may be that the court is thought to be excessively legalistic. I should be sorry to think that it is anything else. There is no other safe guide to judicial decisions in great conflicts than a strict and complete legalism.

But that legalism has been seen as a means of legitimating a conservative approach by the High Court to reformist legislation, providing a brake based on a political view of the Constitution (particularly as a protector of individual enterprise, through section 92) on the aspirations of (in particular) Labor governments. This is examined in great detail in Brian Galligan's *Politics of the High Court* (1987). It has even been the subject of some recent judicial criticism. Sir Anthony Mason, in his University of Virginia paper (1986), said (at p. 5):

> Unfortunately, it is impossible to interpret any instrument, let alone a constitution, divorced from values. To the extent they are taken into account, they should be acknowledged and should be accepted community values rather than mere personal values. The ever present danger is that 'strict and complete legalism' will be a cloak for undisclosed and unidentified policy values. Legalism, when coupled with the doctrine of *stare decisis*, has a subtle and formidable conservative influence. When judges fail to discuss the underlying values influencing a judgment, it is difficult to debate the appropriateness of those values. As judges who are unaware of the original underlying values subsequently apply that precedent in accordance with the doctrine of *stare decisis*, those hidden values are reproduced in the new judgment—even though the community values may have changed . . . Constitutions are documents framed in general terms to accommodate the changing course of events, so that courts interpreting them must take account of community values. Additionally, amending constitutions, while possible, is enormously difficult. Unless the courts openly grapple with the issues they will not be debated.

The strict legalism and literalism which dominated the Court's approach after the *Engineers* case no longer adequately describes the way the High Court works. Form no longer triumphs inevitably over substance: the Court looks to the practical operation of a law to determine validity, not merely to the formal way in which the law has been framed. And the Court is more willing to acknowledge its law-making function. As Chief Justice Mason and Justice Wilson said in *Trident General Insurance Co. Ltd v. McNiece Pty Ltd* (1988) 165 CLR 107, a case in which by a 4–3 majority the Court overturned the common law rule of privity of contract, at least for insurance cases: 'Regardless of the layers of sediment which may have accumulated, we consider that it is the responsibility of this Court to reconsider in appropriate cases common law rules which operate unsatisfactorily and unjustly.' The Court in that case upheld a decision of the New South Wales Court of Appeal, which decided to take the lead in rewriting the privity of contract rule. The leading judgment in the Court of Appeal was written by J. A. McHugh who a year later was made a member of the High Court. In the speech he made on his accession to the High Court, Justice McHugh said:

> In the resolution of difficult constitutional questions, sometimes all that a judge can do in the end is to select the solution which seems constitutionally preferable to other solutions. Although the proper exercise of the judicial function requires that the choice of the preferred solution be justified by a reasoned decision based on considerations external to the judge's own set of values and not by reference to what Mr Justice Jacobs once called individual predilections ungoverned by authority, reason and logic are not always conclusive. As closely split decisions of this Court demonstrate, opposite conclusions are reached because the individual judgments, although logically impeccable, commence with different premises based on different constitutional values, none of which is logically irrelevant or inappropriate to the resolution of the question to be decided.

It is unlikely that all the members of the Court would agree with these views, but the fact that there are several members of the Court prepared to express them means that there will be more pressure on all members of the Court to disclose the respective premises on which their judgments are built.

JUDICIAL LAW MAKING

When Michael Kirby was sworn in as a Justice of the High Court in 1996 he referred to Justice Dixon's 'strict and complete legalism' speech and commented that since 1952 much had changed:

> There will be no returning to the social values of 1952, still less those of 1903 when this Court was established. It falls to

> each generation of Australian lawyers, led by this Court, to fashion new principles of the Constitution, of common law, and of equity, which will contribute wisely to the good governance of the Australian people. There is now a greater public understanding of the limited, but still very real, scope for judicial creativity and legal development. Judges are now more candid about this aspect of their function. Without a measure of creativity how else would the common law have survived seven centuries, from feudalism to the space-age?

The Court's many political critics accept that the common law has to change (though they complain that the Court goes too fast and too far). They utterly reject, however, the right of judges to 'develop' the Constitution, labelling this activity 'progressivism'. Professor Greg Craven, for example, attacks the way the Court has, in his view, revised the meaning of the Constitution in accordance with perceived needs and desires of the contemporary Australian populace. He denounces the literalism which the *Engineers* case brought into the interpretation of the Constitution, and would revert to an interpretation based on the intentions of the founders. Former Queensland premier Rob Borbidge has attacked the Court for its 'dynamic approach to constitutional interpretation' and for failing to observe the traditional limits of the judicial function in a common law country. He proposed changes to the method of appointing judges (giving the States a share of power) and the right to sack judges using a referendum. More significantly, he proposed a new federal constitutional court, two-thirds of whose members would be the State Chief Justices. Presumably such judges would apply a method of interpretation that favoured the political interests of the States.

The judges accept that they see the Constitution differently from the way it was perceived by the first High Court. Sir Gerard Brennan, in his retirement speech in May 1998, said the founding Justices 'read the text of the Constitution through the prism of their experience in securing the approval of six self-governing colonies to bring the Commonwealth into being . . . Reading the text through those eyes, they espoused the doctrine of State reserved powers and implied immunities.' He went on:

> In time, with the First World War, the economic and commercial integration of the States and the growing sense of national identity, the doctrine of reserved powers was discarded in the *Engineers'* case. Changing conditions exposed the true meaning of the text . . . In recent times, this Court has looked to the history of the constitutional text to identify the subject to which the language is directed and the nature and objectives of the federal movement. It has looked to the purpose of a provision so far as that can be elicited from the text. It has sought to examine the Constitution with that strict logic and high technique of which Sir Owen Dixon spoke. That is the judicial method that keeps the law in a state of good repair.

The phrase that stands out in this passage is 'the true meaning of the text'. What the history of the High Court demonstrates is that its perception of what is 'true' does vary over time. And each variation changes political power relationships, either between the Commonwealth and the States, or between governments and individuals.

As the Chief Justice of South Australia, John Doyle, has pointed out (1996):

> The Constitution is neither an exact text requiring of the High Court only that it elucidate the odd verbal ambiguity or uncertainty, nor an empty vessel into which the High Court pours its own version of constitutional arrangements and Commonwealth powers. Developing the theory of how it is to be interpreted, and striking the right balance in the process of interpretation, is an enduring issue, and one perhaps that will never be resolved.
>
> It is interesting, I think, to reflect on the fact that much of the criticism of High Court decisions rests upon unstated conflicts in the theory of interpretation . . . One cannot help thinking that there must be a true theory of constitutional interpretation, and one that is all-embracing, but the reality is that, if there is, neither the High Court of Australia nor the Supreme Court of the United States has yet reached agreement upon its principles.

Nor, it is necessary to add, would it matter very much if the courts could agree on what those 'true' principles should be. The fact is, that there will always be politicians, and judges, who will not accept the current truth.

Reforming the Court

In 1984 the federal parliament, at the request of the High Court Justices, made an important change to the Judiciary Act which in effect allowed the Court to set its own agenda. Previously, there was an automatic right of appeal in cases involving relatively moderate amounts of money—$20 000 or more. This right was abolished. The parliament decided instead that appeals would only be heard if the Court granted special leave to appeal. The conditions for the grant of special leave were expressed in general terms: the High Court 'may have regard to any matters that it considers relevant but shall have regard to whether the proceedings . . . involve a question of law, or . . . is of general importance . . . or . . . is required to resolve differences of opinion between different courts . . . and . . . whether the interests of the administration of justice . . . require consideration by the High Court . . .'.

The High Court has interpreted this as giving it complete discretion as to when it should grant special leave. For example, it has said that normally it will not grant special leave in tax cases, because it regards them as falling within the special expertise of the Federal Court. Similarly, it has said that it normally will not hear town planning cases, as they should be decided by State courts. When it refuses special leave it often says that it does so because the proposed appeal has no prospect of success, or because it believes the decision appealed from is plainly right, or because resolution of the appeal will depend on the facts in the case (it is only interested in resolving questions of law).

Several leading barristers objected to this scheme, arguing that it was unconstitutional because it went beyond parliament's power to regulate appeals. As Ian Callinan QC argued in a paper to the Australian Bar Association in 1986, 'the overall scheme is to prohibit all appeals unless the Court, in its virtually unfettered discretion, considers that such appeals may be brought'.

The problem was that only the High Court could rule on

whether the provision was unconstitutional, and this was a provision which gave it very considerable power. Needless to say, when an attempt was made to overturn the provision, it failed (*Smith Kline & French Laboratories (Aust) Ltd v. The Commonwealth* (1991) 173 CLR 194). The Court unanimously upheld its own power to determine which appeals it would hear.

Although the number of special leave applications brought before the Court rose steadily, its judgment workload, in terms of appeals and other cases heard, barely changed, hovering around the 70 a year mark. In 1996–97 it heard 369 special leave applications (101 of them involving criminal matters), but it granted special leave to appeal in less than one-fifth of them.

The Court also changed its system of dealing with these applications. In the early 1980s it customarily assembled a court of five Justices to hear criminal special leave applications, so that if it thought there was any merit in an application it could treat it as the appeal and deal with it, without holding a later hearing. Civil special leave matters were heard by a Court of three Justices.

However, by the late 1990s it required all applications to be made originally in writing. A few it would dismiss on its reading of the papers. And hearings generally involved only two Justices. Sometimes there would be three 'full' courts, each of two judges, hearing special leave applications simultaneously in different cities. Not surprisingly, many lawyers considered that they did not have a fair chance of having their applications approved. More surprising, perhaps, was the fact that when Ian Callinan QC was appointed to the bench he expressed no public criticism of this machine-like processing of a system which he had earlier denounced as unconstitutional.

Although the High Court's ability to determine what cases it would hear produced some disquiet, the legal profession's main concern about the Court is directed to the mechanics of the way it hears and determines cases. In the 1990s it has adopted a general rule that all litigants must produce written arguments of the case they wish to present, and these have to be exchanged with their opponents well before the Court begins its hearings. The idea is to focus the attention of all sides (and the judges) on the legal and factual issues of the particular case. In some cases the presentation of these written submissions has been used to limit the amount of oral argument that can be presented to the Court. No longer is the length of a hearing determined by how long-winded the counsel might be. The Court can and does set quite strict time limits for most cases, particularly difficult constitutional cases. Where once the Court might have heard argument for weeks, it now considers it an exception to set aside three or four days to hear a complex constitutional case.

The trend to require written submissions reflects the system used by the US Supreme Court. Unfortunately, the High Court has not as yet copied the way the US Supreme Court presents its judgments. Normally the US Supreme Court presents a single majority judgment and a single minority judgment (though individual Justices may add brief comments explaining why they have adhered to, or rejected, particular elements of those judgments. The High Court has not developed anything remotely resembling this collegiate system. There are often unanimous judgments, or joint majority or minority judgments, but more often than not a majority will consist of four or five individual judgments which may vary in point of principle or emphasis. The High Court has resolutely refused to adopt the US Supreme Court system and has resisted the New South Wales Court of Appeal system of allocating judgment writing to specified judges (though this may change). The present system allows every judge to indulge in his or her idiosyncratic views. The understanding of the law (by lawyers and by the public) would undoubtedly benefit if the Justices could be persuaded to submerge their differences in order to reach majority judgments about what the law is and how it is to be interpreted. Parliaments are sometimes accused of producing laws that are obscure, but at least they do not produce different versions of the same law. The High Court can produce seven different interpretations of the one law.

14

POLITICS AND THE COURT

> [I]n this cynical age, when critics are more inclined to look for the canker in the rose rather than to admire the rose itself, it is not surprising that there are some academic lawyers who regard it as unrealistic to take what the judges say at its face value. The real reasons for the decisions, they say, are not those given by the judges; there is a hidden agenda. The decisions are to be explained by the beliefs (or prejudices) of the judges on social, political and economic questions. Since this so-called realist theory is quite at variance with the reasons published by the judges, the natural inference, from which some theorists, particularly those on the left wing of politics, do not shrink, is that the judges are deliberately deceitful in professing to act in a strictly legal way. Other writers of this school show more charity, and suggest that the influence of the values or prejudices of the judges is an unconscious one and that the judges are naively unaware of it and really believe that they are strictly guided by legal rules and principles. Another suggestion made is that the judges adopt legalism as a valuable strategy that enables them to perform a political function without appearing to act politically. (Gibbs 1990, p. 25)

The former Chief Justice said the theory could be tested by looking at what the Court determined in three cases, the *Bank Nationalisation* case, the *Communist Party* case and the *Dams* case.

It would be 'superficially easy' he said to apply the theory to the *Bank Nationalisation* case (*Quadrant*, October 1990, p. 27):

> It can plausibly be said that some of the judges had conservative views and anti-Labor sympathies, although their judgments did not reveal any such sympathies or give the slightest indication that they were affected by them. The theory becomes more difficult to apply to the *Communist Party* case. There, the Court struck down legislation introduced by a Liberal Government and it is very difficult to suggest that it accorded with their prejudices to do so . . . Similarly, there is no reason to believe that, of the Justices who decided the *Dams* case, the four who formed the majority thought that the building of the dam would be more harmful than beneficial or that the three in the minority held the converse view or that the four were, and the three were not, sensitive to contemporary political opinion. The differences of opinion manifested in the various judgments in that case were differences regarding legal principle, not political policy.

The Justices who decided the *Dams* case were very much aware of the political consequences of their decision and at pains to explain that those political consequences—the merits of the political argument about whether or not the dam should be built—did not influence their decision. However, as has been pointed out earlier, the Court does at times take political consequences into account, and it has on occasions allowed what it perceives to be the political consequences of its decision to determine the outcome it arrives at—most notably in its decisions on section 90 and the political impact on the States of outlawing the States' use of artificial licensing laws to impose what are in effect sales taxes on liquor, tobacco and petrol products.

Nor are the Justices of the High Court ignorant of politics and political processes. Some Justices, particularly Chief Justices, use public forums to advance their views about the way governments are approaching such issues as judicial independence, funding of the courts and appointments to the courts (where no doubt they have a legitimate right to defend the interests of their branch of the state apparatus), but also about the virtues or otherwise of particular legislation and of the relationship between governments and parliament. Judges have been known to use their influence with politicians to seek the appointment of particular people to judicial and other posts. They have also been known to delay or advance their departure from the bench, in effect choosing the political colour of the government that will appoint their successors.

This book has not attempted to explore the political proclivities of the judges who came to the Court from a political background (for example Barwick and Latham on the one side, Murphy and Evatt on the other), nor those who came from non-political backgrounds. Ex-politician judges are now out of favour, possibly because it is more difficult now for leading members of the Bar to make the transition into politics, and it is impossible now to have a successful career simultaneously in both politics and the law. But the need for judges to be educated about politics is at least as great as it has ever been, particularly given the trend, for some Justices at least, to acknowledge the policy implications, and sometimes policy motivations, of particular decisions. Most lawyers who appear before the Court are probably less informed than the Justices they address about the policy and political implications of what they are being asked to determine. The exceptions to this are, or should be, the solicitors-general of the Commonwealth and the States who are involved on a daily basis in advising governments of the legal validity and implications of their policy proposals, and who, to do their jobs properly, must be conscious of the political implications of the legal solutions they offer to their governments. Because of the way the legal system works in Australia, it is left to the solicitors-general to provide the Court with a watered-down version of a Brandeis brief (a brief which provides the Court with historic, economic and political facts and arguments, rather than one which only examines strictly legal precepts) in those cases in which they appear. However, the States and the Commonwealth are not always represented as parties or interveners in all the cases that do have important political or policy implications, and there is no tradition in the Court of *amicus curiae* regularly being briefed to provide the Court with as much information as it should have.

The problem is more acute now than it has been, because of the Court's greater willingness to use a 'dynamic approach to constitutional interpretation' (to quote Sir Anthony Mason in his address on 'The Australian Constitution, 1901–1988', 62 ALJ 752, p. 760). When the Court is given a case that allows it to review the current meaning of the Commonwealth's power to make laws with respect to 'trade and commerce . . . among the States' it will need to look at economic facts and arguments as well as arguments based on the US Supreme Court's interpretation of its commerce power, and it will need to get those facts from other than the general (or even specialised) reading which the Justices themselves may have individually undertaken. The Justices would be better equipped to make other decisions too if they had more information at their disposal, but time constraints do not allow the Court as much time as it might need to investigate all the consequences of all of its decisions.

The Court does not decide issues in a vacuum. It makes its decisions about the meaning of the Constitution, about the interpretation of statutes and about the current state of the common law only when relevant cases are brought before it for decision. This is not to suggest that the Court is entirely in the control of those who bring litigation before it. In some of its judgments it has indicated its willingness to tackle particular issues, should a relevant case be brought before it (a signal to the legal profession, rather than to particular litigants). Sometimes a case is argued in a way that does not raise the issues which the Court, or a particular Justice, believes should be raised, and the matter is adjourned until the issue can be properly prepared and argued. In 1991, for example, the Court deferred consideration of a challenge by News Limited to the Industrial Relations Commission's contempt of court protections, so that the Court could consider whether section 92's guarantee of freedom of interstate intercourse was relevant to a freedom of expression argument. The section 92 issue was raised by several of the Justices, not by News Ltd. The case was adjourned by the Court so that this issue could be properly debated at a later time, but News Ltd was never asked whether it wanted to pursue the section 92 point. The Court in fact based its decision on the implied constitutional protection of political free speech—not section 92.

However, the Court is not always in a position where it can

dictate what issues it would like to explore, which areas of the law it would like to clarify or change or which interpretations of the Constitution should be revised. It may be that at some time in the next few years the Court would like an opportunity to look anew at the interpretation of the trade and commerce power, but it won't be able to do so until a dispute arises between litigants that concerns the meaning of that section. This is unlikely to happen in relation to the trade and commerce power, for example, because governments are not at present interested in testing their powers in this area (or, for that matter, in many other areas of constitutional power). The spirit of deregulation currently affects both major political parties, and while that spirit is abroad, there is no need for legislation asserting the Commonwealth's right to regulate and control interstate trade and commerce—though, for example, differences between the Commonwealth and the States on the implementation of national road rules and motor vehicle controls could provide a test case if the new cooperative federalism were to come to an acrimonious end.

But when the test comes and is determined, the outcome of the case is rarely going to depend on what governments think or what lawyers advocate. The young Robert Menzies may have been an exceptional lawyer when he faced the High Court in 1920 and suggested that it had gone astray with its doctrine of implied prohibitions, but it was not the brilliance of his argument which caused the Court to revise and reverse its approach to constitutional interpretation. Nor was it a question of the time being ripe for such changes. It was the High Court, with a new majority, that wanted such a development.

It is inevitable that the Court will continue to change its interpretation of the Constitution as the Court itself changes, as political needs change and as Australia and the world change. The constitutional text may remain fairly static, but its meaning will change with circumstances, though what those circumstances require will be determined by the High Court.

The Court's function as law-maker and as Constitution-reviser is political. It sometimes has a political impact on governments and political parties and on the political life of the nation. This function is carried out by a group of people who are not responsible or accountable in a political sense for their decisions. Indeed they are protected, by appointment until age 70, from accountability for those decisions unless the parliament finds that they are guilty of proved misbehaviour or incapacity. For that reason in particular, it has been suggested that the High Court and similar courts in other countries which exercise the power of judicial review to strike down legislation and place limits on the exercise of power by the executive are anti-democratic. While it may be argued by some of the judges that this 'misconceives what is involved in the exercise of judicial power' (Sir Gerard Brennan 1990), the fact is that the Court is not, and is not intended to be, democratic. Its function is not to bow to the popular will on a moment-to-moment, issue-by-issue basis, but to control the exercise of power by elected and appointed officials where that is necessary according to the Court's interpretation of the Constitution and the law. But the Court must exercise its powers responsibly in a legal sense.

The Court's previous reluctance to acknowledge, except on rare occasions, that what it decides will or may have a political impact makes it imperative that others should highlight the political consequences of what the Court is being asked to do, be they the lawyers who appear before the Court, the clients they represent, or academic or journalist observers. The citizens who have no say in choosing the Court have a right to know what it is doing and what effect its decisions will have on them. The Court rightly rejects the occasional suggestion that the way it approaches a particular legal issue may be affected by its view of the partisan political battle between government and opposition. The Court cannot and does not make decisions based on the current state of public opinion, or parliamentary opinion, but it does need to be sensitive to its role in the political process, just as all those involved in the political process need to be conscious of the Court's proper role.

For there can be no doubt that Mr Glynn was right: the founding fathers did create a judiciary who have become legislators.

Justices of the High Court

The High Court in 1998

Chief Justice, Murray Gleeson. Appointed to the High Court in 1998. Served for nine years as Chief Justice, New South Wales Supreme Court. Educated in Sydney and became a QC in 1974.

Justice Mary Gaudron. Appointed to the High Court in 1987. Solicitor-general for New South Wales 1981–87. From 1974 to 1980 a deputy president of the Conciliation and Arbitration Commission. Educated in Sydney and became a QC in 1981. The first woman to be appointed to the Court.

Justice Michael McHugh. Appointed to the High Court in 1989. A member of the New South Wales Court of Appeal from 1984 until his appointment to the High Court. Educated in Newcastle and entered the legal profession through bar entrance exams rather than through university.

Justice William Gummow. Appointed to the High Court in 1995. Appointed to the Federal Court in 1986. Educated in Sydney and practised as a solicitor before being admitted to the Bar.

Justice Michael Kirby. Appointed to the High Court in 1996. President of the New South Wales Court of Appeal 1984–96. Chairman of the Australian Law Reform Commission 1975–84.

Justice Kenneth Hayne. Appointed to the High Court in 1997. Judge, Victoria Court of Appeal from 1995. Judge, Victorian Supreme Court 1992–95. Educated in Melbourne. Was a Rhodes Scholar.

Justice Ian Callinan. Appointed to the High Court in 1998. Educated in Brisbane. Became a QC in 1978. Playwright and author.

FORMER JUSTICES OF THE COURT

Chief Justice Sir Samuel Griffith. The first Chief Justice (1903–19). Educated in Sydney but practised law in Queensland where he was active in politics for more than twenty years, serving on several occasions as premier and attorney-general. Was the pre-emminent lawyer of the first Constitutional Convention. Wrote the Queensland Criminal Code. Was Queensland Chief Justice for ten years before his appointment to lead the first High Court.

Justice Sir Edmund Barton. Member of the first High Court and remained a Justice until 1920. Educated in Sydney. An active and influential member of the New South Wales parliament for twenty years. Elected to the first Commonwealth parliament and was Australia's first prime minister.

Justice R. E. O'Connor. The third member of the first High Court (1903–12). Educated in Sydney and also an active politician in New South Wales for thirteen years, then government leader in the Senate in the first Commonwealth parliament. First president of the Arbitration Court.

Chief Justice Sir Isaac Isaacs. Justice from 1906 to 1930 and then briefly Chief Justice in 1930–31, from which position he resigned to become the first Australian-born Governor-General. Educated in Melbourne, a minister in Victorian governments in the 1890s and then elected to the Commonwealth parliament. Served as attorney-general 1904–06.

Justice Henry Bournes Higgins. Appointed 1906, died while still a Justice in 1929. Educated in Melbourne, active in the later constitutional conventions. Member of the Commonwealth parliament from 1901 until his appointment to the Court. President of the Arbitration Court 1907–20.

Chief Justice Sir Frank Gavan Duffy. Justice from 1913 to 1931, Chief Justice 1931–35. Born in Dublin, Ireland, and educated in Melbourne. Became a QC in 1901.

Justice Sir Charles Powers. Appointed 1913, served until 1929. Educated in Brisbane. Member of the Queensland parliament for seven years. Queensland solicitor-general 1899–1903. Commonwealth Crown Solicitor from 1903–13.

Justice A. B. Piddington. Appointed to the Court in 1913, but resigned less than a month later without sitting on the Court. Educated in Sydney, served in the New South Wales parliament.

Justice Sir George Rich. Appointed 1913 and served until 1950. Educated in Sydney. Acting judge and judge of the New South Wales Supreme Court 1911–13.

Chief Justice Sir Adrian Knox. Appointed 1919, retired 1930. Born in Sydney, educated there and at Cambridge, England. Member of the New South Wales parliament for four years.

Justice Sir Hayden Starke. Appointed 1920, retired 1950. Educated in Melbourne. Decided not to become a KC.

Chief Justice Sir Owen Dixon. Appointed a Justice 1929, and became Chief Justice in 1952, retiring in 1964. Educated in Melbourne. Acting judge of the Victorian Supreme Court in 1926.

Justice Dr H. V. Evatt. Appointed 1930, retired 1940 to enter the Commonwealth parliament. Later became Chief Justice of the New South Wales Supreme Court. Educated in Sydney. Member of the New South Wales parliament before his appointment, at age 36, to the High Court.

Justice Sir Edward McTiernan. Appointed 1930. Educated in Sydney and a member and minister in the New South Wales parliament before his election to the Commonwealth parliament. Served as a Justice for 46 years.

Chief Justice Sir John Latham. Appointed 1935, retired 1952. Educated in Melbourne. Member of the Commonwealth parliament 1922–34. Served as attorney-general and deputy prime minister, and leader of the opposition.

Justice Sir Dudley Williams. Appointed 1940, retired 1958. Educated in Sydney. Won the Military Cross in World War I. Acting judge and judge of the New South Wales Supreme Court before his appointment to the High Court.

Justice Sir William Webb. Appointed 1946, retired 1958. Educated in Brisbane. Crown Solicitor and later Queensland solicitor-general before his appointment to the Queensland Supreme Court as a judge (1925–40) and then Chief Justice (1940–46).

Justice Sir Wilfred Fullagar. Appointed 1950, retired 1961. Educated in Melbourne. Judge of the Victorian Supreme Court 1945–50.

Justice Sir Frank Kitto. Appointed 1950, retired 1970. Educated in Sydney. First Chairman of the Australian Press Council following his retirement from the Court.

Justice Sir Alan Taylor. Appointed 1952, died in office 1969. Educated in Sydney. Judge of the New South Wales Supreme Court in 1952.

Justice Sir Douglas Menzies. Appointed 1958, died in office 1974. Educated in Melbourne.

Justice Sir Victor Windeyer. Appointed 1958, retired 1972. Educated in Sydney.

Justice Sir William Owen. Appointed 1961, died in office 1972. Educated in Sydney. Acting judge, then judge of the New South Wales Supreme Court 1936–61.

Chief Justice Sir Garfield Barwick. Appointed 1964, retired 1981. Educated in Sydney. Entered the Commonwealth parliament in 1958 and served as attorney-general and then Minister for External Affairs.

Justice Sir Cyril Walsh. Appointed 1969, died in office 1973. Educated in Sydney. Judge of the New South Wales Supreme Court 1954–69.

Chief Justice Sir Harry Gibbs. Appointed Justice of the High Court 1970, and Chief Justice 1981, retired 1987. Educated in Brisbane. Judge of the Queensland Supreme Court 1961–67. Judge of the Federal Court of Bankruptcy, 1967–70.

Justice Sir Ninian Stephen. Appointed 1972, retired 1982 to become Governor-General. Educated in Melbourne. Judge of the Victorian Supreme Court 1970–72.

Justice Sir Kenneth Jacobs. Appointed 1974, retired 1979. Educated in Sydney. Judge and then Judge of Appeal of the New South Wales Supreme Court 1960–74. President of the New South Wales Court of Appeal 1972–74.

Justice Lionel Murphy. Appointed 1975, died in office 1986. Educated in Sydney. Elected to the Senate 1962–75. Served as attorney-general 1972–75.

Justice Sir Keith Aickin. Appointed 1976, died in office 1982. Educated in Melbourne. Senior member of the Victorian Bar when appointed.

Justice Sir Ronald Wilson. Appointed 1979, retired 1989. Educated in Perth. Was Crown prosecutor, Crown counsel and then Western Australian solicitor-general for ten years before appointment to the High Court. Retired to become Moderator-General of the Uniting Church.

Chief Justice Sir Anthony Mason. First appointed to the Court as a Justice in 1972, and became Chief Justice in 1987. Educated in Sydney and became a QC in 1964, the year he was appointed for a five-year term as Commonwealth solicitor-general. Appointed as a member of the New South Wales Court of Appeal, where he served three years before his appointment to the High Court. Retired, aged 70, in 1995.

Justice Sir Gerard Brennan. Appointed a Justice in 1981 and became Chief Justice in 1995. One of the first judges of the Federal Court created in 1976, and the first president of the Administrative Appeals Tribunal. Educated in Queensland where he became a QC in 1965. Retired from the Court, aged 70, in 1998.

Justice Sir William Deane. Appointed a Justice in 1982. A judge of the Federal Court from 1977, and previously a judge of the New South Wales Supreme Court. Educated in Sydney and became a QC in 1966. Retired to become Governor-General in 1996.

Justice Sir Daryl Dawson. Appointed to the High Court in 1982. Was solicitor-general of Victoria from 1974 until his appointment to the High Court. Educated in Melbourne and became a QC in 1971. Retired in 1997.

Justice John Toohey. Appointed to the High Court in 1987. A member of the Federal Court from 1977, and Aboriginal Land Commissioner in the Northern Territory 1977–82. Educated in Western Australia and became a QC in 1968. Retired in 1998.

List of cases

ACF case, see *Australian Conservation Foundation v. The Commonwealth* (1978) 146 CLR 493

Adelaide Company of Jehovah's Witnesses Incorporated v. The Commonwealth (1943) 67 CLR 116

Air Caledonie International v. The Commonwealth (1988) 165 CLR 462

Airlines of NSW v. NSW (No. 2) (1965) 113 CLR 54

Alexander's case, see *Waterside Workers' Federation of Australia v. J. W. Alexander Ltd* (1918) 25 CLR 434

Amalgamated Society of Engineers v. Adelaide Steamship Co. Ltd (1920) 28 CLR 129

Attorney-General (Cwlth), ex parte Rel McKinlay v. Commonwealth (1975) 135 CLR 1

Attorney-General (NSW) v. Brewery Employees Union of NSW (1908) 6 CLR 469

Attorney-General v. R (1957) 95 CLR 529 (Privy Council)

Attorney-General (Victoria); ex parte Rel Black v. The Commonwealth (1981) 146 CLR 559

Australian Capital Television Pty Ltd v. The Commonwealth (1992) 177 CLR 106

Australian Communist Party v. The Commonwealth (1951) 83 CLR 1

Australian Conservation Foundation v. The Commonwealth (1978) 146 CLR 493

Australian Consolidated Press v. Uren (1967) 117 CLR 221

Re Australian Education Union; ex parte Victoria (1995) 184 CLR 188

Australian Railways Union v. Victorian Railways Commissioners (1930) 44 CLR 319

Baker v. Campbell (1983) 153 CLR 52

Bank Nationalisation case, see *Bank of NSW v. The Commonwealth* (1948) 76 CLR 1 (High Court); (1949) 79 CLR 497 (Privy Council)
Bath v. Alston Holdings (1988) 165 CLR 411
Baxter v. Commissioner of Taxation (NSW) (1907) 4 CLR 1087
Black v. The Commonwealth (1980–81) 146 CLR 559
Boilermakers case, see *R v. Kirby; ex parte Boilermakers' Society of Australia* (1956) 94 CLR 254 (High Court); (1957) 95 CLR 529 (Privy Council)
Brambles Holdings Ltd v. Federal Commissioner of Taxation (1977) 8 ATR 108
Brandy v. Human Rights & Equal Opportunity Commission (1995) 183 CLR 245
Ex parte; The Brisbane Tramways Co. Ltd (1914) 18 CLR 54
Broken Hill Pty Co. Ltd, ex parte; R v. Commonwealth Court of Conciliation & Arbitration (1909) 8 CLR 419 (*BHP* case)
Bropho v. Western Australia (1990) 171 CLR 1
Brown v. The Queen (1986) 64 ALR 161
Burgess case, see *R v. Burgess; ex parte Henry* (1936) 55 CLR 608
Church of the New Faith v. Commissioner of Pay-Roll Tax (Vic) (1982–83) 154 CLR 120
Clark King & Co Pty Ltd v. Australian Wheat Board (1978) 140 CLR 120
Coe v. Commonwealth of Australia (1979) 24 ALR 111
Cole v. Whitfield (1988) 165 CLR 360
Colonial Sugar Refining Co Ltd v. Attorney-General (1912) 15 CLR 182
Commissioner of Taxation v. Casuarina Pty Ltd (1970–71) 127 CLR 62
Commissioner of Taxation v. Insomnia Pty Ltd, 13 May 1983, unreported
Commissioner of Taxation v. St Helens Farm (ACT) Pty Ltd & ors (1981) 146 CLR 336
Commissioner of Taxation v. Watson and Gulland (1985) 160 CLR 55
Commissioner of Taxation v. Westraders Pty Ltd (1980) 144 CLR 55
Commonwealth v. Bank of NSW (1949) 79 CLR 497
Commonwealth v. Evans Deakin Industries Ltd (1986) 161 CLR 254
Commonwealth v. Queensland (1975) 134 CLR 298
Commonwealth v. Tasmania (1983) 158 CLR 1 (*Dams* case)
Commonwealth v. Verwayen (1990) 170 CLR 394
Communist Party case, see *Australian Communist Party v. The Commonwealth* (1951) 83 CLR 1
Concrete Pipes case, see *Strickland v. Rocla Concrete Pipes Ltd* (1971) 124 CLR 468
Cooper Brookes (Wollongong) Pty Ltd v. Commissioner of Taxation (1981) 147 CLR 297
Cormack v. Cope (1974) 131 CLR 432
Corporations case, see *New South Wales v. The Commonwealth* (1989–90) 169 CLR 482

Lemonthyme and Southern Forests—Richardson v. Forestry Commission (1987–88) 164 CLR 261
Mabo v. Queensland [No 1] (1988) 166 CLR 186
Mabo v. Queensland [No 2] (1991–92) 175 CLR 1
Macmine Pty Ltd v. Commissioner of Taxation (1978–79) 53 ALJR 362
McCormack v. Federal Commissioner of Taxation (1978–79) 143 CLR 284
MacCormick v. Commissioner of Taxation (1984) 158 CLR 622
McGinty v. Western Australia (1996) 186 CLR 140
McInnis v. The Queen (1979) 143 CLR 575
McKinlay's case, see *Attorney-General (Cwlth), ex rel McKinlay v. Commonwealth* (1975) 135 CLR 1
McKinney & Judge v. The Queen (1991) 171 CLR 468
Melbourne Corporation v. The Commonwealth (1947) 74 CLR 31
Miller v. TCN Channel Nine Pty Ltd (1986) 161 CLR 556
Milirrpum v. Nabalco Pty Ltd (1971) 17 FLR 141
Minister for Immigration & Ethnic Affairs v. Teoh (1995) 183 CLR 273
Minister for Justice (WA) v. ANA Commission (1977) 138 CLR 492
Moran's case, see *W. R. Moran Pty Ltd v. Deputy Federal Commissioner of Taxation* (1939) 61 CLR 735; (1940) 63 CLR 338
Mullens v. Federal Commissioner of Taxation (1976) 135 CLR 290
Municipal Council of Sydney v. The Commonwealth (1904) 1 CLR 208
Murphyores Inc. Pty Ltd v. The Commonwealth (1976) 136 CLR 1
Nationwide News Pty Ltd v. Wills (1992) 177 CLR 1
New South Wales v. The Commonwealth (1908) 7 CLR 179 (*Surplus Revenue* case)
New South Wales v. The Commonwealth (1989–90) 169 CLR 482 (*Corporations* case)
Newton v. Federal Commissioner of Taxation (1958) 98 CLR 1
Onus v. Alcoa of Australia Ltd (1981) 149 CLR 27
Oteri v. The Queen (1976) 11 ALR 142
Pak Siu Ling & ors v. Minister for Immigration (1991) (Federal Court), 15 February 1991, unreported
Parker v. The Queen (1962–63) 111 CLR 610 (High Court); (1964) 111 CLR 665 (Privy Council)
Payroll Tax case, see *Victoria v. The Commonwealth* (1970–71) 122 CLR 353
Peate v. Federal Commissioner of Taxation (1966) 116 CLR 38; (1967) 1 AC 308
Peterswald v. Bartley (1904) 1 CLR 497
Philip Morris Ltd & ors v. Commissioner of Business Franchises & anr (1989) 167 CLR 399
Pincus v. Commissioner of Taxation (1985) 160 CLR 55
PMA case, see *Victoria v. The Commonwealth* (1975) 134 CLR 81
Polyukhovich v. The Commonwealth (1991) 172 CLR 501 (*War Crimes* case)

Bibliography

General

The authorised (by the Justices) reports of judgments of the High Court, together with summaries of the arguments presented to the Court, are published in the *Commonwealth Law Reports* (CLR). Judgments are also reported somewhat more rapidly in the *Australian Law Reports* and the *Australian Law Journal Reports*. Since 1980 *The Legal Reporter* has also published summaries of the judgments within a week or two of them being handed down, and is the only source of reports on special leave applications and Chambers matters. Judgments are available within a short period of being published on the High Court's Web page: *http://www.auslii.edu.au/au/cases/cth/high_ct*

The major text linking the work of the High Court with that of governments and parliaments is Professor Geoffrey Sawer's two-volume *Australian Federal Politics and Law*, the first volume dealing with the period 1901–29, the second with the period 1929–49. Professor Michael Coper's *Encounters with the Australian Constitution* is probably the best general study of the High Court's constitutional work, particularly when read in conjunction with Professor Leslie Zines' *The High Court and the Constitution*, while Dr Brian Galligan's *Politics of the High Court* is a more philosophical study of the way judicial review has been used by the High Court. A brief historical account of the High Court (to 1980), its Justices and some of the problems faced by the Court is contained in *Keystone of the Federal Arch* by J. M. Bennett.

Two further series of publications are invaluable. The first is *The Official Records of the Debates of the Australasian Federal Convention*, republished in 1986 by Legal Books, Sydney, in six volumes, the last of which contains an exceptionally fine index. The second is the *Reports of the Constitutional Commission*, including two volumes of its final report (1988) and five volumes of reports by its Advisory Committees (mainly 1987). The updated version of the Constitution is published widely. Recently the Commonwealth parliament's education office published a small, compact edition which includes the Statute of Westminster and the Australia Acts, for a very low price. The Constitutional Centenary Foundation has published an *Annotated Constitution*, for the use of non-lawyers.

The High Court also makes available, on its Web site, speeches and papers given by Justices of the Court. This is an invaluable resource.

Listed below is a selection of significant books and articles found most useful for the purposes of this text.

Books

Aroney, Nicholas (1998) *Freedom of Speech in the Constitution*, Sydney: Centre for Independent Studies

Australian Institute of Judicial Administration Inc. (1986) *Judges as Royal Commissioners and Chairmen of Non-Judicial Tribunals*, Melbourne: AIJA

Bachelard, Michael (1997) *The Great Land Grab*, South Melbourne: Hyland House

Bates, G. M. (1987) *Environmental Law in Australia* (2nd edn), Sydney: Butterworths

Becker, Theodore L. (1969) *The Impact of Supreme Court Decisions*, New York: Oxford University Press

Bennett J. M. (1980) *Keystone of the Federal Arch*, Canberra: AGPS

Blazey, Peter (1972) *Bolte: A Political Biography*, Milton: Jacaranda Press

Brazil, P. and Mitchell B. eds (1981) *Opinions of Attorneys-General of the Commonwealth of Australia, vol 1: 1901–14*, Canberra: AGPS

——(1988) *Opinions of Attorneys-General of the Commonwealth of Australia, vol 2: 1914–23*, Canberra: AGPS

Brennan, Frank (1998) *Legislating Liberty: A Bill of Rights for Australia?*, St Lucia: University of Queensland Press

Cameron, Clyde (1982) *Unions in Crisis*, Melbourne: Hill of Content

Chisholm, Anthony & Reynolds, Ian (1982) *Heritage Conservation in Australia: An evaluation of economic incentives*, Canberra: Centre for Resource and Environmental Studies

Committee of Inquiry into the National Estate (1974) *Report of the National Estate*, Canberra: AGPS

Coper, Michael (1983) *Freedom of Interstate Trade under the Australian Constitution*, Sydney: Butterworths

——(1987) *Encounters with the Australian Constitution*, North Ryde: CCH

Crisp, L. F. (1955) *The Australian Federal Labour Party 1901–1951*, London: Longmans

Deakin, Alfred (1944) *The Federal Story*, Melbourne: Melbourne University Press

——(edited by J. A. La Nauze 1968) *Federated Australia*, Melbourne: Melbourne University Press

Denning, Lord (1979) *The Discipline of Law*, London: Butterworths

Dixon, Sir Owen (1965) *Jesting Pilate*, Melbourne: Law Book Co.

Downer, Alexander (1982) *Six Prime Ministers*, Melbourne: Hill of Content

Edwards, Colin (1965) *Bruce of Melbourne: Man of Two Worlds*, London: Heinemann

Else-Mitchell, Mr Justice ed. (1961) *Essays on the Australian Constitution*, Sydney: Law Book Co.

Evans, Gareth ed. (1977) *Labor and the Constitution*, Melbourne: Heinemann

Galligan, Brian (1987) *Politics of the High Court*, St Lucia: University of Queensland Press

Gaze, B. & Jones, M. (1990) *Law, Liberty and Australian Democracy*, Sydney: Law Book Co.

Green, Frank C. (1969) *Servant of the House*, Melbourne: William Heinemann Ltd

Griffith, J. A. G. (1977) *The Politics of the Judiciary*, Glasgow: Fontana (5th edn, 1997)

Harris & Dutton eds (1971) *Sir Henry, Bjelke, Don Baby and Friends*, South Melbourne: Sun Books

Hazlehurst, Kayleen M. ed. (1987) *Ivory Scales: Black Australia & the Law*, Sydney: New South Wales University Press

Howard, Colin (1980) *The Constitution, Power and Politics*, Melbourne: Fontana

La Nauze, J. A. (1972) *The Making of the Australian Constitution*, Melbourne: Melbourne University Press

——(1979) *Alfred Deakin: A Biography*, Sydney: Angus & Robertson

Lee, Simon (1989) *Judging Judges*, London: Faber & Faber

Lloyd, Clem (1977) *The National Estate: Australia's Heritage*, Sydney: Cassell Australia

——(1988) *Parliament and The Press: The Federal Parliamentary Press Gallery 1901–88*, Melbourne: Melbourne University Press

MacAdam, Alastair & Pyke, John (1998) *Judicial Reasoning and the Doctrine of Precedent in Australia*, Sydney: Butterworths

McCorquodale, John (1987) *Aborigines and the Law: A Digest*, Canberra: Aboriginal Studies Press

McMillan, John, Evans, Gareth & Storey, Haddon (1983) *Australia's Constitution: Time for Change?*, Sydney: George Allen & Unwin

Marr, D. (1980) *Barwick*, Sydney: George Allen & Unwin

Menzies, Sir Robert (1968) *Central Power in the Australian Commonwealth*, 2nd edn, Melbourne: Cassell Australia Ltd

——(1967) *Afternoon Light: Some Memories of Men and Events*, Melbourne: Cassell Australia Ltd

Millar, T. B. (1978) *Australia in Peace and War: External Relations 1788–1977*, Canberra: Australian National University Press

Miller, Arthur S. (1985) *Politics, Democracy, and the Supreme Court*, Connecticut: Greenwood Press

Official Record of the Debates of the Australasian Federal Convention (6 vols) (1986), Sydney: Legal Books

Pannick, David (1988) *Judges*, Oxford: Oxford University Press

Portus, G. V. ed. (1933) *Studies in the Australian Constitution*, Sydney: Angus & Robertson

Reynolds, Henry (1987) *The Law of the Land*, Ringwood: Penguin Books Australia Ltd

Richardson, J. E. (1973) *Patterns of Australian Federalism*, Canberra: Centre for Research on Federal Financial Relations, ANU

Sawer, Geoffrey (1967) *Australian Federalism in the Courts*, Melbourne: Melbourne University Press

——(1972) *Australian Federal Politics and Law 1901–1929*, Carlton: Melbourne University Press

——(1974) *Australian Federal Politics and Law 1929–1949*, Carlton: Melbourne University Press

——(1977) *Federation Under Strain: Australia 1972–1975*, Melbourne: Melbourne University Press

Scalia, Antonin (1997) *A Matter of Interpretation*, Princeton: Princeton University Press

Scutt, Jocelynne A. ed. (1987) *Lionel Murphy: A Radical Judge*, Melbourne: McCulloch Publishing Pty Ltd

Snedden, Billy Mackie & Schedvin, M. Bernie (1990) *Billy Snedden: An Unlikely Liberal*, Melbourne: Macmillan Australia

Souter, Gavin (1988) *Acts of Parliament*, Melbourne: Melbourne University Press

Stevens, B. & Weller, P. eds (1976) *The Australian Labor Party and Federal Politics*, Melbourne: Melbourne University Press

Thomas, Mr Justice (1988) *Judicial Ethics in Australia*, Sydney: Law Book Co. Ltd

Weller, P. ed. (1975) *Caucus Minutes 1901–1949* (3 vols), Melbourne: Melbourne University Press

Weller, P. & Lloyd B. eds (1978) *Federal Executive Minutes*, Melbourne: Melbourne University Press

Whitlam, Gough (1985) *The Whitlam Government 1972–1975*, Ringwood: Viking

Winterton, George (1983) *Parliament, the Executive and the Governor-General*, Melbourne: Melbourne University Press

Wright, D. I. (1970) *Shadow of Dispute—Aspects of Commonwealth–State Relations, 1901–1910*, Canberra: Australian National University Press

Zines, L. ed. (1977) *Commentaries on the Australian Constitution: A Tribute to Geoffrey Sawer*, Sydney: Butterworths

—— (1987) *The High Court and the Constitution*, 2nd edn, Sydney: Butterworths

Articles

Brennan, Mr Justice (1978) 'Limits on the use of judges' *Federal Law Review* vol. 9, pp. 1–14

——(1979) 'Judging the judges' *Australian Law Journal* vol. 53, pp. 767–70

——(1990) 'Courts, democracy and the law' (The Blackburn lecture), (1991) 65 ALJ, pp. 32–43

Coper, Michael (1979) 'The role of the courts in the preservation of federalism' *Australian Law Journal* vol. 63, pp. 463–73

Craven, Greg (1997a) 'The High Court and the Founders: an unfaithful servant', papers on Parliament, No. 30, pp. 63–92

——(1997b) 'The High Court's democratic deficit', *Policy* pp. 7–13

Doyle, Chief Justice John (1996) 'Balancing Acts' *Eureka Street*, pp. 18–19.

Finn, Paul & Smith, Kathryn Jane (1992) 'The Citizen, the Government and "Reasonable Expectations"', 66 ALJ, pp. 139–51

Gibbs, Sir Harry (1990) 'Law and Government' *Quadrant*, October, p. 25

Gleeson, A. M. (1979) 'Judging the judges' *Australian Law Journal* vol. 53, pp. 338–47

Hanks, Peter (1987) 'The Political dimension of Constitutional adjudication' *University of NSW Law Journal* vol. 10, pp. 141–54

Howard, Colin 'The Constitution as a legal document' in Mayer, Henry & Nelson, Helen (1980) *Australian Politics* 5, Melbourne: Longman Cheshire, pp. 143–9

Lloyd, Clem (1987) 'Not peace but a sword! The High Court under J. G. Latham' *Adelaide Law Review* 11 (1987–88), pp. 175–202

McCorquodale, John, (1983) 'Aborigines in the High Court', *Australian Quarterly* vol. 55, pp. 104–13

Mason, Sir Anthony (1986) 'The role of a Constitutional Court in a federation' *Federal Law Review* vol. 16, pp. 1–16 (This was his University of Virginia lecture, only slightly revised)

——(1988a) 'A Bill of Rights for Australia' paper delivered to the Australian Bar Association, Townsville

——(1988b) 'The Australian Constitution 1901–1988' *Australian Law Journal*, vol. 62, no. 10, pp. 752–60

——(1990) 'Opening of the Centre for Comparative Constitutional Studies, Melbourne' *Public Law Review* vol. 1, pp. 111–13

Meagher, Justice R. P. (1998) 'Civil Rights: some reflections' *Australian Law Journal* vol. 72, pp. 47–52

Murphy, Justice L. K. (1983) Speech to the National Press Club, Canberra

Sawer, Geoffrey 'The Constitution and its Politics' in Mayer, Henry & Nelson, Helen (1980) *Australian Politics* 5, Melbourne: Longman Cheshire, pp. 129–42

Solomon, David (1983) 'The High Court since Barwick CJ', paper delivered to Society of Labor Lawyers

——(1989) 'The High Court's present view of the federal balance' *Canberra Bulletin of Public Administration*, pp. 80–8

Springall, R. C. (1978) 'Stare decisis as applied by the High Court to its previous decisions' *Federal Law Review* vol. 9, pp. 483–503

Whitlam, E. G. (1954) 'The Constitution versus Labor' in *Labor and the Constitution*, Victorian Fabian Society pamphlet

INDEX

Printed in Dunstable, United Kingdom

88180801R00167